MADRIGAL of SEAS and SUMMITS

MADRIGAL *of* SEAS *and* SUMMITS

A LIFE OF SERVICE TO THE NATION

A. DENIS CLIFT

Naval Institute Press
Annapolis, Maryland

Naval Institute Press
291 Wood Road
Annapolis, MD 21402

© 2026 by A. Denis Clift
All rights reserved. No part of this book may be reproduced or utilized in any form or by any means, electronic or mechanical, including photocopying and recording, or by any information storage and retrieval system, without permission in writing from the publisher.

ISBN: 978-1-68247-456-3 (hardcover)
ISBN: 978-1-68247-987-2 (ebook)

Library of Congress Cataloging-in-Publication data is available.

∞ Print editions meet the requirements of ANSI/NISO z39.48-1992 (Permanence of Paper).

Printed in the United States of America.

9 8 7 6 5 4 3 2 1

In chapters 5–13 of this book, the author has added to, condensed, and otherwise revised his previously published With Presidents to the Summit *(George Mason University Press, 1993), all rights of which have reverted to him.*

For Tyrone C. Clift
Beloved son Ty

CONTENTS

Preface ix

Acknowledgments xiii

CHAPTER 1. On the Ice with Penguins: Antarctica, 1960–1962   1

CHAPTER 2. Beginnings, 1937–1960   22

CHAPTER 3. From the U.S. Navy to the U.S. Naval Institute, 1961–1966   32

CHAPTER 4. From London to the National Security Council, 1966–1971   43

CHAPTER 5. National Security Council, 1971–1977   62

CHAPTER 6. Scouting My First Summit: Iceland, 1973   71

CHAPTER 7. Nixon's Diplomacy, 1972–1974   82

CHAPTER 8. Ford's Continuity, 1974   98

CHAPTER 9. Navigating the Mid–Cold War with President Ford, 1975   111

CHAPTER 10. The United States Turns Two Hundred, 1976   129

CHAPTER 11. First Year as Assistant to Vice President Mondale for National Security Affairs, 1977   137

CHAPTER 12. Building Toward the Camp David Accords, 1978   151

CHAPTER 13. Shuttle Diplomacy with Mondale, 1979–1981 171

CHAPTER 14. From the White House to the DIA and Joint Commission on POW/MIAs, 1981–2009 192

CHAPTER 15. Serving as President, National Intelligence College, 1994–2009 215

CHAPTER 16. Full Circle: U.S. Naval Institute, 2009–2023 241

Appendix. Staff Schedule, Nixon and Pompidou in Iceland, 30 May–1 June 1973 247

PREFACE

"Name a highlight," I am asked when I say my more than fifty-year career was dedicated to service to the nation. We are at Arlington National Cemetery for a burial. A forty-one-year-old mother with children in arms weeps when a B-52 thunders low overhead in salute to her father. She was six months old when he disappeared while flying an Air Force mission off the far east of the Soviet Union. As she grew up, there was a void where there should have been knowledge and family life. Now, thanks to our work, she stood at her father's gravesite. I answered the question: "My role as presidential commissioner on the U.S.-Russia Joint Commission on Prisoners of War and Missing in Action."

With a full and fascinating career behind me, all of which I have the honor to say was dedicated to service to nation, I look back in this memoir at the continual march of activity and demands, and on what was for me the parallel joy of shaping a stable and loving home life. The adventure has been nonstop, and in writing about it I reflect on the critical importance of the work done by those in the U.S. government helping to carry out its foreign policy.

After serving in the Navy and attending the London School of Economics and Political Science, I started on the National Security Council as foreign operations officer in spring 1971. In 1974 I was promoted to lead President Gerald Ford's NSC staff for the Soviet Union and Eastern and Western Europe and NATO, which kept me busy through 1976. As a "summit sherpa," I helped presidents and a vice president interact with other heads of state throughout the world while learning, again and again, that diplomatic skills apply on every level of human interactions. This knowledge remained invaluable after those years.

In 1977 I left the NSC—and moved from the third to the second floor of the Old Executive Office Building—to become Vice President Walter F. Mondale's assistant for national security affairs. I held this job for his full term, until 1981.

My next career chapter was at the Defense Intelligence Agency (DIA), which I joined as defense intelligence officer-at-large in 1981. Here my first step was a big one, becoming the founding editor in chief of the Department of Defense's new, highly authoritative report *Soviet Military Power.* Over ten years from 1981, I guided the shaping and production of this series of publications as it became annual, informing the public and winning defense and presidential awards. In 1982 I became assistant deputy director for external affairs; in 1985 deputy director for external relations; and finally, in 1991, chief of staff, where I remained until 1994, having attained the highest rank of Senior Executive Service, SES-6, in 1993.

I next had the honor to help guide the evolution of the Joint Military Intelligence College, first into the National Defense Intelligence College, the flagship degree-granting education and research institution in the U.S. Intelligence Community, serving as its president from 1994 to 2009. During those years as college president, I was elected to serve on the Middle States Commission on Higher Education from 2000 to 2005. And from 1992 to 2009, I served in parallel as Presidential Commissioner on the U.S.-Russia Joint Commission on Prisoners of War / Missing in Action. Created by President George H. W. Bush and President Boris Yeltsin, this commission aimed to account for servicemen still missing from past conflicts—for me, another great honor.

All of these positions were demanding and tremendously rewarding on a personal level. But possibly the role of which I remain most proud was my work at the nonpartisan, nonprofit, independent forum for national security matters, the U.S. Naval Institute. I served as editor in chief of *Proceedings* from 1963 to 1966, and in 2009 I rejoined the Institute to become vice president for planning and operations, retiring in 2023.

This book reports the above and aims to inspire others with the value of public service. To capture the experience, I have both added to and revised my previously published *With Presidents to the Summit* (1993), to which I hold all rights. That book's focus was on the in-depth details of my career as a summit sherpa—the making of successful summits—with occasional forays into my personal perspectives. In this new book, I've added my own story: where I came from, the U.S. Navy background and how I came to be a sherpa, and what I did beyond.

Throughout, I've focused more on the personal side of my trajectory, how it affected me and my family, and lessons that were driven home. It is my hope that these will be of use to others who set out on a path of working for the betterment of the globe as a whole.

ACKNOWLEDGMENTS

I must first thank Vice Admiral Pete Daly, USN (Ret.), and his wife, Jane, for their enthusiastic, strong support for this work. Next I thank Annie Rehill, who played a central, both inspirational and editorial, role in the realization of this work. Annie urged me to write the tale of my life when I first recounted to her some of its episodes many years ago. She helped with both the new writing and the transformation of some of the accounts that appeared in earlier published works.

My son Tyrone, a most talented and hardworking professional, bridged the gap between his home and work in Austin, Texas, and my workplace in Annapolis. Thanks to him we have been able to locate, assemble, and include the book's photography.

At the Naval Institute Press, I thank, in turn, my editor, Susan Brook, a nonstop, hardworking believer in the value of the work; the publisher, Rear Admiral Raymond Spicer, USN (Ret.); and the director, Adam Kane.

CHAPTER 1

On the Ice with Penguins

Antarctica, 1960–1962

In 1961, I walked around the world.

As a Navy lieutenant junior grade, I had flown on a four-engine C-130 ski-plane to the geographic South Pole with my commanding officer, Rear Admiral David M. Tyree, for the fiftieth-anniversary commemorative ceremonies of the first attainments of the Pole by the Norwegian team of Roald Amundsen and the U.K. team, led by Captain Robert Falcon Scott. We had also flown in delegations from Great Britain, Norway, and New Zealand. I was the on-scene correspondent reporting and filing the October 30, 1961, news report that would run in media across the United States and overseas.

It was minus 40 degrees. Gleaming icy surface snow spread in every direction as far as the eye could see. The speeches—first in the Pole Station mess hall, then out at the Pole—were short. "The deeds of Amundsen and Scott half a century ago are of greatest significance in man's brief Antarctic history," Tyree said. "Both men stand proudly in the front ranks of those who, in their different ways, have made such vital contributions to the exploration and opening of the Antarctic continent. Amundsen and Scott laid bare the hinterland of this white continent. They demonstrated that no matter how bitter the elements of nature might be, valiant men could still achieve their goals. Scott and Amundsen added to the sum of man's knowledge; more important, they added immensely to the sum of man's inspiration."

U.S., British, and Norwegian flags were on display. With the ceremony's conclusion at the tall pole erected by the United States marking 90 degrees south, a marble plaque was laid with the names of the first arrivals, their dates, and the words "A tribute from Great Britain and Norway, 1961, presented to the U.S. Amundsen-Scott South Pole Station."

Some two hundred to three hundred feet out, a large, half-buried ring of empty fuel drums circled the tall pole, placed there by our scientists and station crew in recognition of the very slight variations in the precise site of 90 degrees south as the world turned. The precise geographic South Pole was within that circle. With the ceremony over, I quickly headed outside the ring. In my polar boots and parka, breathing a bit heavily at the 10,000-foot polar elevation, I hiked all the way around the ring, crossing each of the earth's 360 degrees of longitude—a nonstop journey all the way around the world.

That circumnavigation was part of a life of derring-do, adventure, and accomplishment. I was in the second year of my Antarctic Operations Deep Freeze 1960 and 1961 expeditions. Almost a year earlier, November 7–9, 1960, I had been a member of the Marble Point–McMurdo Trail Party, assisting and filing a news report on nine Navy Seabees and their Finnish American leader, Army Major Antero Havola, driving enormous D-9 tractors sixty miles across the surface ice of McMurdo Sound from Marble Point to McMurdo Station.

After many days of planning, the trip had taken thirty hours. The tractors, weighing forty and forty-four tons, had originally been brought to Antarctica from the United States by ship in 1957 and offloaded on the west side of McMurdo Sound at Marble Point. They had been used to carve and grade an experimental rock-earth runway and then left there because their enormous weight had made it impractical to transfer them to a new location.

Major Havola and his driver, Navy Construction Mechanic Second Class Willard Cunningham, had examined the cross-ice route three days earlier in their treaded Weasel vehicle, keeping a constant watch for ice cracks and flaws and stopping every third mile to bore holes, hand-coring seven and eight feet and more down through the ice. Havola had decided that seventy-one inches of ice would be the thinnest his safety margins would permit.

At Marble Point, the Seabees lubricated and changed the oil on the D-9s. Their cabins were removed as a safety measure should one of the big machines start to break through the ice with a driver at the controls. Four seventy-five-foot lines were attached to the controls of each D-9 and run out behind the tractors. When the tractors were underway, one man could control each machine with these lines, or reins, while walking in relative safety seventy-five feet behind.

Major Havola welcomed me to the operation. I boarded his Weasel, and just before we departed McMurdo, he had the driver swing by sick bay to pick up a case of brandy miniatures for medicinal purposes. We headed out. On the evening of the 7th, we were with the Seabees as the two D-9s were eased out onto the ice of McMurdo Sound. There were four drivers operating in one-hour shifts as teams of two, with one pair walking behind controlling the reins and the other two resting in the cabin of an accompanying treaded Sno-Cat.

Havola was trailblazing. Ranging a mile and a half ahead of the D-9s, he searched out the best passages through the snow and pressure ridges of the ice. Every two miles he stopped, and he and Cunningham, with me an able third hand, hand-cored down through the ice to ensure we had sufficient thickness. As we hand-cored, lubricating the deepening hole with antifreeze, all that could be heard in the incredible silence of Antarctica was the distant roar of the approaching D-9s.

At 2:00 the following morning, the sun was bright, and we spotted the tracks made by our Weasel on the trip out. We now paralleled those tracks. The men manning the D-9s would know they were on a tested trail. By 6:00 a.m., the tractor train had passed over the thinnest ice, seventy-eight inches, and our trail party stopped to rest. Food arrived by helicopter, the tractors were refueled, and we moved out again. We were on old ice now, more than nine feet thick, and the drivers rode their brute D-9s, which could now move faster. The Sno-Cat broke down, but one of the D-9s took it in tow without a blink. We were on the concluding multihour leg of our successful return to McMurdo.

It was just half a year earlier, in spring 1960, that the compulsion had hit: "Go to Antarctica." I had completed more than a year's duty at the Fleet Intelligence Center, Pacific (FICPac), Ford Island, Hawaii, as an air intelligence officer. I had been growing professionally in my first-tour intelligence work, and—bachelor's life—enjoying the great bodysurfing, the best of rum, and lovely ladies everywhere. Then I watched a TV documentary on Antarctic exploration during the 1957–58 International Geophysical Year, narrated by Rear Admiral George Dufek, U.S. Navy. There is more to Navy life, I thought, and set my sights on the great white continent down under.

A check through official channels with the Bureau of Naval Personnel brought the quick response that there were no intelligence billets in Antarctica and advised that I apply myself to my current work. I requested and received permission to speak to my intelligence center commanding officer, Captain Brendan Moynahan. He had been a Navy Catalina seaplane pilot in the Pacific in World War II and was now in his final active-duty assignment. His wife was a member of a well-to-do island sugar family. He planned to retire in Hawaii, and his deep tan spoke of his love of golf. He heard me out, was intrigued by my audaciousness, and gave me permission to write directly to Rear Admiral Tyree, Dufek's successor. Moynahan wished me well and advised that he would inform the intelligence center's personnel officer that he had granted his permission.

On May 22, at my manual typewriter and satisfied with draft number three—no manual erasures—I signed and mailed a two-page letter to Admiral Tyree, underlining my college journalism degree, my newspaper and writing experience, good record at FICPac, good physical fitness, eagerness to serve, and belief that I would make a strong contribution to his mission. Into the mailbox it went, and the work at FICPac proceeded. By then I was sharing a rental home and sleeping on a screened porch under palms, with steps down to the beach on the Pacific near Diamond Head. The weeks turned into months. I heard nothing and told myself to keep surfing and forget Antarctica.

On August 29, 1960, I received an official letter from Lieutenant Commander R. E. McCloskey, the Operation Deep Freeze personnel officer, advising that the Bureau of Naval Personnel would be issuing orders to me to join the Antarctic Support Staff, Operation Deep Freeze 1961, to serve as assistant public information officer. The letter continued,

> My purpose in writing is to let you know that in executing your orders it will not be necessary or desirable for you to report to Washington headquarters. We have you booked from Hickam Air Force Base to New Zealand on a MATs special-mission aircraft (SARD mission 2566 trip number 171). The itinerary for the flight is not yet firm, but the aircraft should be at Hickam about the 19th of September. If you check with the Navy Air Traffic Control Officer in a week or two he should have the info by then.
>
> While in New Zealand you will need civilian clothing and both khaki and blue uniforms. You will be furnished cold weather clothing in Christchurch prior to departure for Antarctica.

For the first time in my life, I was floating. I had levitated. My feet were not touching the ground. The thrill of the letter was absolute. On September 7, 1960, I received official orders detaching me to join the Antarctic command. My Hawaiian co-tenants and landlady accepted my departure. I sold my beloved convertible, put my few belongings in storage, and headed deep, deep south.

Immediately upon landing in Christchurch, New Zealand, I reported to the Deep Freeze New Zealand headquarters at Harewood, on the grounds of Christchurch International Airport. My new immediate boss, Captain Arthur Ashton, welcomed me and introduced me to Admiral Tyree, whose welcome was even warmer. He told me, first off, that I would attend his daily morning senior staff operations and planning meeting.

September meant the coming of spring in Antarctica and the launch of the first Deep Freeze flights from New Zealand to McMurdo Sound ice runway, more than two thousand miles to the south across the unforgiving Southern Ocean, the pack ice, and the mountains, snow, and ice of the Antarctic landmass. Scheduling and launching the flights south were the Tyree staff's top priority and challenge. To me, the aircraft supporting the operation were lineal descendants of Waldo Pepper's flying circus, each with a specific mission—R4D Marine Corps variants of the venerable DC-3, with names like *Semper Shaftus*, fitted with skis and JATO (jet-assisted takeoff) bottles; Navy P2V Neptunes, the photo mappers; Air Force double-decker Globemasters hauling bulk cargoes, people, helicopters, and, yes, loaded inside the cargo space, smaller fixed-wing aircraft, wings detached; Super Constellations, Willie Victors; and the pride of the Navy's VX-6 Squadron 6, four of the new four-engine, turboprop C-130 Hercules transports, each fitted with three skis weighing a total of 7,500 pounds, known as Ski-130s.

Weather forecasts were vital to flights-south mission accomplishment. Admiral Tyree had to rely on fragmentary information from widely separated Antarctic stations and one lonely Southern Ocean picket ship in trying to outguess potentially deadly headwinds, storms, and blinding whiteouts. Crews and passengers on aircraft that were lost or out of fuel stood little chance of survival and recovery. I can picture the Harewood senior staff meeting when the meteorologist, a Navy captain, strode into the conference room, a smile from ear to ear, with the first photo printouts from the first satellite weather bird—the TIROS (television infrared observation satellite) launched earlier that year. Tyree at last had a picture of the current and incoming weather over the entire route, from takeoff to landing.

I was issued my full kit of Antarctic gear, and within days was southward bound to McMurdo Sound on board our Super Constellation, a flight ironically remembered for its heat. All passengers had been ordered to don rubber survival suits over all of our Antarctic wool in case the plane had to ditch in the ocean. The saying was that the Navy wanted us to die dry.

Captain Ashton stayed in New Zealand. I would be his hardworking assistant forward. I was to be the staff liaison officer looking after the foreign diplomatic, military, and academic visitors flying in and out inspecting our far-flung Antarctic research operations. I was to look after the work of our Navy enlisted journalists operating from our McMurdo press office, and with them look after incoming journalists from the United States and abroad. As time permitted, I was also to contribute as many of my own news articles as possible.

The foreign visitors were central to the new spirit of international cooperation. In 1958, during the International Geophysical Year, President Dwight D. Eisenhower had proposed to the eleven nations engaged in research on the Antarctic continent that all enter into a treaty preserving the continent for research and other peaceful purposes. The treaty was quickly negotiated and entered into force. Included in its fourteen-article provisions, treaty-state observers were granted free access, including aerial observation, to any area and—with advance notice given—allowed to inspect all stations, installations, and equipment.

The United States attached importance to the confidence-building nature of these treaty provisions. Every aspect of our research and Navy/military support for that research was open for inspection, and we were proud of that research. Years later, when I would be working at high U.S. levels with the Soviet Union on strategic and conventional arms issues, I was impressed by the fact that in Antarctica we had set the precedent for the subsequent on-site U.S.-Soviet arms inspection agreements.

Admiral Tyree and other senior staff members kept a close eye on my handling of the first foreign visitors to Deep Freeze 61, and the feedback was "Good job. Keep it up." When a visitor was inbounding on a flight, I boarded my treaded orange Weasel vehicle and drove the two miles from McMurdo Station to the over-water, eight-foot-thick-ice runway out on the Sound. Each of my visitors, always over-swaddled in heavy clothing, having landed and with baggage in hand, clambered into the Weasel's rear seat. Through the rearview mirror I could see eyes gazing in awe at the plumed snow-capped volcano Mt. Erebus high on the horizon. The vehicle was noisy; conversing was not easy. Halfway to the station, I would shout over my shoulder to ask if I might place a forty-ounce imperial quart of gin or scotch in his quarters. Each visitor was now a believer in U.S. research—and a new friend. I would ensure that each had desired run of our stations at McMurdo, Byrd, and the South Pole. I would often escort them. The result was a plus for our scientists, the Navy, and U.S. diplomacy.

Such station-to-station travel was not that easy. On one flight to Byrd Station, my two visitors and I were on board a Navy two-engine R4D peering out of portholes, flying high over the white of Marie Byrd Land. Suddenly, one engine, then the other, stopped—silence. I shouted to the visitors to strap themselves into their bucket seats, and as we coasted through the air, three sets of silent prayers were said. After what seemed a long time—it wasn't—one engine coughed, then the other turned and started again. Propellors spinning, welcome return of noise, we were flying! The plane chief, who had been forward, told us that the pilot and copilot had forgotten to throw the switches to the next fuel tanks when the first tanks ran dry. Ever the escort, my face was calm and smiling.

Having just been a division officer at the intelligence center in Hawaii, my responsibilities running our four-man McMurdo press office were a snap. The enlisted journalists were capable self-starters. One of them, a veteran chief, liked to do his typing Kerouac-style, with a long roll of paper on the bulkhead feeding down into his typewriter. They would check quickly with me on proposed stories, do their travel, digging, and writing, then back to me for a quick edit, and out the stories went. The work was equally smooth with our Navy photographers. Visiting journalists were dependent on us for support; we served them well and made lasting valuable contacts. Sid Scales, a visiting New Zealand artist and cartoonist, did cartoons of the operation, including one of Admiral Tyree as a stately emperor penguin. Just before he boarded his return flight, Sid gave me an inscribed-with-thanks, penciled head-and-shoulders portrait of a bearded Denis Clift hard at his typewriter in the press hut.

My stories began appearing regularly in American and New Zealand newspapers and magazines—the *Los Angeles Herald*, *New York Mirror*, *Stars and Stripes*, and *Navy Times*. I rode a C-130 to report on the first flight of the new season to open Byrd Station, with 15,000 pounds of cargo on board and a very warm reception from twenty-one happy scientists and support crew who had wintered over. On such flights to Byrd and the South Pole, when the C-130s arrived, landed, and were offloading, the crew kept the four big turbo prop engines running, props spinning—an incredible screaming sound. They did not want to risk engine oil and lubes congealing in the deep cold with engines unable to restart; we stayed well clear of the props. Another story with wide coverage, one that included a long, extremely hard, leaping up, down, and sideways helicopter flight, was on the delivery and installation of a 280-pound Grasshopper unmanned weather station. We were deploying several in remote parts of the continent.

My news stories were part of Admiral Tyree's daily reading file, and I had regular contact with him at his senior staff meetings. He had directed that my liaison responsibilities be expanded to include congressional and White House visitors—some good adventures there. Planning was going forward in those meetings for a two-icebreaker expedition to the Amundsen Sea. I recommended that he assign me to the expedition as liaison for reporters and foreign officers who would be observers on the two ships, and as the Navy's news correspondent on the expedition. Captain Ashton didn't want to lose all I was doing at McMurdo. Tyree gently overrode him and directed Captain Edwin A. McDonald, the icebreaker expedition's commodore, to include me on his staff on board the flagship USS *Glacier* (AGB-4).

Commissioned in 1955, the 8,600-ton *Glacier* was the pride of the Navy's icebreaker fleet. Her ten diesel engines generated 24,000 horsepower flowing to two giant electric motors spinning shafts powering twin, three-bladed propellors, each 17.5 feet in diameter. This gave her the muscle to break through ice up to twenty feet thick. With this muscle, her job at the beginning of each Deep Freeze Spring season was to open a channel from the Ross Sea to the ice-locked McMurdo Station. She would charge like a bull. The sloping forefoot of her bow would ride forward sliding up onto the ice, and her weight would crush the ice downward. She would back off and charge again, with the thick broken ice smashing and churning around her, gradually moving mile after mile, cutting a channel three ships in width. One or two of our smaller World War II–vintage *Wind*-class icebreakers worked well behind her breaking the ice just smashed into smaller pieces and coaxing it to move north and seaward, clearing and widening the channel for the inbound resupply transports.

Damage to the *Glacier* was expected and occurred in this process, damage to her propellor blades as they reversed and forwarded, with large chunks of ice colliding and wedging temporarily between blades and hull. By the time the channel had been opened in Deep Freeze 61, *Glacier* was missing half of one blade on the port propellor and half of two blades on the starboard. As this had been anticipated, a Navy cargo ship had already delivered replacement blades to a commercial shipyard in Wellington, New Zealand. The *Glacier* would have to go into drydock to have the new blades fitted before she could depart and lead the expedition in late January.

On December 24, 1961, I was on board the *Glacier*, and the ship was underway for New Zealand. As we moved up through the Ross Sea, the turning, unbalanced, uneven propellor blades produced a constant *bang, bang, bang* thudding through the steel hull. By the next morning, we were steaming through one of the building open-ocean storms for which the waters of the Southern Ocean circling the globe are famous. If the *Glacier* had a sloping forefoot bow for icebreaking, she also had a classic polar ship's rounded hull from bow to stern so that she would be squeezed upward intact rather than crushed if trapped by masses of ice. Now, she rolled and rolled as she plunged and rose through the mounting waves.

Commodore McDonald had spacious quarters on board the ship, including a dining saloon manned by the best of stewards. He had invited several of his onboard guests to Christmas breakfast: the renowned "artist-of-the-Navy" Arthur Beaumont, South African Naval Commander Jack Netterberg, and Dr. Brian Roberts of Great Britain's Scott Polar Institute—all of whom would sail on the expedition. Roy Champion, the harbor master of New Zealand's Port Lyttelton, along with me, *New York Herald Tribune* correspondent Wadsworth Likely, and Lieutenant Commander Jim Peeler were also among the assembled.

A wave of waves produced a mighty roll to port that had the ship hanging over, standing on her ear. We all went flying, finally staggered to our feet, and began regrouping. My head smashed a glass-framed painting on a bulkhead, and the knock brought my folk-singing guitarist's instincts to the fore. Following some quick sick bay patching, I dropped down to my cabin, cranked a sheet of paper into my typewriter, and composed an instant song:

CHRISTMAS BREAKFAST WITH COMMODORE MCDONALD

It was a grey, young Christmas morning
High on the icy Ross Sea,
When the *Glacier* without forewarning
Interrupted morning tea.

Limbs akimbo, plates were flying
When she heeled a hard 50 degrees,
On the deck stout Beau was lying
Bedecked in Christmas trees.

A pastoral painting hung broken
Done in by Clift's head with a rap,
While the Commodore's breakfast potion
Flew straightaway into his lap.

Jack Netterberg clung to the bulkhead,
Roy Champion balanced coffee,
And pineapple juice was liberally spread
As we tossed in the wrath of the sea.

Peeler grabbed for Likely
As the *Herald Tribune* sailed past
And wedged him ever so tightly
T'ween sofa and sideboard at last.

> Below Brian Roberts lay sleeping
> As the waves at length set us free.
> Above, the Commodore rising said
> "That's quite enough breakfast for me!"

This opus was performed with guitar accompaniment in the same saloon with the same company later in the day and was greeted by the bruised with laughter and applause.

Wellington, the capital of New Zealand, is a strikingly attractive ocean harbor city, its waters surrounded by tall green hills lined with residential districts. I kept my quarters on board the *Glacier* while the yardwork proceeded. There was time to enjoy the local sites, restaurants, and pubs ashore with new friends in pleasant summer weather at the same time I was preparing for the expedition.

Two members of the media with us on the *Glacier* were a feature writer from the *Boston Traveler* and a photographer from *National Geographic*. Neither would be filing stories while the expedition was underway. There would be no media on board our second ship, the icebreaker USS *Staten Island* (AGB-5). Not only would I be the Navy's correspondent, I would also be the only news correspondent sending stories from our ships. I did some more Antarctic research. I also made sure that all was in order for the expedition's four foreign observers. Commander Netterberg and Dr. Roberts would be with us on the *Glacier*. A Chilean army major and Argentine navy lieutenant would be on board the *Staten Island*.

New Zealand friends invited me to their home to listen to President John F. Kennedy's January 20 inaugural address being broadcast on the BBC. At much the same time, the last maintenance touches were completed and the *Glacier* prepared to leave drydock and move pierside to take on supplies. We sailed for Antarctica on January 29, 1961. It took me a day to regain my sea legs as the *Glacier* settled into her wallowing rolls and pitches on open ocean waters.

Our expedition leader, Commodore McDonald, was an engaging senior officer, a veteran icebreaker sailor at his happiest and in his element when sailing toward and in the formidable unknowns of Antarctica. I would learn in years to come that he was also an author and a contributor to the U.S. Naval Institute's journal *Proceedings*. He told me that I had complete freedom, the run of both ships and their crews, in my reporting on the expedition. While he noted that it would be his formal Navy responsibility to initial each of my stories before it left the ship, he would be surprised if he ever changed a word. The stories would move from the *Glacier*'s communications shack to the U.S. naval attaché at our embassy in Wellington, who would use the embassy's communication channels for further dissemination to the Navy and media in the United States and New Zealand.

As the expedition got underway on January 29, I described the ships, their leadership, and the scientific and exploration goals: "to push through the pack ice to the Antarctic coastline at a point off Cape Flying Fish and then swing westward into the frozen Amundsen Sea. At this time, the two ships will find themselves confronted by a sea as yet unpenetrated because of the imposing density and strength of the ice flows in its waters." From then through March 10, 1961, my reporting flowed:

> **February 13:** After several days of probing, ramming, backing, it has quickly become apparent that the ice is too thick for penetration of the Amundsen Sea. The ships have altered course for the Bellingshausen Sea and found almost equally difficult ice conditions. For the past seven days the expedition led by Captain Edwin A. McDonald has been working along the Antarctic coastline. Excellent weather has allowed for numerous scientific returns from the previously unknown Eights Coast region. Surveyors and geologists have been flown by helicopter from the USS *Glacier* to establish four field camps ashore. From these camps, the new lands are being studied and accurately positioned for future mapping.
>
> **February 15:** Bellingshausen Sea, Antarctica, 15 Feb 1961. Four men, marooned three nights and two days by a savage Antarctic blizzard, were flown to safety this morning in a brilliant rescue by helicopters.
>
> The scientific field party had been trapped on the unexplored Eights Coast by freezing, hurricane-force winds of over 100 miles an hour.

The winds, so violent that they snapped ice ax handles, made the erecting of a tent impossible. Led by Dr. Brian Roberts, Great Britain's official observer to Operation Deep Freeze 1961, the men made their way to the most sheltered part of the outcropping and built a crude stone windbreak. "We owe our lives to that fine Englishman," Lieutenant Commander James Peeler said.

Aboard the icebreakers the expedition could only wait as the buffeting winds and snows made rescue impossible. Twice during the first night, ships' lines parted and the icebreakers had to be maneuvered to avoid perils from surrounding icebergs.

By three this morning, the snow had stopped and the winds had lessened. Captain McDonald ordered the recovery helicopters into the air from the *Glacier* and the *Staten Island*, and the bright red aircraft rose vertically and quickly disappeared to the southeast. First LT j.g. Fluke and LT j.g. Thorpe and then LT j.g. Price and Lt j.g. Calder set their fragile craft down on the 20-degree rocky slope still lashed by 35 knot winds, and the field party members struggled stiffly to climb aboard and returned to the ships. The four men described their 60-hour ordeal, their spirits high, but the strain of the experience showing in their cracked hands and lips, and black-rimmed eyes.

I would learn that this was the first of my stories to run in the *New York Times*, February 17, 1961, and in the Associated Press.

February 16: One of two U.S. Navy helicopters which yesterday rescued a scientific field party today crash-landed and burned on an ice-capped island off the Eights Coast of Antarctic. No one was injured in the accident, but flames engulfed the engine and adjoining compartments of the craft, which had been attached to the icebreaker *Staten Island*. Excessive engine smoke had been spotted. The pilots made their descent from 3,000 feet and were hovering at 20 feet searching for suitable landing space when an engine head burst and the helicopter dropped to the icy hillside. The crew members leapt clear as the burning aircraft slid sideways and backwards 300 feet down the crevassed slope. Help arrived, and all useable parts were salvaged before the burnt red machine was abandoned to Antarctica.

February 21: With work completed in the Eights Coast region, Captain McDonald directed the icebreakers to return as they had entered along the northern edge of the Thurston Peninsula. However, storm-driven ice had closed in behind the expedition and the pack was proving quite heavy to the West. The icebreakers began steering a more northerly route to circumnavigate the impassable floes.

The pack, countless tons of floating sea ice encircling the Antarctic Continent, is in constant flux. Winds and coastal tides are ever at work from above and below reconfiguring the shifting white mass. At one moment, the pack will appear as an area of ice floes each separated from the next by leads of open water. With a change in the winds the floes may close, and if the same winds persist, the edges of the ice jam together and are forced grinding and cracking upwards into pressure ridges. These ridges remain as hummocks on the surface until once again new pressures alter the face of the pack.

The expedition, now at 71 degrees 43 minutes South, 92 degrees 53 minutes West, continues its battle against the floes. A few slush-covered leads appearing to the Northwest may mark the beginning of a favorable shift in the pack.

When our big ship lay almost immobile in the ice, just a bit of open water—a *polynya* in Russian—around the hull, Dr. Roberts and I regularly took long walks around the helicopter flight deck. I had some favorite visitors occasionally: whales who rubbed along the icebreaker's underwater hull, then surfaced to blow before again submerging. The loud *phoosh* and very fishy smell when they blew was unique and exciting.

March 8: The Bellingshausen Sea Expedition yesterday won a crucial battle in its 20-day struggle against the Antarctic ice pack and is now steaming North to the freedom of the open seas. The ships have been lying hemmed in by ice along the coastline of the Thurston Peninsula.

Early on the morning of the 7th, a mile-wide lead of open water some 500 yards to the North appeared beyond the solid ice. It was decided that the *Glacier* must attempt to punch her way through the 25-foot-thick ice to take advantage of the open water before a new shift in the pack could close the lead.

Hour after hour, from eight in the morning on, the big ship backed and rammed, then backed and rammed against the tough floe, which could be crossed on foot in five minutes. Ever so slowly, the *Glacier* narrowed the distance. By two in the afternoon, radar showed that the ice was closing, and that the area of open water had begun to shrink. A six-man party with 1,500 pounds of explosives was placed on the ice by helicopter. Holes were bored and the charges dropped through and suspended 25 feet beneath the undersurface of the ice. With a push of the plunger and detonation, the white surface heaved, a plume of snow shot skyward and then settled a discolored grey with little change apparent in the pack. Three times the procedure was repeated before the men returned to the ship.

By sunset, the *Glacier* had worked her way to the area of the explosions and was within 100 yards of the lead, which had narrowed to a band 500 yards wide. The ship charged, rode high on the floe, and then for the first time in 12 hours continued forward pushing the broken ice aside and entering the open water. The explosives had done their job—the *Glacier* was steaming free.

The 6,000-ton *Staten Island* lay 10 miles to the Southwest unable to penetrate the massed floes barring her entry into the lead. Rather than attempting to ram on a direct line, the *Glacier*'s captain attacked the ice from alternate angles, breaking off wedge-shaped massive chunks and nosing them seaward. The ship's carbon-arc lights danced over the pressure-twisted ice as the *Glacier* continued to chew away at the pack. The *Staten Island* worked back and forth until at four in the morning she was able to break free. With both ships again underway, Captain McDonald directed them to keep steaming north for the final push through the pack.

Friends would later give me this clipping from the *New York Times*.

March 10: The icebreakers USS *Glacier* and USS *Staten Island* have worked northward to ice-free seas through 150 miles of Antarctic pack, successfully concluding the 1961 Bellingshausen Sea Expedition. The two ships parted company early this afternoon steaming on to new assignments for Operation Deep Freeze 1961, while en route to their homeports.

Throughout the expedition, I had been seizing moments to don parka and wool hat and go up on open decks with my nine-by-ten-inch spiral-bound sketch pad, good black pencils, charcoals, and pastels to capture some of the remarkable scenes, such as the night, carbon-arc rescue of the *Staten Island* and, in an earlier sketch from the foredeck of the *Staten Island*, the *Glacier* and *Staten Island* lying in pack ice at the edge of the Eights Coast ice shelf. The work was cold but rewarding—one could not sketch with polar mitts on. Years later, I would make high-quality copies of the art and the carbons of my news dispatches and give the originals to the Pritzker Military Library in Chicago for display and long-term safekeeping. Just before our ships parted company, I wrote to my parents:

> I think I can safely say that we, the members of this fine expedition, have barely averted spending the winter in the ice. The whole expedition has been very dramatic, and it shall be a pleasure to describe it when I finally return to the States. I am dashing this off quickly as the ships are now halfway through the pack ice on their way north, and the *Staten Island* has come alongside the *Glacier* for a while. She will take our mail and leave us as soon as we are out of the pack and proceed to her homeport in Seattle by way of Chile, stopping at Valparaiso where the mail will be dropped off to continue by airmail.
>
> We on the *Glacier* are heading for the Palmer Peninsula, which I am told is quite magnificent to see. The ship's party will be spending a lot of time positioning various islands. We will then pick up two

Canadian bug-catching biologists at a Chilean base and head East for the South Sandwich Islands. From there to Montevideo and it won't be until that time that I am finally to learn when I am to leave the *Glacier*. As it stands now, I shall either ride her all the way to Boston, which would get me home about the first of May, or get off her in Rio, flying home and shortening the time by two weeks or so. I hope that you have been able to follow the expedition in some paper. I seem to have been able to create quite a furor through a few papers with my releases.

After we departed Palmer Peninsula we steamed across the South Atlantic for the South Sandwich Islands, where we were to measure the depths of the islands' enormous ocean-floor trench. I enjoyed standing alone on an upper foredeck beneath the bridge, taking in the seascapes. I can still see shafts of sunlight cutting through the clouds and turning accompanying schools of penguins and the rolling ocean into a gleaming silver.

As it would turn out, I would stay on board the *Glacier* homeward bound via Montevideo, Rio de Janeiro, and San Juan, Puerto Rico, debarking when she called at Naval Ammunition Depot, Earle, New Jersey, to offload her ammunition in late April. During this northward passage there was another footnote to history. On April 17, when we were out in the Atlantic having just departed San Juan, the *Glacier*'s captain received orders to heave to until further instructed. It was pleasant spring weather. We waited several hours and then received fresh orders to get underway again and continue on our original course. We could not know that the Bay of Pigs invasion of Cuba was taking place just to our west and that the *Glacier*, with her helicopters and large sick bay, had been identified by the Navy for a possible contingency role.

The summer of 1961 brought good shoreside Deep Freeze work, new opportunities, and another key career decision. We had our Washington, DC, summer headquarters in a creaky, white, two-story wooden building on the Mall in the place now occupied by the Smithsonian's Hirshhorn

Museum. It was one in a maze of such buildings long since demolished that had been built for the surge of civilian and military workers during World War II.

On May 9, I was with Admiral Tyree, having written his address on Antarctic operations for delivery to the National Press Club. The chief steward on the *Glacier* had cooked steaks from a Weddell seal caught off the Palmer Peninsula, now served on toothpicks as bite-sized chunks to the correspondents and others assembled. It was quite a hit. My assignment for the summer—another marvelous challenge in my Antarctic operations—was to direct the production of a motion picture.

I commuted by bus variously from headquarters and my apartment in Georgetown through the city and across the Anacostia River to Naval Station Anacostia, the home of the Navy Photographic Center. There, in a setting of windowless tile-walled rooms steeped in the smell of developer chemicals, I began screening more than forty hours of 16 mm color film shot by our Navy photographers in the most recent and earlier expeditions. My goal was to move from this forty-hour pile of reels to a thirty-minute documentary. As ever, there were talented new civilian and Navy people to meet and work with at the center.

When I had a sense of the overall coverage, I did an informal penciled draft of how a good visual sequence might flow. Then, working with my new colleagues, I started retrieving specific reels and putting them on a hand-cranked Moviola machine, which allowed me to view slowly, go back and forth, and select the exact lengths of film I wanted from each. With that finished, photo technicians put together a rough cut of a visual. I set to work on a script that a narrator would turn into the documentary's audio. Additional lab technicians would help me with more precise cutting, appropriate sound effects, and background music sequences.

In two months' time, I found I had directed the production of what others would consider a fascinating look at Antarctic science and Navy support operations in the early 1960s. A copy of the film, *Portrait of Antarctica*, would be with Admiral Tyree when we returned to Christchurch for the jump-off to Deep Freeze '62 that September, and I would be with him for the first formal screening in a packed theater with the mayor of Christchurch in attendance. The film would then go on to be selected for screening at the 1962 Venice Film Festival.

My formal commissioned officer's active-duty contract with the Navy committed me to three years' service and was nearing completion. In midsummer 1961, as I was pushing ahead with the film, Admiral Tyree called me into his office. The big Chicago-based mapmaker and publisher Rand McNally had approached him with a proposal. Would he produce a book rich in photography on the Deep Freeze operations in Antarctica? Another publisher, Burdette and Company, specializing in Navy cruise books, had approached Rand McNally and wanted to purchase a good number of copies of the new book and bind in additional sections on the men actually serving in different Navy Antarctic units. Admiral Tyree's question to me: Would I like to be the Rand McNally book's author? If so, would I be willing to extend my active-duty service for three months, to January 1962, to ensure that the project was good and seen through to completion?

I was single. What an opportunity. I did not hesitate. My answer was yes twice over. Tyree was pleased. Such a book would be good for his command and the Navy. I was pleased. That evening, in downtown Washington on my way home, I dropped into two venerable used bookstores, searched the shelves, and found and bought four more books on Antarctic history—to get my writing mind into a higher gear. I researched and began writing at the same time that I was again packing and seeking another landlord's forbearance—not easy—on the balance of another lease.

Down we went to Christchurch; I kept writing. On to McMurdo Station, where I found a new place to hole up in the corner of one of the station's Jamesway huts. The thin floors built over packed snow were freezing. The hut's ribbed, padded fabric walls curved up and then back down again in a vertical semicircle. There was a stove. My author's retreat was hot at the top. I wrote wearing Alaskan insulated boots, padded pants, and a T-shirt. But eventually all this writing would result in *Our World in Antarctica* (1962), in which I included this poem:

Cold to the touch,
All but void of
Taste and smell,
Antarctica shares her
Polar beauty with
Man
Through his sense
Of sight.

I'd learned to love writing from my mother, which brings us to my origins and influences.

CHAPTER 2

Beginnings, 1937–1960

Ann Brewer Clift gave birth to me in Manhattan's Women's Hospital on April 24, 1937, in the midst of the Great Depression. There was excitement—the airship *Hindenburg* flew over the hospital just days before its final disastrous voyage to Lakehurst Naval Station, New Jersey. I was taken home to Greenwich Village, where we lived at 136 Waverly Place in a large eight-room apartment just off Washington Square. From our windows, we could see the Empire State building. My parents had a maid, who was friends with Eleanor Roosevelt's maid. In Mrs. Roosevelt's Washington Square apartment, while the maids visited, I played on the plush carpet, tossing social invitations piled in a large silver punch bowl.

In my own family, my mother had worked as reporter for *Time* magazine and then managing editor of *Art News Illustrated*. Her poems appeared in the *Herald Tribune* and the *New York Post*. My half-sister, Jean, from my father's earlier marriage, was three years older than me, and my brother, Scott, was three years younger. Our father, Arthur Henry Clift, had dropped out of Yale to hop trains across America while dodging the railroad cops and learning the life of a hobo. He would write a novel he never was able to publish, "The Click of the Wheels." His other early adventures included the sea—I have his 1926 Sea Service Bureau card, which sets his rating as a Deck Boy, his nationality as "Pennsylvanian," and his ship as the SS *American Shipper*.

On his first voyage out of New York, ordered to stand night bow watch, Dad had to look out for ships and hazards. He also had to regularly check that the ship's running lights were operating, and cry out, "Lights bright!" So all by himself, he stared into the night sky, turned to check the lights, and sang out, "Lights okay!" Then he turned forward again to watch in front of the ship. But suddenly he was knocked onto the foredeck. The mate had kicked him. "It's lights bright!" he barked, "not lights okay. It's lights bright." Lesson learned.

With his wanderlust satisfied, Dad went back to school and graduated from Columbia University. In the early 1930s, he opened a liquor store on Rector Street, two blocks from Trinity Church near Wall Street and the Port of New York's Battery. In 1945, when I was eight years old, Dad bought two war bonds to take me aboard the captured German U-boat *U-505*. I still see the rungs of the ladder we climbed down, and the gray-green of the submarine's interior.

Growing up in that major port city, listening to sea stories, looking at the ships moored at the piers on the Hudson River, all these nautical images and impressions helped shape my subconscious draw to the Navy. The beautiful ocean liner SS *Normandie* ended her life in the Port of New York, and I saw her lying on her side in 1942, when I was five years old.

By then the United States had entered World War II, which took its bloody course as my young mind evolved into awareness. My parents' friends in the Army or Navy would visit between assignments, telling their stories over drinks and food. I listened.

The lines for food rationing were always long. We waited—Jean, Scott, our mother, and I. Real butter was in short supply, so we were rationed squeeze-bags of white lard and a yellow coloring capsule to mix in.

Sounds of the seafaring life filled my childhood from the start. From my bedroom, the windows faced west, toward the Hudson River and the Port of New York. As ships reached and left the piers, their great steam horns blared into the skies and my consciousness. My windows shook from their sonorous force. On weekends I loved going down to the piers, feeding seagulls while watching all the excitement of this international port. New York teemed with liners, tugs, freighters, and warships.

Journalism was another big influence in my early life; my parents had many friends who were reporters, writers, or editors. Foreign correspondent Sam Pope Brewer, my mother's older brother, especially inspired me. Having joined the *Chicago Tribune* in 1936, Sam was in the Balkans in 1941, with German bombs dropping on Yugoslavia. Serbians seized him, thinking he was a German spy. He survived that mistake and moved with British forces and other correspondents to the frontlines of the North African campaign. After the war, Sam worked for the *New York Times* covering Palestine from 1947 to 1949, while Israel was planted in its midst, with deadly consequences that still reverberate today. He was bureau chief in Madrid, covered Beirut in the mid-1950s, and filed stories from Lebanon as Middle East bureau chief. My uncle told stories of drinks at the St. George's Hotel bar, where he met England's Kim Philby, later known as one of the Cambridge Three spies for the Soviet Union.

All of this high drama was lost on me at the time, as I graduated from Stanford and joined the U.S. Navy. After finishing junior high school at Friends Seminary, I'd attended Phillips Exeter Academy. My first year there was not enjoyable, at age thirteen. When I received a periodic five-dollar allowance check in the mail, I added it to a stack ready for my escape. But I never did attempt a getaway, and finally I graduated from Exeter, in 1954. (I returned, ironically, as a guest of honor in 2003 to address the entire Exeter Assembly.)

I spent the summers of 1954 and 1957 as a *New York Daily News* copy boy, working in the East Forty-Second Street building of Superman fame, with its big globe revolving in the lobby. My job was to sit on the editorial floor's long benches and jump up when a reporter or editor yelled, "Copy boy!" I ran news stories from one desk to another and carried out other tasks that today are accomplished by a "send" button. I learned journalism literally from the ground floor up.

The best part of the job was accompanying *News* photographers to the racetracks and baseball parks. The Yankees, Giants, and Dodgers were all in action at Yankee Stadium, the Polo Grounds, and Ebbets Field. Most of the photographers were heavy-smoking, heavy-drinking guys with a sense of humor and no desire to lug their heavy equipment. The copy boy was the mule, carrying the long telephoto lens and the big Speed Graphic cameras in their wooden boxes. I sat with the photographers in the parks' photo boxes hanging out over the crowds, and had the job of writing a rough caption each time I heard the click of a photo being shot. Around the seventh inning, I jammed the exposed plates into a big brown envelope, hopped a subway back to the *News* building, and rushed the glass plates to the photo lab with my scrawled captions. From there the tabloid's professional writers transformed them into news copy.

When Stanford University sent my letter of acceptance, at Exeter the gray-faced, gray-haired, tweed-jacketed prep school administrators were dumbfounded. I had earlier announced it would be either Stanford or the Navy for me, as I had no interest in the Ivy League. They'd told me I did not stand a chance.

From the moment I arrived in Palo Alto, California, the Stanford years were as rich, rewarding, and enjoyable as the prep school years had been drab and demanding. Good friends early on; I was elected a member of the freshman council. I did have to admit that, to Exeter's credit, I was better prepared than many for my classes.

Greek letter societies were new to me, but friends maneuvered me into pledging with them at Alpha Tau Omega. We played and studied hard, with lots of singing. Amazing music was available in San Francisco just a short drive away. Back on campus, we enjoyed listening to the music of another Stanford undergrad's group that he was forming with two Menlo Park Junior College students—they decided to call themselves the Kingston Trio.

In my junior year, I was elected president of Alpha Tau Omega, "Worthy Master" in fraternity parlance. With that grand title, I was surprised to receive an invitation to lunch from Stanford President Wallace Sterling. This would turn out to be my first summit—a summit of three, including Sir William Deakin, warden of St. Antony's College, Oxford, who had told Dr. Sterling he would like to meet me. Deakin, a friend of Winston Churchill, who had had a swashbuckling career with British Special Operations in World War II, parachuted into Montenegro to work with the Yugoslav partisans led by Joseph Broz Tito. There he had met my uncle Sam covering the fighting for the *Chicago Tribune*. When Sam had learned that Sir William would be visiting Stanford, he had told him to be sure to pass his best to his nephew.

I took pleasure in my journalism major, even the practical work of covering local court trials. Department head Professor Chilton R. "Chick" Bush was a good mentor, and through him I did an internship with the *San Francisco News*. The New York Giants had just moved to San Francisco, and the Dodgers to Los Angeles. At the *News*, the sports editor, intrigued by my experience at the *Daily News* as a copy boy, published a piece on May 12, 1958, with my major-league insights.

Our fraternity house, one of those with spreading lawns that reached from the main campus along fraternity row, was a handsome old stucco-covered, three-story building. One afternoon, I was out on the lawn with two or three brothers. A short, elderly man with a trim, gray crewcut passed by and asked me if he might have a word. He was curious about the almost nonstop row of windows on the third floor. That entire floor was a communal sleeping porch, I explained, and invited him in to have a look. We had completed our tour, and I was seeing him out when he introduced himself. "I am Alexander Kerensky."

I had been entertaining a principal player in the 1917 Russian Revolution. Kerensky had been prime minister of the Russian Provisional Government until he was ousted by Vladimir Lenin and went into exile. Kerensky was now at Stanford's Hoover Institution, working on his papers. Long after graduating from Stanford, as I worked with first Soviet and then Russian diplomats, admirals, and generals through the 1970s–90s,

I regaled interlocutors with that campus encounter. Invariably, the reaction ranged from disbelief to amazement to delight.

Thanks to my parents, I had been privileged in my earlier education to attend excellent schools—Friends Seminary, Phillips Exeter Academy, and Stanford University. I had learned, pried open a young mind a bit, but had not been a great academic achiever. If I enjoyed a course I earned top grades, as for journalism at Stanford. If I did not enjoy the course, I did what I had to do to pass. But as I entered my Stanford senior year in the fall of 1957, a big issue before me was not academic achievements; rather, it was military service. I had my draft card. I wanted to serve. It was plain and simple patriotism.

Four or five Alpha Tau Omega brothers were preparing for Navy service as members of the Naval Reserve Officers Training Corps. I was impressed by what they were doing, the specifics of their training, their positive commitment. I was also a bit envious. Had I been better mentally organized when I entered college, I might have applied to join their ranks. Now, on the final lap to graduation, I decided to apply for a Navy commission via Officer Candidate School (OCS). I completed the initial paperwork and received instructions in early March to proceed to an interview at Moffett Field naval air station, near the Stanford campus. Its enormous hangars had been built in the early 1930s for naval airships such as the 785-foot USS *Macon* (ZRS-5). The interview went smoothly. I asked about the possibility of serving in naval intelligence and was told that the first hurdle would be to be accepted to OCS.

After next passing the physical exam, I had to wait several weeks before receiving the good word on May 20, 1958, that I had been accepted for naval service. In the meantime, *Newsweek* magazine's executive editor, Malcolm Muir Jr., had come to Stanford to interview me and several of my classmates. Soon thereafter I wrote to him that I was joining the Navy and would seek my commission via Officer Candidate School upon graduation. He replied in a letter dated June 12, 1958, "Thank you for your letter of June 5, good luck in the Navy, and do get in touch upon your return. For your information, you were one of those who had been tentatively selected for a job. I hope we will hear from you. Sincerely, Malcolm Muir, Jr." So that was one job possibility in my back pocket following Navy service.

I graduated from Stanford and drove back to the East Coast. With one of my fraternity brothers as copilot, we made the drive nonstop. On June 23, 1958, I was sworn in to the Navy at the Naval Recruiting Center, Federal Plaza, in downtown Manhattan. My report date to Officer Candidate School in Newport, Rhode Island, was June 30 for four months' training.

On the appointed day and hour, I arrived by train in Newport and boarded a Navy bus. It was crowded. I stood next to a fairly heavy-set guy about my height. He had a big smile, thinning hair, and a loud Hawaiian sports shirt. This was Peter Boyle, the future movie star of *Young Frankenstein* fame. We immediately struck up a friendship that would stretch into the years to come.

Inside the naval station, the bus stopped and a loud voice barked, "All you stragglers line up over here!" Stragglers? But we were right on time, I thought. Chief Boatswain's Mate Scales was letting me know that Seaman Apprentice Clift was no longer in charge.

Boyle and I were assigned to Lima Company, an open barracks for eighty with a center row of back-to-back lockers and twenty double bunks on either side. We had a railed balcony looking out on Narragansett Bay. Every so often during the summer, we would see 12-meter yachts on the water preparing for the America's Cup, good visual relief from the work at hand.

There were about six hundred in our OCS Class 39, with dawn-to-post-dusk training and class work. The Navy's goal in sixteen weeks was to give us a cross section and sampling of the military and professional training that the Naval Academy and Naval Reserve Officers Training Corps graduates would receive over four years—the bare minimum to prepare us for entering the Fleet and working alongside our regular Navy contemporaries. Marching—fundamental for order and teamwork—was a must. Dawn marches in fog had a charm, as we prepared for parades. But apparently the OCS administrators had a very limited number of recordings to boom out over the loudspeakers. I know every rip, toot, and thunder of "Colonel Bogey's March" to this day and hour.

Halfway through the training, a barracks mate one bunk over—Ivy League graduate and member of one of New England's finest blueblood families—was dropped from the program. We were required to make our bunks with the sheets so taut that a quarter would bounce on them. His bunk always looked distinctly unmade. We also had to shine our black work boots to a mirror finish on the toes. He would sit cross-legged by his bunk rubbing his boots softly with expensive shoe cream and a sock. The result was no more than a warm, black glow. Peter Boyle, by contrast, was great with his boots. A born comedian, he would stop shining for a few moments, put his hands in his boots, pretend they were puppies, and have them climb all over him, jumping, licking, carrying on. In the end, the Boyle boots always had that mirror shine.

I kept my head low and worked hard. Weeks and months passed quickly. My parents came up to Newport at the end of October for graduation and commissioning. Ensign Clift in his Navy blue uniform with gold stripe and gold star on each sleeve had orders to air-ground officers training at Naval Air Station, Jacksonville, Florida. If that went well, I would have my choice of air intelligence schools at either Norfolk, Virginia, or Alameda, California. I looked forward to returning to the Bay Area.

At Alameda, another eight-week course awaited me. I was seeking certification as an air intelligence officer—intelligence for the Navy's aircraft carriers, carrier aircraft, and other air wings. I graduated well up in my class, with a choice of follow-on assignments. Having decided to keep pushing westward, I was bound for the FICPac. Ford Island / Pearl Harbor, Hawaii, would be the first operational assignment.

On January 8, 1959, I received a formal letter from FICPac's commanding officer, Captain Moynahan, extending the traditional aloha and welcome aboard. I arranged for initial housing at bachelor officers' quarters (BOQ) 11, Naval Station Pearl Harbor. I arrived in mid-March and spent my first day in the Waikiki resort area of Honolulu swept up in a huge celebration—Congress had just passed the Hawaii Statehood Act.

FICPac was located in Building 75 on Ford Island in the middle of Pearl Harbor, with Navy shuttle boats moving passengers back and forth between Landing C, Pearl Harbor, and Landing A, Ford Island, twenty-four hours a day. The remains of the battleship USS *Arizona* (BB-39) lay submerged off to starboard as the boats approached Landing A; the *Arizona* memorial would not be built until 1962. It was a short walk from the landing to FICPac past buildings still scarred by bullets from the Japanese attack. My new professional home, Building 75, was a pre–World War II trapezoidal industrial structure in the southeast quadrant of the Island.

Our mission was to provide intelligence in written, photographic, and briefing formats to the officers and crews of the ships and aircraft of the U.S. Pacific Fleet. We were in the depths of the Cold War, with most of our work highly classified. The Soviet Union was the nuclear superpower adversary. Because of my degree in journalism, it was decided to put me in charge of the Printing and Publications Division. FICPac published a large volume of books, pamphlets, reports, and folio-size documents.

Chief Lithographer's Mate Storch ran the print plant and accompanied me on an early tour. The presses gleamed; the concrete floor was buffed to a near-mirror gleam. The plant was spotless, with the lithographer's mates at attention when I arrived. I met each of the men, toured the plant, and the chief turned to face me. "Sir, thank you. These men do an outstanding job. We take pride in our work. We hope you will let us do that work." Now that was a nicely crafted message from an old pro to a brand-new ensign. Translation: We'll get the job done for you. Don't you mess it up.

From the outset, I enjoyed my division officer's responsibilities. I fully believed in the importance of the intelligence we were publishing. At the same time, I went about my junior officer administrative duties and stood my night and weekend watches. Ashore, I found two other officers with whom to rent a house in the Manoa Valley Hills above Waikiki. I bought an aging Chevy convertible to make the commute to and from Pearl along Kamehameha Highway, which was a pleasure. My friends and I had a favorite bodysurfing haunt on the eastern shore of Oahu and a nice social life, with lovely ladies galore. When December 1959 rolled around, I counted my first year of commissioned service a good one and took leave to fly to New York City to be with my parents and siblings.

In March 1960, I was notified that I would be promoted to lieutenant junior grade, effective May 1. At sea, I participated in an operational readiness inspection on board the aircraft carrier USS *Hancock* (CVA-19). I also had the chance to fly. Because senior naval aviators on the FICPac staff had to log hours for flight pay and proficiency, every few weeks they would take me along in twin-prop planes, handing me the controls periodically between islands out over the ocean.

It was in Hawaii that I got a glimpse into what would become a revolutionary new era for U.S. national intelligence. On May 1, 1960, Francis Gary Powers' U-2 spy plane was shot down while on a strategic reconnaissance mission over Sverdlovsk, USSR. The downing of the plane came just 110 days before the first successful recovery of a Corona orbiting satellite, the nation's first photo reconnaissance satellite. The space reconnaissance age had begun. While I was not cleared into the Corona program, I was privy to the gossip about the exotic missions being flown by Air Force twin-boom C-119 aircraft out of Hawaii, then trailing trapezes designed to snag payload parachutes descending over the Pacific—payloads that, I would learn, were the first returning Corona film capsules with their space-reconnaissance photography of the USSR.

As FICPac life continued, I began to find the work routine and Hawaiian climate sameness less exciting. I had been bitten by the Antarctic bug.

CHAPTER 3

From the U.S. Navy to the U.S. Naval Institute, 1961–1966

Seven chapters were planned for *Our World in Antarctica*, and by early October 1961, I had three of them in draft, huddled at my typewriter in a Jamesway hut as a member of Operation Deep Freeze 1962.

Then, on October 5, I received a letter from the U.S. Naval Institute in Annapolis, Maryland. Frank Uhlig Jr., who would edit its annual publication *The Naval Review*, asked if I might be interested in working as an editor for the Institute's flagship periodical, *Proceedings*. I had not known previously that there was a professional publishing house called the Naval Institute. I wrote back expressing interest, and the managing editor, Roger Taylor, replied that he looked forward to meeting me when I returned stateside.

I learned that the Institute had asked the Navy's Chief of Naval Information to recommend candidates for the editorial staff. My name had come up because of my news articles from the *Glacier* on the

Bellingshausen Sea Expedition. President John F. Kennedy had read some of them and told his naval aide to keep him posted on the expedition. Unbeknownst to me, then a young lieutenant junior grade, my name was recognized on high rungs of the senior Navy staff.

December 1961 bustled as I pushed to finish the book manuscript while also falling in love with a beautiful lady from Christchurch, Gretchen Anne Colombus, a graduate in geography from Canterbury University and a schoolteacher. These positives were suddenly countered by the 1961 culmination of the Berlin Crisis, with the construction of the infamous Berlin Wall. With the surrounding uncertainty as to what the fallout would be, the Navy extended my active duty for an additional twelve months, to January 1963. I was directed to leave Antarctica immediately for service in the Office of Naval Intelligence (ONI) at the Pentagon. The Bureau of Naval Personnel order was a masterpiece of brevity: "Orders 15 May 1961 as modified 28 August 1961 cancelled. When directed in Jan detached duty; report CNO duty. ACDU extended acd PL 87–117 and NAVACT 7. New tentative RAD date 31 Jan 1963."

Our courtship had been swift. I had been living off base and enjoying parties at her sister Averil's house in Christchurch. Gretchen and I met there. At first I just noticed how pretty she was, with her shining blond hair and bright smile, but as we began to talk, her wit captivated me. Happily, she also seemed to enjoy my company, and the courtship blossomed. I shared the shocking news with her. We'd already planned to be married, but now there was no time for a Christchurch wedding. She would have to follow me to Washington as soon as she could, and we would be married in the States. In the meantime, I would find us a place to live.

Some in Gretchen's family had their doubts about this "Yankee sailor skipping out." Luckily for me, my fiancée had no doubts. She got her passport and visa, packed two trunks including her mother's sewing machine, and set sail for Miami on a Dutch ocean liner in mid-December.

I wrote to the Naval Institute's Roger Taylor that I was on the move in uniform, saying I looked forward to being in touch again as soon as the situation permitted. Along with the interest *Newsweek* had expressed before I'd graduated, I now had the security of two intriguing job possibilities after my naval service.

On Saturday, February 10, 1962, Gretchen and I were married in a side-chapel service at my mother's church, the Church of the Ascension, in New York. Back at their apartment, a wedding cake and a case of chilled champagne awaited us all. Gretchen and I spent our one-night honeymoon there, in their spare bedroom. On this same day at Berlin's Glienicke Bridge, the Soviets exchanged Francis Gary Powers for their spy Rudolf Abel. We drove back to Washington in my new rear-engine Chevy Corvair.

By March, I was a junior ONI officer serving in the fifth deck of the Pentagon. The job was deadly dull after Antarctica, message-shuffling desk work. The book manuscript was in draft, and I'd brought a box full of photographs. I spent evenings and weekends selecting photos and writing captions. The future with my bride glimmered with potential— but an actual career change was going to happen only with action by me. By now the Berlin Crisis was abating, and the Bureau of Naval Personnel was having better second thoughts. I was given the option of bringing my active-duty service to a close in early June 1962. This would bring my total active service to four years to the day rather than three. There was good in that.

I contacted *Newsweek*'s Malcolm Muir Jr., only to learn he had departed and no job awaited me. It was time to bring life to the Naval Institute channel.

On May 24, Gretchen and I made an early evening drive from Georgetown to Annapolis. We had the news on the radio and learned that Mercury astronaut Scott Carpenter had been orbiting Earth in the *Aurora 7* spacecraft earlier that same day. With too much capsule fuel expended, his ocean landing site had been overshot by more than two hundred miles. The air-sea search was on as we drove. He and the capsule were recovered, and the drama added to the dinner conversation.

We met the Institute's leadership over dinner at the Chesapeake Inn, one of the finest local seafood restaurants. Three weeks later, in a letter dated June 18, 1962, Roger Taylor offered me the position of assistant editor for *Proceedings*, with a start date of July 9. By now I'd shipped the manuscript, photos, and captions for *Our World in Antarctica* to my editor at Rand McNally; the next step would be page proofs for me to review.

Roger Taylor agreed to nudge the *Proceedings* salary up a notch, and I detached from active duty on June 23. Gretchen and I found a small, white-framed house to rent in West Annapolis at 3 Shiley Street, a comfortable walk away from the U.S. Naval Academy. At the time, the independent Naval Institute had a long-term lease with the Naval Academy to occupy the second floor of its naval museum, Preble Hall. In 1999 the Institute moved up the hill to the Academy's Hospital Point, which also houses a historic graveyard and expansive athletic fields. Today the Institute resides in the renovated Beach Hall, named for famed submariner Captain Edward "Ned" Beach Jr. I would work there too, many years later, after serving on the National Security Council under four presidential administrations, and then as president of the National Defense Intelligence College. But none of that could have been known to the younger me in 1962, as I walked on July 9 from our home to Preble Hall, excited to begin my new career in journalism.

There was work to be done. As the voice and debating platform for the Naval Institute's independent forum, *Proceedings* welcomed new ideas and ideas that challenged the common wisdom—provided they met our nonpartisan standards. But the staff was in disarray, and the editor would depart before the end of the year. Stacks upon stacks of unread manuscripts spilled across my desk and an adjoining long counter. A pink editorial sheet covered each one, with unchecked little boxes and blank spaces awaiting comments from two assistant editors and the editor. In what I would dub Operation Augean Stable, I set to reading and commenting, well aware that a near-legion of unhappy, well-intentioned authors were drumming their fingers as they waited for *Proceedings* to break its silence and render judgment on their works.

As I dug out from under the stacks, I also broadened my responsibilities. The articles scheduled to be published in the September 1962 issue were the first I had a chance to put an editorial pencil to—what a privilege.

The lead story was an excerpt from Marine Colonel Robert D. Heinl Jr.'s forthcoming Naval Institute Press history, *Soldiers of the Sea*. In a powerfully written chapter, "The Right to Fight," Heinl describes the Corps' post–World War II battles for its very existence in the halls of the nation's capital. Exemplifying the Constitution's executive and legislative checks and balances, Heinl calls Commandant General Alexander A. Vandegrift's famous May 6, 1946, Bended Knee Speech to the Senate Committee on Naval Affairs "a body blow—a kick in the groin some felt—and when Congress adjourned in August the merger bill [into the U.S. Army] was unacted on."

The September 1962 issue also carried "The Strange Assignment of the USS *Lanikai*," by Rear Admiral Kemp Tolley, USN (Ret.). Tolley recounted his mission in late 1941, on orders from President Franklin D. Roosevelt, to commission the schooner *Lanikai* in the Philippines and sail her into the path of the Japanese fleet. Clearly, Tolley had come to believe that the mission was designed to draw the Japanese into sinking her and triggering the U.S. entry into World War II. The *Lanikai* set sail to the southeast and finally dropped anchor in Perth, Australia, on March 18, 1942, eighty-two days out of Manila. "My God! What are you doing here?" cried Rear Admiral William Purnell, Chief of Staff to Commander, Southwest Pacific. "You're supposed to be dead!"

On September 10, *Our World in Antarctica* was published. I was happy to read in a letter from publisher Andrew McNally III that he believed the book would "enable its readers to become more aware of the research being carried out in this most barren and isolated continent and the men and equipment that make this research possible." A positive review in the November 4 *New York Times Book Review* further bolstered my spirits, especially as it was written by Captain William R. Anderson, USN (Ret.), who had commanded the nuclear submarine USS *Nautilus* (SSN-571) on her historic first under-ice transit of the North Pole. To my elation, this was followed by reviews in newspapers across the country, several by reporters who had visited us in Antarctica.

I seemed to be on a streak of success, and at age twenty-seven, I looked forward to a future that was hazy but brimming with potential. Recognizing the new responsibilities that came with these opportunities, I applied myself and worked hard. My efforts were rewarded: The Naval Institute promoted me to editor in chief of *Proceedings* in 1963.

The first Institute year went very well. In February 1963, Superintendent of the Naval Academy Rear Admiral Charles Kirkpatrick invited me to his office to present a commendation citation and the Navy Achievement Ribbon awarded by Secretary of the Navy Fred Korth for my Antarctic work, recognizing both *Our World in Antarctica* and "Portrait of Antarctica."

On October 18, 1963, an Annapolis *Capital* headline read, "Clift New Editor of *Proceedings*." The story reported, "A. Denis Clift has been named editor of the United States Naval Institute *Proceedings*, and his appointment has been confirmed by the Naval Institute Board of Control headed by Admiral David L. McDonald," who would go on to serve as Chief of Naval Operations from 1963 to 1967. The *Capital* piece went on, "Clift is one of the youngest men ever to head the 90-year-old professional magazine. Clift joined the staff of the Naval Institute in July 1962 as an assistant editor after being released to inactive duty by the Navy."

What was it that I was now commanding? *Proceedings* was a monthly professional journal in 6¼-by-9½-inch format. It ran 170 to 200 pages per issue, two columns per page, with twenty-five to forty monthly ads on average and with a circulation of 65,000 copies.

Our printer, the George Banta Company in Menasha, Wisconsin, produced a handsome product—heavy, glossy, clay-coated white stock paper, each print character of Baskerville type individually set in monotype. The covers used heavier LusterCote stock for four-color printing. Each of the thirty-two-page signature of pages was sewn into each issue, just as in high-quality hard-covered books. I would learn that the sewn bindings had been introduced during Fleet Admiral Chester W. Nimitz's second tour as president of the Naval Institute's board of control. As a young officer, in 1912 Nimitz had published his first *Proceedings* article on submarine warfare. He used the journal as a reference and groused one day that it would not stay open to the page he had turned to. Stitching the signatures solved the problem.

As *Proceedings* editor, I had overall responsibility, set editorial policy, and oversaw the selection of articles, layout, and final editing of each issue. I supervised a staff of nine—four assistant editors, two associate editors, one administrative assistant, and two secretaries. On any given day, we had three months' issues in different stages of production. While guiding the review of unsolicited manuscripts, I also solicited manuscripts.

Active-duty officers served as directors on the Institute's board of control. They met every month with the Institute's executive secretary, editorial director, and me to comment and pass judgment on the article we had earlier mailed to them with our recommendation for publication. I prepared thoroughly for the board meetings and was honored to be in the company of the sharpest naval professionals: two successive Chiefs of Naval Operations and extraordinary officers such as Captain Edward L. Beach Jr., who in 1955 had published *Run Silent Run Deep*, and then–Rear Admiral William P. Mack, who would later publish books including a World War II destroyer series and naval officers' guides, and in 1972 would become superintendent of the Naval Academy.

Our guiding philosophy was that the essays we selected must be authoritative, and not written by our staff. To provide useful information for Naval Institute members and the broader professional readership, we sought the views of those in the Sea Service, prime participants, and experts in their fields. My responsibility was to work with authors to ensure that their work met our high professional, nonpartisan standards. Good substance and high quality were my imperatives, in an editing process that sometimes meant working with rough writing to produce a smooth, easily understandable essay.

As part of this job, I also became a senior leader in a professional society treasured by its members. One of my great pleasures was regular personal contact I had with authors and members, including senior service leaders, foreign officers, academicians, and policymakers specializing in naval and national security affairs. People liked to drop by my office, usually with a smile. I learned from them, and *Proceedings* benefited from their interaction with us.

The importance of networking had been clear to me since my Stanford days as president of Alpha Tau Omega, and the Navy and Naval Institute reinforced that foundation. Fresh from my cooperation on Antarctic expeditions, I invited the Soviet naval attaché for lunch at a Washington restaurant on the shores of the Anacostia River. As we broke bread, a destroyer came upriver en route to the Washington Navy Yard, dressing the scene very nicely. My goal in the meeting was to explore the possibility of finding an author in their Navy who might wish to write for *Proceedings*. The idea must have come as something of a shock to my luncheon partner—and been reported to Moscow—coming as it did a little more than a year after the Cuban Missile Crisis.

A few months later, I was invited to a reception at the Soviet embassy, where I met Assistant Secretary of the Treasury for Law Enforcement James A. Reed. As we shared a drink and chatted, I learned that in March 1943, he had shared a stateroom with Lieutenant John F. Kennedy while sailing for the Pacific on board the transport USS *Rochambeau* (AP-63). During the long westward passage, they debated politics and became friends. Both fought the war from PT boats. When Kennedy was elected president, he named Reed Treasury assistant secretary in the policy post overseeing the United States Coast Guard. In just a few months, Reed would have the president on board the tall ship cutter *Eagle* to address the importance of the Coast Guard mission and launch the funding for a new generation of medium-endurance and high-endurance cutters.

In 1965, I wrote Reed to invite him to contribute the lead article for the August issue of *Proceedings*, which would focus on the 175th anniversary of the Coast Guard. He wrote "Renaissance of the U.S. Coast Guard," which opened, "Like Proteus of Greek legend, the Coast Guard must be capable of assuming many different shapes on short notice." Our correspondence continued after he departed the Johnson administration to return to private law practice in New York.

I was still in my twenties, with networking skills that I'd learned earlier and was now continuing to develop. While on active duty in ONI, one of my jobs had been to screen incoming diplomatic cables from around the world and route them to the right desks. There had been a crisis in Argentina at the time, and I had been impressed by the under-pressure reporting of Robert McClintock, the U.S. ambassador to Buenos Aires. Now at my *Proceedings* editor's desk, I learned that he had been one of our authors for several years. To my delight, I found he was in Newport, Rhode Island, serving as State Department adviser to the president of the Naval War College. I had on my desk an article that had not been up to our standards, but its ideas were worth examining. The unsolicited manuscript called for the creation of a new numbered U.S. Navy Fleet, with the mission of operating off Central and South America. I made contact with Ambassador McClintock and told him of the pros and cons I wanted examined, and he accepted the challenge.

He wrote the lead article for the October 1965 *Proceedings*, "Latin America and Naval Power," a nicely researched and thoughtful essay that concluded, "We should ask ourselves whether there is a requirement for an additional numbered U.S. Fleet, similar to the Sixth Fleet in the Mediterranean. I should say unequivocally that *the answer is no*." There were no challenges to this from our readership.

Rob McClintock, some thirty years my senior and a fellow Stanford alumnus, became my good friend. He would serve as one of my principal references when I applied to the London School of Economics and, later, when I applied from London for my first position in the Johnson White House.

I was recruiting high-profile individuals, but I was also determined to find more of the best thinking and writing of naval officers still "below the horizon," who were moving up in their careers. Research papers were a formal requirement at the Naval War College. I felt that many of those papers, including the good ones, were being read, graded, then filed away, never to see the light of day. I arranged with the college president that I would visit Newport at the end of the academic year to screen the completed research. The papers would stay there, but I was then able to contact the authors and recommend that they submit their work to *Proceedings* for consideration. Good authors emerged and were published.

I enjoyed so many privileges as *Proceedings* editor, and I took none of it for granted. I was and remain filled with gratitude for the opportunities. I went to sea on the world's first nuclear-powered merchant ship, the NS *Savannah*, which had luxury passenger quarters and accommodations—an Atoms-for-Peace initiative of the Eisenhower administration. I gave an address to the Maritime Bar Association in Washington, and I represented both the Institute and the Academy when the tall ship Indonesian barquentine KRI *Dewaruci* made a midsummer port call in Annapolis. I even had my own corporate credit card!

Meanwhile, on the home front, Gretchen was enjoying life in America. Exceedingly talented and creative, she built sets and designed costumes for the Children's Theater, studied watercolor, and before long was producing sought-after paintings. Her mother's sewing machine, now with a U.S. electrical transformer, whirred as Gretchen created elegant new clothes.

I was enjoying the job mightily, but in late 1965, Gretchen and I had a heart-to-heart talk. There was a big world out there, beyond Annapolis. We were having such a good present-day life that we risked just doing more of the same, sliding deeper into a comfort zone instead of expanding on our lives and professional accomplishments. It was time to explore.

From my Antarctic explorations and my work as editor, I had developed a growing interest in the law of the sea and major international oceans issues, both of which were at the time rising in importance, nationally and internationally. But to get into this field professionally at what was now an appropriate level, I had to have better credentials. This meant doing more of my own research and writing, as part of earning a first-class graduate degree in international relations and politics. But where and how?

In late 1965, I had given hard thought to the graduate school that would be the very best in terms of challenge, reward, and professional credentials. My chosen field of study was international relations. As I researched, the London School of Economics and Political Science continued to rise in appeal. It had long since outgrown its late nineteenth-century Fabian

Society offshoot roots, and in the 1960s was a highly selective university highly regarded internationally for teaching and guiding research across the entire spectrum of social sciences. Its student body—with sharp young men and women from every corner of the world—was its particular charm. How better to study international relations than with foreigners in a foreign setting of great acclaim?

CHAPTER 4

From London to the National Security Council, 1966–1971

On September 8, 1966, Gretchen and I set out on our new adventure, excited and surprised by my acceptance into the University of London's renowned London School of Economics and Political Science (LSE). Our ship—the SS *United States*—towered above Manhattan's pier No. 86 on the Hudson River, with a long black hull and white superstructure sweeping aft. Colossal raked smokestacks crowned the ocean liner, glowing against the sky in red, white, and blue. This was the champion, and we walked up her gangway for our transatlantic passage. Family and friends from New York and Annapolis came on board to give us a champagne sendoff. We were on top of the world.

Back at the Naval Institute, retired Navy Commander R. T. E. Bowler Jr. had given me a good sendoff. He announced my departure in *Proceedings*, thanking me for a job well done since I'd joined the Institute in July 1962. The Institute had done well for me too, sparking curiosity about the international politics of the oceans. The interest had over time grown to the point that I was inspired to pursue in-depth studies through working on a master's degree at LSE, cofounded (apparently reluctantly) by George Bernard Shaw. LSE, I thought, would offer a solid good preparation for service in government.

I'd learned through a letter dated March 2, 1966, that I would be a candidate for the MSc degree in international politics. Dr. Anne H. Bohm, secretary of the graduate school, informed me that the 1966–67 academic year would comprise three terms: Michaelmas, October–December; Lent, January–March; and Summer, April–June. I was advised to be in London for registration between September 12 and 30. We would be funding the entire year abroad with our meager savings—a working budget for the year of $7,500.

Gretchen and I had booked a tourist-class cabin just off the bar—at a cost of $458.50 for us both (a hefty amount in 1966 for a young couple of limited means). As the liner got underway outside New York harbor, we breathed in salty breezes on the deck, leaning over the railing while marveling at the transparent blue-green waves that crashed onto the pointed bow as it plowed through Atlantic swells.

On a whim, I pulled from my wallet a *Proceedings* business card and found the tourist-class head purser. Handing it to him, I asked that he have it sent to the ship's commodore, Rear Admiral L. J. Alexanderson, USNR. He snatched it from me coolly, clearly disdainful of this presumptuous economy-class passenger.

Still, he took the card. And the frost melted as he glanced at it. "Mr. Clift! You have resigned as editor of the Naval Institute *Proceedings*. I just read it in the new issue. I get it every month! Of course I will send your card up to the commodore—right away."

Late the next morning, the *United States* steamed at her cruise speed of more than thirty knots. Out on the Atlantic, she was driving steady as a rock, producing a strong wind aft from her bows—no pitching, yawing, or rolling, just a slight tremble in the pale-green steel decks beneath our feet as the ship's great hull cut through the ocean.

Gretchen and I were enjoying a pre-lunch Bloody Mary at the bar when a uniformed staff member approached us. "Mr. and Mrs. Clift?"

"Yes."

"The commodore extends his compliments and invites you to move to a first-class suite on the sundeck, if that is satisfactory."

Indeed it was. In our new, spacious quarters, we could relax on a sofa or armchairs, with a thick rug underfoot. Cut flowers on the coffee table brightened the suite, with sun streaming in through portholes from the sundeck. There was a big private bath, and the double bed was enormous. Later that day, we joined Commodore Alexanderson for cocktails. We would also be his guests for dinner. The voyage was a joy, and we arrived in Southampton exhilarated, ready for our year in the British Isles. We had deeply enjoyed our years at the Naval Institute, now with a fresh appreciation of the high respect that *Proceedings* had earned amid its audience.

I had no way of seeing then that much later in life, in 2009, following a very rewarding forty-three-year federal career, I would rejoin the Institute and stay there for fourteen more years. But now, in 1966 on board the *United States*, Gretchen and I shared an excitement that reverberates still today in my memory.

We arrived in Southampton, England, on September 13 midday, after a quick 2:47 a.m. stopover at Le Havre. The passage from New York to France—3,197 miles—had taken four days, seven hours, and forty-nine minutes, at an average speed of 30.79 knots. But now our admiration for the ship's efficiency, and our own serenity, transformed quickly into focus as we bustled through the packed British customhouse. We found our trunks as they came ashore, marshaled our luggage (temporarily minus a typewriter), cleared customs, and caught a cab to the train station. We were bound for London.

We arrived at Waterloo Station late, about 9:30 p.m., and got a cab. The Chesham Hotel had been recommended by a lifelong friend of my father, Arthur Stull, who was there to welcome us with food and drink and send us off to bed. Next morning we woke to the sound of horse hooves clopping. The Chesham, on Belgrave Square, was just a stone's throw from Buckingham Palace, and members of the Queen's Royal Horse Guard were en route from their stables to morning exercise.

I made my way to the LSE, muttering about the opposite flow of traffic. The "campus" was just more city buildings squashed together just off the Strand on Houghton Street. This was not the sprawling Stanford campus. I was pleased: This new life aimed at a much higher career.

After collecting the papers that would be needed for registration, I received directions to the student union in St. Clements Building "to inquire about flats" to rent. I was advised to buy a copy of the map book *Geographic London A–Z* and to make an appointment at the University of London Union Accommodations Bureau.

A day or two later, Gretchen and I located the London Accommodations Bureau at 390 Oxford Street and climbed two flights into a long, colorless office packed with people. We were given a card, waited, and then called forward by a young woman. Her first question: "How much are you willing to pay?" We proudly announced our agreed-upon budget figure, eight to nine guineas, to which she replied, "Oh dear." When we told her Gretchen was expecting our firstborn in January, she said, "Oh dear. I'm afraid you won't get a flat." She called a landlady, and they talked about the baby. "The landlady says no."

We left with her list in hand, had a sandwich, and then walked to a real estate agent on Cromwell Road—not a single flat in our price range. We visited several more agents in the Kensington area, with "No" as our answer. Finally, an agent said he had a flat at thirteen guineas on Old Brompton Road. We went to a street roaring with traffic, into a house that was being torn apart. On the third floor, we stepped from a large, empty room into a bedroom full of Victorian furniture. No kitchen, just a shallow closet hiding a one-burner hotplate and an icebox about the size of a wastepaper basket. The toilet and bath were shared, half a floor down, on the landing. This was a "No" for us.

We looked in Hampstead on London's north side, where the underground, elevated in Golders Green, clattered by right outside the window. Another "No thank you."

Our week's reservation at the Chesham was ending. Gretchen was almost five months pregnant and needed to stop marching around the city. The calendar was not waiting either, as the academic year rapidly approached. It was now September 19, and classes started in October.

Under pressure, we found a tiny short-term rental in Knightsbridge, off an alleyway just around the corner from Harrods Department Store. Apparently Audrey Hepburn had once stayed there—if that was true, it would definitely have been short term. This was a dark studio that combined a sitting room and bedroom. I think there was a window, but it was behind a heavy curtain that opened onto a brick-wall air shaft. The place was cold. We fed shillings into the meter of a gas-fueled fireplace burner decorated with red leather flames. There was one other combined room: a closet-sized kitchen and bathroom. A tiny stove, refrigerator, and sink lined two sides of this mini-space, with the toilet sitting on the third. The door accounted for the room's fourth side. In the middle, a shower drained into the center of the floor, with showerhead, circular shower rod, and pushback curtain hanging from the ceiling.

We were young. We laughed—and kept up the search.

Luck for the lucky comes to those who persevere. We watched the newspapers' classified ads relentlessly and early. Suddenly there it was in *The Times*, two lines: a flat in Kensington. Out we charged. The second-floor apartment at 37 Rosary Gardens was beyond our dreams, newly restored, with high ceilings, a white living room and dining room with new gold carpeting, and two big windows that overlooked the quiet residential street. The large, white-tiled bathroom with full porcelain shower and tub also faced the front of the building, shielded by frosted glass. The bedroom, furnished with a double bed, closet, dresser, and ample space for a crib, was in the back, where another large window looked out on a peaceful scene of backyard gardens. The kitchen was in an alcove to the right as we entered the flat—small as always by American standards, but comparatively grand to us, especially given our recent lightning education on housing availability.

The absentee landlady wished to rent immediately. The price was half again what we had planned to pay, but we grabbed it. This was in one of the loveliest residential parts of central London, halfway between the greens of Kensington Gardens / Hyde Park and Chelsea on the Thames.

Just two blocks away, there was a direct underground line to the London School of Economics. We would scrimp and trim elsewhere. We signed the lease for 37 Rosary Gardens, our new home.

It hadn't been nonstop stress while we'd searched. We'd also enjoyed some tourist time, including on Sunday, September 18, when we joined a grand congregation of some three thousand at Westminster Abbey to attend the Service of Thanksgiving for the Victory achieved in the Battle of Britain in the Year 1940. The Central Band of the Royal Air Force played as the audience was stirred with hymns, prayers, lessons, and pageantry. The service concluded with a blessing, the "Call of the Royal Air Force," "The Last Post," and finally "Reveille." The Ensign of the Royal Air Force marched with the band to the Abbey's west end as the famous bells rang.

But it was time now to turn my attention toward academia. Graduate studies at the LSE were typical: coursework, research papers, written exams. Aside from scheduled classroom hours and heavy readings, I met periodically with a tutor. Before arriving in London, I'd decided to make a point of attending classes, even though this was optional in Britain. As a naval officer and then an editor, I'd been away from the academic world for eight years; now I had to retool myself into a student.

I was paying for everything this time. To succeed, it was essential that I earn high grades and the degree. I had to become a consummate scholar. This necessity was etched into my mind by the head of the International Relations Department, who informed our class at the end of the first term, just before exams, that we would be sorted into three categories depending on how we fared. Those who did poorly would be asked to leave. The next tier, those who did fairly well, would be allowed to sit exams for the degree after two years of study. Finally, those who did well would be allowed to sit the exam after one year. The Clifts were on a one-year, make-or-break budget.

My tutor and the LSE library were major inspirations. The influential nuclear-age strategic thinker Dr. Coral Mary Bell was my tutor. We hit the right notes from the beginning. She looked positively on my relative worldliness and background as an author and editor. Pointing to important real-world research subjects close at hand, Dr. Bell assured me I was on the right track while also guiding me through the intricacies of the master's program.

Large deposits of natural gas had been discovered off the Netherlands beneath the North Sea. The nations bordering the North Sea—Great Britain, Norway, Denmark, West Germany, the Netherlands, and Belgium—were hard at work negotiating their exact national seabed boundary lines. This would be my first major research project. When I turned in my paper, Dr. Bell had high praise and guided its submission to the journal of the Royal Institute of International Affairs, *The World Today*. "North Sea Gas: A Case Study in International Cooperation" was published in April 1967. I was of course delighted, especially as a graduate student, to see my article second in the issue, right after "Sterling and the Common Market" by George Rowland Stanley Baring, Third Earl of Cromer and banker.

The LSE library was as disorganized as Dr. Bell was effective. It was noisy, with books scattered everywhere and a card catalog that was irrelevant—a far cry from my memories of hiding away in Stanford's library stacks for some essential hours of reading and cramming, retreating from the joys of fraternity life.

In search of peace and quiet, I developed a network of other libraries. Eventually this grew to eight across central London, starting with the reading room in the Geological Museum, quiet and an easy walk from Rosary Gardens. There was also a good Royal Navy reading room a bit west of our flat. The highly authoritative Institute for Strategic Studies was just a short walk up the Strand from the LSE, and its director, Alistair Buchan, welcomed me warmly as the former *Proceedings* editor. At the same time, this wealth of London libraries increased my contacts and research resources, so that overall, the hopeless LSE library did me a good turn.

While I was reading and writing, Gretchen was receiving good prenatal care. Our beloved son Alexander Eugene was born at Queen Charlotte's Hospital on January 12, 1967. I rushed to obtain his U.S. citizen's papers from our embassy, and we successfully negotiated with the landlady to keep our new Hyde Park pram in the lobby. Life was a joy, and extremely busy.

Looking to the future, I kept networking, wangling an invitation in early spring to the Cunard Line's Royal Festival Hall reception to unveil a five-foot model of the *Q4*, its new ocean liner being built in Scotland. Again pulling out my *Proceedings* card, I next persuaded the John Brown Shipyard to fly me up to Glasgow to walk the decks of a great new ship, the future *Queen Elizabeth II* still abuilding. I would repay this act of good faith by publishing a major piece on the ship, ". . . Long Live the Queen," in the April 1968 *Proceedings*.

With the third and final term's exams looming, while Gretchen and I both battled infectious hepatitis that had been passed to us by a weekend host in Cambridge, I sat down at the typewriter to address the Honorable Hubert H. Humphrey, vice president of the United States, on our 37 Rosary Gardens letterhead:

June 5, 1967

Dear Mr. Vice President:
I am taking the liberty of writing you in your capacity as Chairman of The National Council in Marine Resources and Engineering Development, as I wish to serve the U.S. government in the direction of its national and international oceanic program and feel qualified to provide valuable service in a responsible, executive way.

By way of brief personal introduction, I am 30 years old, a graduate of Phillips Exeter Academy and Stanford University (A.B. 1958), a former U.S. naval officer (Lieutenant, USNR), and holder of the Secretary of the Navy's Commendation for Achievement. I am the author of *Our World in Antarctica*, Rand McNally & Company, 1962. From 1963 to mid-1966 I was Editor of the United States Naval Institute *Proceedings*. During the years of my editorship I took intense interest in America's rapidly expanding oceanographic/oceanologic program and in its scientific, industrial, national security and foreign policy implications. Considering man's use of the seas and the fact that such use could only increase radically as technologies evolved, more money was invested, and nations' needs for space and resources continued to grow, it seemed to me that we were on the threshold of an era in which more and more governmental attention would have to be given to national and international oceanic activities.

With the above considerations in mind, I resigned from the *Proceedings* in order to undertake the present year of postgraduate study (M.Sc. degree) at The London School of Economics and Political Science in the field of international politics, with a view towards applying such knowledge in its oceanic context. At the same time, I have been continuing independent research on international maritime activities, and during the current year I have published or will soon be publishing the following papers: "North Sea Gas: A Case-Study in International Cooperation," April 1967 issue, *The World Today*, monthly journal of the Royal Institute of International Affairs; and "North Sea Gas and Oil Exploration," scheduled for publication as the lead article in the September/October issue of *Oceanology International*.

Mr. Vice President, I stand ready to provide whatever references, personal or professional background information, or examples of published work that the Council on Marine Resources and Engineering Development might require of me. I sincerely hope that it will be possible for me to serve the government in this field.

And off the letter went.

I boned hard for the final exams at the LSE, and did well. Dr. Bell advised that I had come within a whisker of graduating with distinction; only one person in our class would receive that honor. Formal University of London mimeograph notification of the award of degree arrived in August, and the elegant, full-color, engraved MSc diploma several months later.

In mid-April, I went to the embassy to obtain our son Alex's passport. With schoolwork over, we were planning a trip to the Netherlands, and then back to America. From the splendid experience of our sundeck suite on the SS *United States*, I had learned that with the new commercial jets flying the wealthy across the Atlantic first class in a matter of hours, the big ocean liners were struggling to fill their first-class accommodations. I went to the Cunard Lines booking office to inquire about costs and accommodations for a return passage for three on the majestic RMS *Queen Mary*—on what would be her third-to-last crossing ever. To my delight, I was offered a first-class suite at an economy-class rate, with an August 2 sailing.

Meanwhile, my letter to the vice president produced a June 15 response from one of his assistants, Dr. Edward Wenk Jr., advising that while there were no staff openings on the National Council, he had forwarded my letter to the Interagency Committee on Oceanography. That committee's executive secretary, Dr. Edwin Shykind, wrote on June 27, "There is a distinct possibility that a position may become available on ICO staff in the very near future. It would involve working in the international aspects of U.S. oceanography especially as they influence our scientific and political relationships with other countries." He invited me, if interested, to submit my résumé and Federal Form 57, or its equivalent, at my earliest convenience.

There was excitement at 37 Rosary Gardens, not only about the possibility of a job but about one I had dreamed about almost two years earlier. I wrote back immediately stating my interest and requesting a Form 57. On July 18, 1967, Dr. Shykind again wrote enclosing the form, requesting its completion, and asking me to be in touch upon my return to the United States to see if the committee was still interested. If so, an interview would be arranged in Washington. One reads and rereads every word of such correspondence carefully. His concluding paragraph gave hope: "In the meantime, we look forward to further correspondence with you. Again, our thanks for your interest."

Packing, closing up the flat, and preparing to leave London had left us very tired. We were still regaining strength from the ravages of hepatitis months before. We did not realize that we had not yet plumbed the depths of exhaustion. Two to three days before the sailing, our scheduled port of departure was closed. British dockworkers went on strike. Shepherding our trunks and other baggage, we made our way with a fairly orderly mob from the train in Southampton to a terminal where, after a few hours, we would board a ferry for the overnight English Channel crossing to the port of Cherbourg, France, where the *Queen Mary* awaited us.

It was dark and the ferry was packed. People were jammed together, in my view to the point of unseaworthiness and danger. I was desperately worried about Gretchen and seven-month-old Alex. There was smoke and noise; the bars were roaring. I inched and inched my way to the ferry's staff office, where people were clamoring for attention. A good ship's soul lent an ear. I described my wife's health, noted that we had a young baby—and, once again, politely offered that magical *Proceedings* card. The ship's officer and I navigated our way back to Gretchen and Alex, and he led us discreetly through the masses to a tiny cabin with a single bunk for the night.

The voyage home on the *Queen Mary* was elegant, culminating an extraordinary year. Our wood-paneled suite, with its dressing table, sofa, alcove for the crib, double bed, and private bath, had two large brass-rimmed portholes we kept open to the sea. The design and details of the *Queen Mary*'s great rooms spoke to the care the Cunard Line's shipbuilders gave to a queen in the 1930s. During one of our strolls on her long decks, the ship's commodore hailed us and told Alex he was a fine young lad.

My father, Artie, was pierside with his pickup truck for all our gear when we disembarked and cleared customs in New York. Mother Ann was at the front door to welcome us to the 136 Waverly Place apartment, my childhood home, and now our temporary abode. My parents were thrilled to meet, hold, and hug their grandson.

I was soon on the phone with Dr. Shykind. Yes, they felt my background and qualifications warranted their further consideration. He and members of his staff wanted to schedule an interview. We set a date for a meeting in their Washington Navy Yard Offices. If all went well, that was where I would be working. But where would we live?

When we sailed for England, we had left our hearts in Annapolis. On a wild chance, I called our former landlady. She welcomed the call. The dentist who had rented 3 Shiley Street for the year away had not renewed his lease. He had been dissatisfied with the lack of central heating. She said she would be pleased to have us as tenants again. The house was available whenever we wished to move in; the rent, of course, would have to go up—from $125 to $140 a month. Dame Fortune had again smiled on us.

Life at Shiley Street was a great part of our overall major transition. Gretchen was a first-class chef. Her table held greens from her garden, and throughout the entire house, vases of flowers she had grown brightened the spaces.

The new professional world I was entering in 1967 had just been shaped by legislation that Congress had recently passed: the Marine Resources and Engineering Act of 1966. The mood in Washington and in informed circles across the land was that the nation should be giving as much priority to the oceans—inner space—as it was giving to the Apollo program and our drive for the moon.

The law required the president to develop and conduct a comprehensive and coordinated program of marine science, engineering, and resource activities. A cabinet-level National Council on Marine Resources and Engineering Development, chaired by the vice president, was to guide this work. In parallel, the law created the Commission on Marine Science, Engineering, and Resources, to be chaired by Ford Foundation Chairman Julius A. Stratton—the Stratton Commission—to prepare a report for Congress evaluating the nation's ocean needs, best future direction, and best future governmental structure. The common wisdom was that because there was a National Aeronautics and Space Administration for exploration of space, there should also be a new national-level agency, a wet NASA, for the oceans.

With the new law in force, the Interagency Committee on Oceanography, which had reported to the Federal Council on Science and Technology, now became the Committee on Marine Research, Education, and Facilities reporting to the Council on Marine Resources and Engineering

Development. Although we were in the Executive Office of the President, we were housed in the Washington Navy Yard's Building 159E, a hulking old warehouse overlooking the Anacostia River, converted for office use but with giant freight elevators for vertical transport.

As soon as I started the new job in October 1967, I was assigned as executive secretary of the committee's Panel on Interagency Programs and International Cooperation in Oceanography (PIPICO), chaired by an official at the Department of State. There was a warm welcome by all. I soon had a second desk at State and shuttled back and forth between the offices by foot, cab, and buses. This was a busy time, in the United Nations and in national capitals. There was growing international interest in international versus national ownership of unexploited mineral wealth such as manganese nodules thanks to the notion that untold billions could be earned from such metals.

There was a growing movement toward more cooperative exploration of the oceans, with a call for an International Decade of Ocean Exploration. Preparatory work was underway for sweeping new law of the sea negotiations, with a call for a new international law of the sea convention. A group headquartered in Paris, the Intergovernmental Oceanographic Commission (IOC) of the United Nations Educational, Scientific and Cultural Organization (UNESCO), was the international focal point for scientific exploration of the oceans. Our PIPICO panel was the body that prepared for and staffed U.S. participation in the commission. By early 1968, I was readying for my first IOC mission to Paris. This work would continue to grow through the summer of 1969, and our chairmen of delegations sometimes double-hatted me with both U.S. responsibilities and much-appreciated on-loan responsibilities to the IOC International Secretariat.

Throughout this period, I was writing and publishing on oceans issues. I gave permission to have my LSE essay on North Sea gas published as a college textbook chapter. The Mexican publisher Limusa/Wiley produced a Spanish-language edition of *Our World in Antarctica*. *Proceedings* published my analytical essay on law of the sea and seabed issues, "Of Diplonauts and Ocean Politics," in the July 1970 issue.

Meanwhile, by mid-1968, the Stratton Commission had moved from field trips, research, and hearings to preparation of the first draft of its report to Congress. The executive director of the commission staff, Dr. Samuel Lawrence, aware of my writings and the fact that I had been *Proceedings* editor, made a formal request through my chain of command that I be seconded to the commission on a part-time, overtime basis to help with the report, selecting its photographs and illustrations and preparing the captions. I was given a desk—my third office—in the New Executive Office Building across Pennsylvania Avenue from the White House.

As drafting of the commission report proceeded, staff and commissioners were not pleased to discover that they had virtually ignored national security issues in their chapters. This was not accidental. The Navy had taken great care to keep the commission from dabbling in defense issues that were beyond its charter. However, now that the text of the report was emerging, the omission was glaring. I was given the additional assignment of writing a bylined commission report staff paper, "Defense Interests and the National Oceanographic Program," that would be published by the Department of Commerce Clearing House for Federal and Scientific Information and referenced in the commission's final report to Congress.

Our Nation and the Sea: A Plan for National Action, Report of the Commission on Marine Science, Engineering and Resources, the Stratton Report, was published in January 1969. On February 19, a letter from Julius Stratton arrived at our 3 Shiley Street home.

> Dear Mr. Clift:
> This morning there arrived on my desk, fresh from the press, the final copy of *Our Nation and the Sea*. As I leafed through the pages, I felt a sense of satisfaction that I am sure will be shared by everyone on our wonderful team that made this report what it is. There were times for all of us that it seemed impossible that the task would ever be finished. But we did finish, and I think we can all be proud of the result.

I am very conscious of how much we owe to you for your contribution to our effort and most especially for the skill with which you selected the pictures that have so enlivened the whole report. I know that I speak for every member of the Commission in expressing our deepest appreciation for your help and loyal support.

With my own warmest thanks and good wishes,
Sincerely yours, s/Julius A. Stratton

When the commission was established, the original timetable for delivery of the report had been autumn 1968, prior to the presidential election. Why was there a slippage of months in the delivery date? If there is formal documentation, I have not seen it, but for those of us laboring in the vineyards at the time, the explanation is a classic Washington political tale.

With the commission well into its work in mid-1968, Vice President Hubert Humphrey, a champion of greater priority for the national ocean program, received the Democratic presidential nomination. Why not hold publication of the report until after he was elected? He would work with Congress and act on its recommendations swiftly and most favorably. He would push through the commission's key structural recommendation that a new national-level agency, the National Oceanographic and Atmospheric Agency (NOAA), the wet NASA, be established.

But Humphrey's Republican opponent, former Vice President Richard Nixon, won the election. By the spring of 1969, Nixon's administration let it be known that the president's priority was the environment, not the oceans. He established an environmental council in the Executive Office of the President and launched work on the creation of the Environmental Protection Agency. The proposed NOAA faded into the shadows, and would eventually reemerge to be established as a much-diminished subset of the Department of Commerce.

As I neared the two-year mark in my Navy Yard life—a veteran Annapolis-to-Washington commuter by now—Dr. Wenk, executive secretary of the National Council on Marine Resources and Engineering Development, wrote to invite me to join the staff of the council as executive secretary of its centrally important Committee for Policy Review (CPR), reporting directly to him with other additional assignments as he might decide. This would be work of a higher profile, another promotion—with more pay, of importance to a growing family. On January 7, 1969, late at night, it had been snowing and we had driven carefully to Anne Arundel Hospital. We shared the joy of the birth of our second son, Tyrone Christopher Clift.

I would have a grand office in the council's suite of offices in the New Executive Office Building at Seventeenth Street and Pennsylvania Avenue NW—but without a parking space. Against all odds, in the talks leading up to my acceptance of the assignment, I negotiated a highly coveted parking spot in the building's basement garage.

The new role had me hustling with the Committee for Policy Review, where most of the real, high-level interagency work of the council took place. With my great visibility in the post, I was also walking through fresh portals. In May 1970, the chairman of the National Academy of Science's Committee on Oceanography wrote to the council's executive secretary to request that I be loaned part-time to participate with the academy's International Marine Science Affairs Panel in the writing of its "broad-scale report on tasks pertaining to the ocean and its use that need to be done through international cooperation, mechanisms required to accomplish such tasks, and needs for United States government policy in this regard."

My principal collaborator would be the panel's chairman, University of Washington Professor of Law William T. Burke, one of the nation's leading authorities on law of the sea. There was good teamwork. The report was completed and went to press, to emerge as a National Academy of Sciences softcover book. In February 1971, I received a warm letter of thanks from Bill Burke expressing his gratitude for the Clift chapter on global services.

On September 25, 1970, a letter on White House letterhead from Counselor to the President Daniel P. Moynihan was hand-delivered to my office. I was invited to serve as secretary of the U.S. delegation to the Conference on Pollution of the Sea by Oil Spills, being held by the Committee on the Challenges of Modern Society (CCMS) of the North Atlantic Treaty Organization (NATO) in Brussels in early November.

Moynihan, distinguished Harvard professor and future senator from New York, had a wide-ranging portfolio as one of the most senior members of President Nixon's staff. The NATO Alliance, now just over twenty years old, had been losing steam. Member nations were split and arguing over the conflict in Vietnam. A fresh sense of purpose was required. The CCMS, addressing land and sea environmental issues, urban problems, and other modern problems, was created, with Counselor Moynihan one of its architects.

Pollution of the sea by oil spills was a real and growing problem. Much of the world's oil traveled by sea in giant tankers. Once the cargo was delivered, it was cheapest for the tanker owners to have the empty tanks hosed down and the discharge pumped into the oceans—millions of gallons of oil were involved. The seas were being fouled.

Secretary of Transportation John Volpe was named chairman of the delegation. Counselor Moynihan was deputy chairman. There were several scientific and maritime experts. I was the delegation's right hand. In his opening address to the conference, Secretary Volpe sounded the call: "My government proposes that NATO nations resolve to achieve by mid-decade a complete halt to all intentional discharge of oil and oily wastes into the oceans by tankers and other vessels. This is a fundamental and major goal. It may involve steps such as improved ship design aimed at clean ballast operations and the development of adequate port facilities to receive waste, oily bilge and ballast waters." The conference adopted these recommendations, and they moved next to the Intergovernmental Maritime Consultative Organization en route to becoming accepted international standard and practice.

By late 1970, it was becoming clear that the work laid out by Congress in the Marine Resources and Engineering Development Act of 1966 had just about run its full course. The Stratton Commission report had been delivered, and with its completion, the commission ceased to exist. The work of the council, which had flourished under Vice President Humphrey, was waning under Vice President Spiro Agnew. There were fewer meetings at either the council or the CPR level. The new administration had shifted Executive Office of the President priorities. For lack of new funds, the council would cease to exist on April 30, 1971.

During its existence, the council prepared a report each year, *Marine Science Affairs*, from the president to Congress tracking the nation's oceans policies and programs. As my last major council staff assignment, I guided the preparation of the 1971 report.

At the same time, I set to work on the next chapter in my career, in which the years 1967–70 had been extraordinarily valuable. The Executive Office of the President experience and the work with U.S. and foreign officials, some at the highest levels inside and outside government on a broad range of forward-looking, policy-level issues: All of this had given me a real-world education and credentials that went well beyond ocean affairs. My published writings over the past four years had further enhanced my credentials.

In making the move from the London School of Economics to Washington, I had written Vice President Humphrey. On February 1, 1971, to launch what hopefully would be the next giant leap forward, I wrote the assistant to the president for national security affairs, Dr. Henry A. Kissinger. On February 4, the National Security Council (NSC) staff secretary, Jeanne W. Davis, a senior, highly capable foreign State Department official on loan to the White House, sent a response that opened the door a crack. There were no openings on the NSC staff at the present time, she wrote, but the NSC personnel situation was flexible, and they would be interested in talking to me. She suggested that I call her office to arrange a mutually convenient time.

Three interviews followed over the next two to three weeks: the first with Jeanne Davis; the second with Colonel Bob Behr, U.S. Air Force, who headed the NSC's science and technology (S&T) staff; and the third with Dr. Kissinger's deputy, the deputy assistant to the president for national security affairs, Brigadier General Alexander M. Haig Jr., U.S. Army. The first two were exploratory, polite, and noncommittal.

The meeting with General Haig took place in his White House West Wing office. He was a West Pointer, a warrior who had experienced combat in Vietnam. He had the reputation of being smart, savvy in the ways of the Pentagon and Washington, and highly capable. President Nixon trusted him and admired his performance. My personnel folder was open on the desk in front of him with notes on the top, probably from Jeanne Davis and Bob Behr. He was blunt, to the point, and positive. I had a good background. They liked what they saw. The initial thinking, given all the oceans work, was that I should go to the S&T staff, but they had a real need on the NSC's European staff. He thought I'd be a good fit. Give them a few days, and he would be back in touch.

The calendar had now moved from February into March. The Marine Sciences Council would still shutter its doors forever at the end of April. I waited two weeks and heard nothing. I contacted Jeanne Davis and was asked to be patient. Truly it was a time of hope, tension, and anxiety. With less than four weeks to go before I would be out of a job, I put in a call to General Haig. He had a few choice words for me, and told me to hang on.

The NSC job offer came in mid-April 1971. The professional leap was a great one, opening an incredible new door to the future. I closed up the old shop—keeping, in a brilliant stroke, my parking space—and migrating a block south from the contemporary red-brick New Executive Office Building to a Victorian-style structure, the monumental Old Executive Office Building, with its great, many-windowed granite sides and columns. This had once been the home of the State Department, the Navy, and the War Department. I was assigned to the NSC European staff. I would be on the NSC payroll, not that of another agency. My title would be foreign operations officer.

CHAPTER 5

National Security Council, 1971–1977

I started on the National Security Council as foreign operations officer in spring 1971. Because the State Department's Helmut Sonnenfeldt was my immediate supervisor, my office was in his suite, Room 368, overlooking the West Wing and residence of the White House. I shared this office with CIA Soviet expert William G. Hyland, who was on loan to the NSC staff and would become both friend and mentor.

President Richard Nixon had taken office in 1969 determined to be fully in charge of his administration's foreign policy and broader defense/intelligence, international-economic, and national security policy. Under Nixon, the NSC was a uniquely powerful staff instrument—indeed, at a height of power never attained before or since in the history of the National Security Council.

Hal Sonnenfeldt, my boss until early 1974, was NSC senior staff member for the Soviet Union, Eastern and Western Europe, and Canada, reporting directly to Dr. Henry Kissinger, Nixon's assistant for national security affairs, and to Kissinger's deputy, General Haig. Very early each morning, the NSC secretariat in the Old Executive Office Building prepared a stack of the most recent diplomatic, intelligence, and defense cables, telegrams, and reports for reading by each of the geographic and functional units on the NSC staff. My colleagues and I on the European staff would plow through the stack quickly, selecting key developments to be summarized with our own analysis and comments added. With Sonnenfeldt's approval, these would go over to the NSC staff offices in the West Wing of the White House for further action.

As members of the National Security staff, we participated in the formal work of the NSC, the high-level, invariably contentious interagency meetings that shaped policy and strategy papers on a range of issues for review by the NSC principals and decision by the president, and oversaw implementation of the policies and strategies once decided by the president. We also handled the papers preparing the president, Kissinger, and Haig for their meetings with foreign chiefs of state, heads of government, ministers, and ambassadors. There was a large volume of these visits and meetings. At the same time, we prepared our principals for their foreign travels.

In 1973, when Dr. Kissinger became secretary of state as well as national security adviser, he took Hal Sonnenfeldt and Bill Hyland to State. I tossed my hat in the ring for the top NSC Soviet Union, Eastern and Western Europe, and Canada position. The competition was high-level and spirited. My winning advantage, as it would be told to me, was that I was a known and valued player in the arena. As President Ford took office on August 9, 1974, I was entering the new and lofty post. Two of my most important assistants on the NSC staff bear special mention here.

Nixon's major foreign policy accomplishments in the early 1970s had included the top secret preparations for the breakthrough to China and the summits of détente with the Soviet Union. Our NATO and European allies had felt so neglected as these twin strokes were unfolding that fresh summit initiatives were required to heal bruised feelings. So I had to address Soviet and Western European audiences simultaneously.

Because there were already more than enough State foreign service officers on the NSC staff, I was not interested in bringing more to work for me. I explained this to retired Air Force Lieutenant General Brent Scowcroft, who had replaced General Haig as deputy assistant to the president for national security affairs; he wholeheartedly concurred with my reasoning. My assistants' posts were advertised, one to work with me on the USSR and Eastern Europe, the other for the Western Europe, Canada, and law of the sea portfolios. The résumés came in and were sorted; I interviewed candidates; and I picked two winners.

I was very impressed by the young CIA analyst who was just finishing a tour supporting U.S.-Soviet Arms control negotiations. He had the right background and experience, the right skill sets, and he came across as someone who would work well with me. His name was Robert Gates. I selected him. We did great work together for the next two years before his career path called him back to CIA headquarters in 1976. When President Jimmy Carter took office in 1977, I recommended Bob to the new deputy national security adviser, David Aaron. Bob Gates was selected and would work for David and Zbigniew Brzezinski before returning to the CIA. From there, he would soar from assistant director of Central Intelligence to director, to deputy national security adviser to the president, to president of Texas A&M University, to secretary of defense. Not a bad choice.

My second key choice was Captain Gerrish "Jerry" Flynn, U.S. Navy, a very sharp Harvard grad recommended by Assistant Secretary of Defense Robert Ellsworth. Jerry joined me fresh from destroyer command, and following his NSC staff years would become one of the key assistants to the chairman of the Joint Chiefs of Staff, and squadron commander of Destroyer Squadron 23, the Little Beaver Squadron, made famous by then-Captain Arleigh Burke in the World War II Battle of the Pacific. He, Bob, and I formed a great team that stood the 1974–77 watch well.

Part of our work was preparing the president for meetings with foreign leaders, the summits that played a singularly important part in the role of the United States as a global superpower. From the outset, staffing summits became a very important, continuing part of my role under

Presidents Nixon and Ford, and, with the coming of the Carter administration, would lead to my selection as national security adviser to Vice President Walter F. Mondale.

Throughout my government service, I had to keep my finger on the national pulse and how the president responded to key developments. As we kept watch on the international scene and developed updates and advice pertaining to developments and potential U.S. engagement, it was imperative that those of us working on national security also remain keenly aware of and responsive to domestic interests. In this perennial juggling act, goals could change at a moment's notice, a moving target. To achieve national objectives, the president had to be completely up to date as he entered each summit, armed with diplomatic tactics continually being honed and readjusted. We were the behind-the-scenes machinery that made all this possible—for me, the perfect job.

On the home front, meanwhile, the late 1960s and early 1970s were parallel years of joy for Gretchen. Our splendid sons, Alex and Ty—my pride and her absolute treasures—were moving along through nursery, then preschool and kindergarten, on to elementary and the first grades, from early games to sports. Gretchen and I were also thrilled with the historic house we found to buy in West Annapolis, overlooking the Severn River and within pleasant walking distance of the Naval Academy. These were very happy years, years of growth for all of us. Mom was becoming the classic kids' chauffeur, mastering the switch from the left side of New Zealand roads to the right side of those in the States.

U.S. international involvement increased throughout the twentieth century. The nation's leader is ultimately responsible for the conduct of foreign policy—and this has placed mounting demands on the president's time in office. It was my job, as a member of the National Security Council staff, to help the administration navigate this perennial situation. The responsibilities involved demanded diplomacy, evenhandedness, and equal measures of confidence and flexibility. Doing the job engaged all of my skills and educational background. I learned more with every new challenge—and the challenges did not take a break. I handled the nonstop demands of this complex, fascinating, all-consuming career thanks to a stable home base, with Gretchen in happy command of the home front.

Looking back, it's also clear that letters addressed to people in power at key points in my career helped me to attain goals that otherwise would not have been within my reach. I knew these were audacious moves, but my initiative was bolstered by the belief that I had nothing to lose. And I had expertise to offer, as well as a growing network of acquaintances.

The pivotal importance of networking had been made clear to me at Stanford, and then in the Navy, my ONI duties had included screening international diplomatic cables. As *Proceedings* editor, my global network expanded continually, and the London School of Economics cemented all these building blocks into a solid foundation for U.S. government work. Linking all of these steps was my developing expertise in matters pertaining to the world's oceans. Even if the letters produced no results, each time I fired one off I already had good work. Operating from this position of strength, my hope was to improve my situation by making direct contact with people for whom I wished to work, people who otherwise may not have known (a) that I existed, or (b) that I was very interested in what they did. In each case, the letters worked their magic in one way or another.

Throughout my seven years on the NSC, and then for four more years as Mondale's national security assistant, every time the president or vice president attended a summit, I traveled. Gretchen could not have been more supportive, understanding, and enthusiastic. Our house was surrounded with expansive, various gardens. Gretchen's green thumb was well known in Annapolis, with articles and photos appearing in the press and an array of ribbons, mostly blue, emerging from contests.

To help myself prepare for my daunting duties, I read. I studied the history and effects of summitry, analyzing its anatomy and how it had arrived at this point of détente in the early 1970s. At the end of World War I, President Woodrow Wilson, the first true American summiteer, headed the U.S. delegation to the Paris Peace Conference. Before making that historic journey, he had laid the ground for success through years of thoughtful, deliberate foreign policy practices, staffing, information-gathering techniques, and diplomatic probing.

Wilson entrusted to Colonel Edward Mandell House the unprecedented role of White House personal diplomatic emissary and foreign policy adviser. The job continued under President Franklin Delano Roosevelt, carried out by Harry Hopkins. In 1947, the National Security Act institutionalized it. Of all the successive national security advisers, Henry A. Kissinger under Presidents Nixon and Gerald Ford brought it to full prominence.

But even though presidents invite and need close advisers, ultimately they are the leaders. Presidents also believe seriously in their right to weigh alternatives to their governmental departments' status quo. They believe they have the right to make their own decisions following consultations, and to enact those decisions at the time and place of their choosing. In practice none of this is an easy process, however well intentioned the government's bureaucracy may be.

A president's word carries authority, and it must be delivered to the desired audience with precision or risk misinterpretation—often with the most interesting results. I had seen this for the first time in Antarctica, when Kennedy tracked our icebreaker expedition.

As part of my official duties during the 1961 Bellingshausen Sea expedition with the icebreakers USS *Glacier* and *Staten Island*, I wrote news dispatches that ran regularly in the New Zealand press. Wire services picked these up for release in the United States, which led to the new president, Kennedy, taking an interest in the expedition's stories of danger and rescue. He asked his naval aide to keep him updated. This expression of interest rippled down through the Navy's chain of command, and by the time it reached our two ships it had been bent into a stern, clipped order that our expedition's commodore get his ships out of the pack ice immediately to avoid being trapped for the winter. We had been biding our time, as polar seamen must, awaiting a shift in the winds that would produce open leads of water in the sea permitting us to exit. What was thought to be a direct order from the president changed that plan dramatically, resulting in officers and men going onto the ice with dynamite to blast a path through the ice to open water. For more than a day, they blasted with little effect, because ice, which is elastic, easily absorbs the force of an explosion. Eventually, though, the winds did shift, freeing us to be on our way.

Such misinterpretations of a president's instructions are not always accidental. Those entrusted with carrying out policy may dislike the change in direction, or oppose it and do their best to block or undercut a directive. They could just be testing the waters. Woodrow Wilson's brilliance as a statesman was matched by his innovations in diplomacy and summit staffing. He had the State Department handle the government's daily foreign policy business, while sending Colonel House on repeated overseas missions from 1914 to 1917, directing him personally as they sought how to mediate the war's end.

Wilson dedicated more than six months to the Treaty of Versailles, setting sail for Paris on December 4, 1918. He held negotiations preliminary to the Paris Peace Conference; visited Great Britain, Italy, and the Vatican; participated in the Peace Conference; returned briefly for business in the States; then back to Paris from March through mid-June, signing the treaty that would bring an uneasy peace and create the League of Nations. He addressed the Parliament in Belgium on June 18–19 before returning home.

Successive presidents handled summitry according to their respective styles and preferences, and by 1947, the United States found itself responsible for the security and well-being of the entire "Free World." Such a status brought an urgent requirement to streamline and modernize the foreign policy and defense structure of the executive branch, to provide the president and nation with the needed mechanisms for America's new global role. The wartime, largely independent operations of military services had to be meshed with the peacetime requirements of civilian control in the nuclear era. Because the world, at peace, was now a far more dangerous place, the United States felt an urgency to obtain ever-increasing intelligence about the activities and intentions of other nations. U.S. cabinet departments could no longer make major decisions independently, because the actions of one affected those of others as well as the interests of the entire nation.

The National Security Act was passed in 1947, creating the cabinet position of secretary of defense, in addition to the service secretaries. The act created a Central Intelligence Agency and a National Security Council to steer overall coordination.

In 1949, President Harry S. Truman requested, and Congress passed, an amended National Security Act of 1947, which consolidated and strengthened the role of the secretary of defense over the military services and trimmed down members of the National Security Council to the president, vice president, secretary of state, secretary of defense, and a full-time civilian executive secretary and supporting staff. The director of Central Intelligence and the chairman of the Joint Chiefs of Staff would serve as advisers. According to section 101 (a) of the act, "The function of the Council shall to be to advise the president with respect to the integration of domestic, foreign, and military policies relating to the national security so as to enable the military services and the other departments and agencies of the Government to cooperate more effectively in matters involving the national security" (Public Law 216, Section 2, 81st Congress, August 10, 1949). Writing in his 1956 *Memoirs*, President Truman reflected on the National Security Council as "a badly needed new facility," one that established a "place in the government where military, diplomatic and resources problems could be studied and continually appraised. This new organization gave us a running balance and a perpetual inventory of where we stood and where we were going on all strategic questions affecting the national security" (Doubleday, vol. 1, p. 337).

When I joined the NSC staff in 1971, I appreciated immediately the degree to which the system also enabled the president to control the pace and direction of foreign affairs and his meetings with foreign leaders, regardless of how complex or contentious the issues were within the U.S. government. The NSC system placed effectively in the president's hands the reins of foreign, defense, and international economic and resources policy. It harnessed State, Defense, and other executive branch departments, keeping them continually pulling in the traces as needed. Through the NSC, the president had a professional national security staff to produce a constant flow of professional assessments and other substantive support enabling him to absorb and master the details of complex issues, often under tremendous time pressure, and to digest the range of options required for decision in a thorough, objective manner—more so than might have been possible if the same information were coming from the cabinet secretaries.

As the system evolved and matured, it reinforced successive presidents' confidence in their ability to take charge of thorny foreign policy issues and pursue them in face-to-face contact with other leaders. At the same time, in summitry the risk of international miscalculation always accompanies national calibration of judgment. One among myriad examples of this occurred during the October 1962 Cuban Missile Crisis. At this point, there was no longer any illusion that face-to-face diplomacy alone would resolve the situation. Late in the evening of October 23, with Soviet ships steaming toward Cuba, only hours before a U.S. quarantine would take effect, the president, his brother and the attorney general Robert F. Kennedy, and Ambassador Ormsby-Gore of Great Britain informally weighed the president's tactical choices. The attorney general later recalled in his memoir *Thirteen Days*, "The President talked about the possibility of arranging an immediate summit with Khrushchev, but finally dismissed the idea, concluding that such a meeting would be useless until Khrushchev first accepted, as a result of our deeds as well as our statements, the U.S. determination in this matter. Before a summit took place, and it should, the President wanted to have some cards in his own hands" (Norton, 1969, pp. 66–67). The calculation was correct, the Soviets withdrew their missiles, and the United States prevailed.

But setbacks continued, with only an occasional positive step forward in the exceedingly difficult effort to find a more constructive road of U.S.-USSR cooperation that would increase security and ease world tensions. Progress included the post–Cuban Missile Crisis introduction of the U.S.-Soviet Hot Line, the 1963 signing of the Limited Test Ban Treaty, and the 1968 Nonproliferation Treaty. This was the sobering legacy that the two superpowers brought to the 1970s, a new era of détente—and of my participation in the National Security Council.

CHAPTER 6

Scouting My First Summit

Iceland, 1973

May 1973 found me in Iceland, in the midst of a volcanic eruption that lasted from January 23 until July 3. The entire island of Heimaey was evacuated, and the town of Vestmannaeyjar was ravaged. This was far from Reykjavik, our destination, to which many evacuees were flown. Our Air Force pilot had taken us low over the island as we approached Iceland's southwestern tip. We saw the fishing community's red and green roofs, with many homes engulfed by lava and vital approaches to the harbor narrowed. Ash and debris were everywhere. U.S. Navy personnel from Keflavik's NATO base had assisted with the evacuation, and during the summit, President Richard Nixon offered further U.S. assistance.

The 1973 U.S.-French Nixon-Pompidou summit gave me my first adrenaline rush being overseas as we paved the way for the president. I was one of twenty in the pre-advance party. At Keflavik International Airport, a stiff spring breeze greeted us with the pungent smell of fish works.

Reykjavik was about thirty-two miles away. While being driven into the city, I watched in fascination the fields of black lava from Iceland's long volcanic history, dotted with ancient cones on either side of the two-lane highway. Soon the two presidents would follow us on this route.

While Gretchen cared for our two sons back home in Annapolis and pursued her own passions of costume creation, gardening, painting, and more, I focused tightly on making my first White House / NSC staff tour a success. Aside from the family I loved, my life was consumed with work—on which I aimed my sharpest focus, as the job demanded. I continued to be amazed that I was actually here, helping the White House with international policy and decisions. But there was no time to navel-gaze on thoughts of how fortunate I'd been. There was always major thinking to be done, and I never took this or any other job lightly. I gave it my fullest effort.

Reality that day in Iceland was grim, not just because of Iceland's volcano. In Washington, Watergate had already done its damage to President Nixon's ethos, with musings growing ever louder about whether the scandal had diminished his ability to drive a hard bargain. At issue was the U.S. desire to return its attention to Europe in the wake of Vietnam, and to convince France to join in developing a revitalized declaration of Atlantic principles.

But Georges Pompidou was not well, as rumored in Paris and reinforced by his puffy appearance (he would die a year later, of blood cancer). Thus, both presidents had problems that affected them both personally and professionally, and both were in a weakened state as negotiators. On both sides of the Atlantic, there were more doubters than believers in the proposition that the United States could engineer the Europeans into signing a new Atlantic Charter.

None of this affected me or my work. Dedicated to making the charter become reality, I felt a spirit of tremendous adventure as I scouted my first summit. Our advance team included the head of the president's Secret Service detail, the head of the White House Communications Agency, military aides, doctors, National Security Council staff (me), and the lead and supporting advance personnel, specialists in the business of technical preparations for meetings between sovereign chiefs of state.

Preparing for a summit starts with a spark of inspiration for the national result to be realized. From this point of departure flows detailed planning for the substance of the talks, the structure and content of the desired documents, and the accompanying components of private talks and public rhetoric of the summiteers.

While all this planning is going on, parallel arrangements focus on the logistics. The technical side includes transportation, shaping events to each president's advantage, ensuring safety and a full program, and much more. Meeting the double-edged requirements of the press is critical—and extremely challenging, because with every summit comes a torrent of media coverage. If the arrangements for all this have not been thorough, even the finest substantive plans can be undercut in talks between world leaders. Faulty interpretation, scheduling foul-ups, any of a thousand snags can lead to flawed negotiations, embarrassment for the leader, and setbacks—whether minor or major—for the nation. A checklist to avoid such pitfalls is the summit staffer's constant companion. And the first item on this list of essential needs is the pre-advance party.

In Reykjavik, we launched ours by meeting with the U.S. ambassador, Frederick Irving, who, as the president's full-time representative on-scene, would play a vital role in the summit. Being fully aware of both parties' objectives and cultural nuances, he would help set the tone through pre-summit talks with his host country. Irving was a superb ambassador, as I would learn after working with many more—including some who refused Washington's proposals for a visit, and others who tried to impose their own agendas on the meetings. Such situations are rare but very possible: There are ambassadors who, either purposely or inadvertently, turn out to be problem makers rather than problem solvers. The summit pre-advance must spot these issues, try to resolve them ahead of time, and, if unsuccessful, advise Washington that this embassy needs some gentle counseling. A skilled, experienced pre-advance team leader seldom resorts to Washington—but must maintain a constant vigil on the problem diplomat.

An effective ambassador, on the other hand, opens almost every door for the pre-advance team, the advance team, and most important, the summit party. A good embassy is an integral part of the entire process of preparation. It is essential that those heading the pre-advance and those supporting the summit from Washington get to know the ambassador and staff and work together in partnership from the beginning.

Our party drew fully on Irving's expertise as we reviewed our planned sequence of meetings involving bilateral talks with the Icelanders, meetings with the Icelanders and the French pre-advance party concerning the U.S.-French talks, and the social events that would involve the leaders from Iceland, France, and the United States.

Gaullist protocol still set an extremely formal tone for the U.S.-French relationship in the early 1970s. President Pompidou had succeeded General Charles de Gaulle in 1969 following six years as his prime minister, and was, like him, wary of U.S. policies. Then in 1970, during a visit to the United States, he and his wife found it insulting that demonstrators protested France's sale of combat jet aircraft to Libya. He would never return to America until its president had reciprocated with a formal visit to France.

President Nixon looked forward to such a visit—but not until fall 1973. The chess game of summit maneuvering involved island-hopping sessions between the U.S. and French presidents: a quick 1971 Nixon-Pompidou consultation in the Azores, this Iceland summit of 1973, and then December 1974 talks between President Gerald Ford and President Valéry Giscard d'Estaing in Martinique.

This island strategy largely accommodated U.S.-French interests, but in 1973 it also needlessly complicated the talks by injecting Iceland and its interests into the summit scenario. Those interests would turn out to be considerable—underscoring once again the need for extreme care in selecting a summit site. From every conceivable angle, it had to be neutral.

But Iceland in 1973 was not neutral. It was taking a stand. All of its political factions and virtually its entire population of 209,000 agreed that British and other foreign trawlers should not fish within fifty miles of the nation's coastline. With this, the U.K.-Icelandic Cod War was at its peak. The problem went to the heart of Iceland's economy, with fish accounting for 85 percent of export earnings. The issue also went to the heart of the Icelanders' sense of justice. They cited the 1958 Geneva Convention on the Continental Shelf, which gave coastal states sovereign rights over their continental shelf's seabed resources, including marine life. They argued that the shelf and the waters above were, for Iceland, an organic unit. In 1972, they formally announced that their fisheries jurisdiction would be extended to fifty miles. They denied the World Court's jurisdiction in the matter and sent the *Thor*, the *Aegir*, and the *Arakvur*, their diminutive coast guard vessels, to cut the nets of British trawlers and engage escorting Royal Navy frigates in day after day of rammings, bumpings, and near-collisions.

Iceland looked to the United States, France, and the other NATO nations for support and protection from the British "aggressor." Having gained independence from Norway only in 1944, after seven centuries of Danish and Norwegian rule, Iceland was fiercely protective of its recently won freedom. With its own armed forces, Iceland joined the North Atlantic Alliance and, as of 1951, provided Keflavik as the base for NATO's U.S.-manned Iceland Defense Force. Until May 1973, the United States had taken great pains to avoid being dragged into the Cod War, urging that Britain show restraint and that Iceland forgo unilateral claims and instead pursue its fisheries interests in the ongoing U.S. Law of the Sea Conference. But in Reykjavik, subtlety and distance would no longer work. The Icelanders would press their case vigorously with Presidents Nixon and Pompidou—detracting from the primary public purpose of the summit.

By early 1973, the United States and its Western European allies had taken to increasing squabbles over issues including trade competition, monetary policies, and differences over what constituted an equitable sharing of the collective defense. In the wake of the 1972 U.S. summits with China and the Soviet Union, Europe and Japan were feeling grossly overlooked. These frictions had become part of my daily professional life as a member of the National Security Council staff for European Affairs.

In his January 1973 foreign policy report to Congress, President Nixon signaled his heightened interest in Europe, and then launched a fresh round of consultations with European leaders, aiming to quickly restore the relationship and return to a more positive, cooperative spirit on firmer footing. Then, in April 1973, following the president's talks with Prime Minister Edward Heath of Great Britain and Chancellor Willy Brandt of the Federal Republic of Germany, Dr. Henry Kissinger, my boss and the president's national security adviser, sought to place this U.S. diplomatic effort in full conceptual perspective in an address titled "The Year of Europe."

Looking back, it is easy to see how that title might have annoyed Europeans. The address itself called for a high-speed effort to set the U.S.-European house in order, painting a vision of all the benefits to be realized. In tones that alternately exhorted and chastised, Kissinger proposed a new Atlantic charter that built on the postwar blueprint "without becoming its prisoner," addressed problems created by previous successes, and formed a new Atlantic relationship for progress shared by Japan. Europe, Canada, and "ultimately" Japan were invited to join in this effort. "This," concluded Kissinger, "is what we mean by the Year of Europe."

He then put a further positive spin on U.S. goals in a press conference immediately preceding the president's departure for Iceland, saying America wished to "lift the Atlantic debate out of the rut of purely technical controversies where for about a decade public attention has been concentrated."

But Paris saw the U.S. initiative very differently. Longtime close Pompidou aide Michel Jobert, recently named minister of foreign affairs, believed the U.S. position was driven largely by Nixon's domestic difficulties. To the French ear, portions of Kissinger's speech had been erroneous and patronizing. They had no interest in supporting a vision that could suggest France would accept a subordinate role in shaping some sort of collective relationship between Europe and the United States.

Nevertheless, the French pre-advance team was with our American party on May 10 in Reykjavik to prepare for the talks. We were all in perpetual motion, as always while pre-advancing a summit. After an early morning huddle on May 9, our technical experts had fanned out to begin weaving the supporting fabric of the summit. They initiated contacts with Icelandic counterparts, surveyed sites, and launched plans for every aspect of summit support that would be implemented by the advance team that was to follow us and remain until the summit. Air Force personnel would make technical arrangements for the arrival, handling, and security of Air Force One, the *Spirit of '76*; communicators would ensure that the president and his party had the same swift, sure communications as in Washington; White House medical staff would survey hospitals and clinics to determine which facilities could best handle the range of possibilities, from mild illness to stroke or gunshot; and Secret Service personnel would track every aspect of the planning from day one, to ensure the president's security.

On the Icelanders' side, our hosts had a number of pressing, detailed questions. In the big picture, they conveyed that Iceland's third president (1968–80), Kristján Eldjárn, would receive Presidents Pompidou and Nixon for a dinner at his residence. Details for that event needed to be worked out, and did the visiting presidents wish to meet for talks with Prime Minister Ólafur Jóhannesson? In the smaller picture, equally in need of careful, thorough planning, the Icelanders asked about precise timing of the presidents' respective arrivals and the size of their parties: How many senior officials were in each, what were the security arrangements, how many reporters would attend, did we have our own interpreters? Most Icelanders spoke English as a second language, but what about French? What program events did we anticipate in addition to the actual talks? Would there be sightseeing, salmon fishing?

On most of these points, we had arrived with specific instructions. The Icelanders, led by their undersecretary for foreign affairs, were thoughtful, solicitous, and eager to be the best possible hosts. The morning session unfolded smoothly, after which we enjoyed a luncheon of rack of lamb garnished with local hothouse vegetables. Outside, spectacular spring snow squalls swirled against the distant long, low face of Mount Esja.

In Reykjavik, a small city of parks, ponds, and gardens, handsome residential streets built on gentle hills overlooked the main harbor.

Sculptures and statues adorned the greens in a sort of apology for the lack of trees, while witnessing the culture and creativity of its population. Its half-dozen hotels, though modern and comfortable, could not accommodate the security deemed necessary for the presidents of France and the United States, because we could not reserve several floors of two entire hotels at a time when every room in the nation would be booked.

Eventually the team decided that the presidents would be lodged in their nations' respective official diplomatic residences. The U.S. secretary of state, secretary of the treasury, and all the other members of the American party, including Ambassador Irving and his family, would stay at the Loftleidir Hotel, while their French counterparts would take the Hotel Esja. Most of the press would stay on board a chartered cruise ship in the harbor.

We planned for President Nixon to have substantive talks with Iceland's leaders on the evening of his arrival, and then, on May 31, President Eldjárn would host a black-tie dinner for the two visiting presidents at his eighteenth-century Bessastadir Bay residence, a pastoral setting overlooking the capital ten miles distant, and the former home of Denmark's governors. Additional pieces for the three days of talks fell into place, but we still had to identify a site for the U.S.-French talks. Neither the hotels nor any of the government buildings offered what our pre-advance party was looking for. We had to provide not just for the two presidents but also for concurrent meetings at the cabinet and ministerial levels on issues of international finance, trade, and foreign affairs. And the site would have to be clearly presidential!

President Nixon's advance men had by 1973 earned a swashbuckling reputation. A year earlier, on the eve of Nixon's visit to Ottawa, they had proposed (unsuccessfully) changing the color of Prime Minister Trudeau's office furniture from tan to blue to provide a "more congenial" background for television coverage. After that the advance Nixon men had won several duels with Soviet protocol over the complex scenario for the first Nixon-Brezhnev Moscow summit. Now, our highly capable, quick-witted, gregarious pre-advance leader, in charge of his own pre-advance mission, carried this can-do spirit to Iceland.

The solution emerged when he took stock of Iceland's newly constructed cultural treasure, the Kjarval Art Gallery, Kjarvalsstadir. This handsome architectural success, set apart on large grounds in the center of the capital, offered a commodious office off the main floor—just the right setting for the presidents' tête-à-têtes, in an atmosphere sparkling with freshness and taste. Security would be excellent. The only problem was that there were no separate chambers for meetings between Secretary of State William Rogers and Foreign Minister Jobert, or between Secretary of the Treasury George Shultz and Finance Minister Giscard d'Estaing, with all their supporting casts. But our fearless Nixon man was able to arrange for the construction of two large conference rooms within the gallery, complete with walls, doors, conference tables, and chairs, solely for the purpose of the summit. The gallery would become a conference center for the last day of May and the first of June. With this, our pre-advance mission was completed, and we returned to Washington.

On May 27, the White House Advance Office distributed detailed schedules—"bibles"—for the trip. I was to travel in one of two Air Force Boeing 707s reserved for the president. Our staff schedule, which reflected the key items in our pre-advance negotiations, is included in the appendix of this book, offered as an introductory guide that summit sherpas, those who toil behind the scenes preparing and facilitating international summits, could find useful.

As the schedule reflects, the entire focus of the summit was on those hours set aside for the substantive talks, with an absolute minimum of ceremonial events. This was because of the previously noted Cod War, in which Iceland tried unsuccessfully to involve the United States; U.S. interests were not advanced by Nixon's presence in Iceland in the middle of this dispute. Eventually it would be resolved, with all three countries remaining NATO allies.

The U.S.-French talks produced a result that appeared to be minimal but that in fact would make a positive contribution to the Year of Europe process. The French had arrived in Iceland determined to make no concessions to that initiative, and accordingly, after the first day of talks, Pompidou authorized the U.S. side to state only that during the review of relations within the Atlantic Alliance, the French president had stressed the important role played by U.S. forces in Europe and the danger of unilaterally reducing those forces.

French Foreign Minister Jobert in particular was wary of U.S. initiatives. From my vantage point at Secretary Rogers' left during the talks, I watched him approach the situation with droll good grace. Every time the U.S. secretary of state attempted to engage him on a central U.S.-European issue, Jobert would smile and dismiss the topic with a comment like "But of course, Mr. Secretary, that is being discussed down the hall."

Still, despite the lack of agreement on specifics, the very fact of the summit constituted its success. The United States had taken another highly visible step in the larger process of reasserting its influence on the direction of U.S.-European relations. The president's commitment to this process highlighted the U.S. prioritization of the nation's relationship with Europe, and each new step in the process emphasized to Europe's governments that the U.S. voice would be heard and that U.S. influence would be increasingly felt. By 1974, NATO ministers would reach new agreement on a Declaration of Principles to guide the relationship, new U.S.-European mechanisms would be developed to grapple with the mounting energy crisis, and new summit-level multilateral forums—so resolutely opposed by France in 1973—would be established with the first of the new annual Economic Summits of the seven most influential industrialized democracies, held in 1975 at Rambouillet, France. For America, the launching of this process during the U.S.-French summit at Reykjavik represented the accomplishment of its most important objective.

On the flight back to Washington on board 26000, I had the pleasure of entertaining Haraldur Kroyer, Iceland's ambassador to the United States, who was about to be reassigned to Geneva. This would mean a sacrifice for his son, who would have to give up his precious four-foot yellow rat snake, Tiger Eye. So to close the 1973 Reykjavik summit, the ambassador and I toasted the conclusion of our agreement that my family would adopt Tiger Eye. I acted knowing how fascinated my son Alex was with snakes. He loved to handle them. Tiger Eye moved right into West Annapolis, where I have lived ever since, outliving Tiger Eye.

I would encounter more serpents in my sherpa's travels, and many of these adventures and lessons are shared in the following chapters. Throughout this fascinating career, I continued to learn about the significance of official travels abroad by U.S. presidents, and about how summit diplomacy evolved as an instrument of America's foreign policy.

CHAPTER 7

Nixon's Diplomacy, 1972–1974

President Richard Nixon's legacy was forever tainted by the Watergate scandal, an unfortunate executive-level decision that has obscured his diplomatic expertise and accomplishments. Nixon's extensive foreign travel experience included eight pathfinding years of overseas missions as Dwight D. Eisenhower's vice president. This background launched him on the summit trail early in his first years as president. He repeatedly consulted, in person, with European and Asian allies, the leaders of Canada and Mexico, and South Vietnam's President Nguyen Van Thieu.

As president, Nixon, along with National Security Adviser Kissinger and the NSC system, controlled the pace and direction of preparations for the Strategic Arms Limitation Treaty (SALT I) negotiations. During the 1972 Moscow summit, Kissinger explained the process to reporters at the now-demolished Hotel Intourist. Represented by "an extremely able delegation and a very able negotiator who conducts the ordinary business of the negotiations," the U.S. system relied on studies and information provided from committees in Washington. When the inevitable impasses occurred, the U.S. president and Soviet leaders communicated directly to reach fair compromises.

At this point in my career as sherpa, I was one of those laboring behind the scenes, helping to guide the lengthy, thorough, multifaceted preparations for the 1972 and then the 1973 summits. Having not yet matriculated to summit delegate or participant, I did not interact directly with the important new Soviet contacts. I was still learning—through direct experience—that summits' deadlines and imperatives drove each nation's bureaucracy to ramp up its speed as well as its proficiency. In 1972, these conditions contributed to the newly emerging détente.

The work involved in helping to shape U.S. positions for international negotiations is draining, time-consuming, and contentious. I already knew this when I joined the National Security Council in spring 1971, having served on interdepartmental committees in the presidential executive office since 1967 during the Johnson administration.

At my new NSC job, preparations were already underway for the 1972 U.S.-Soviet summit, and the atmosphere was intense. I had to tap into my staff-level interagency coordination background as never before. At the top of my list of responsibilities, outside of the daily staff routine on across-the-board issues, was preparing the United States for negotiations with the Soviet Union aimed at ending the Cold War. For this I had to work closely with the Departments of State and Defense and the Intelligence Community, initially focusing in particular on U.S. and Soviet warships and military aircraft.

Negotiations pertaining to incidents at sea had a much more tangible, immediate purpose than did the talks about the overall problem of how to curb the nuclear arms race. That would lead to SALT I, the first U.S.-Soviet anti–ballistic missile (ABM) treaty. Within that larger framework, our sea-related concern was hostile actions at sea, with U.S. and Soviet Navy ships steaming at close, dangerous quarters, while the two nations' patrol and reconnaissance aircraft buzzed the other's warships mast high.

The relationship between the two navies was unyielding, in a manifestation of the Cold War stalemate.

John W. Warner, first as Undersecretary and then Secretary of the Navy, chaired the interdepartmental team that developed the U.S. position under the aegis of the NSC. Warner led the U.S. delegations to two rounds of talks with Soviet naval counterparts, in October 1971 and mid-May 1972. These led to the structure of a mutually beneficial agreement based on the International Rules of the Road, the maritime code of conduct already in use by the world's mariners.

On May 25, 1972, with Secretary of State William Rogers and Foreign Minister Andrei Gromyko in attendance, Secretary Warner, and Admiral of the Fleet Sergey Gorshkov signed the U.S.-Soviet Incidents at Sea Agreement as one of the first formal actions of the 1972 Moscow Summit. It was a solid agreement, still in effect today. And it augured well for the broader objectives of the 1972 summit.

Some of our U.S. team members focused their full attention on SALT, the ABM Treaty (which had eluded President Lyndon Johnson at the 1967 Glassboro Summit), and a statement aimed at reducing tensions and creating opportunities for cooperation, the "Basic Principles of Relations between the United States of America and the Union of Soviet Socialist Republics." In support of those efforts, my own concentration was on bilateral agreements intended to take U.S.-Soviet relations from stalemate to an interconnecting web of mutually beneficial bilateral programs. Building on the new spirit of détente, our work culminated in Moscow with the signing of agreements on environmental protection; a joint commercial commission; the Incidents at Sea Agreement; and cooperation in the fields of medical science and public health, science and technology, and the exploration and use of outer space for peaceful purposes.

None of these agreements came easily. Draft revisions flew between Washington and Moscow while the presidential party was still en route to the Soviet capital. But on May 24, the agreement was signed.

After the Moscow summit, President Nixon flew to Iran for two days of talks with Shah Mohammad Reza Pahlavi, and then on to Poland for a formal East-West dialogue with First Secretary Edward Gierek. World summitry was like a goldfish bowl, and Nixon knew never to treat as lesser-than another any Warsaw Pact member that wanted to participate in détente. In another manifestation of the Nixon administration's diplomatic savoir faire, in parallel with the Soviet summits, regular consultations with Poland and Romania also moved forward.

The 1972 summit was one of Nixon's signature diplomatic accomplishments. In addition to thawing U.S.-Soviet relations, the Interim SALT I Agreement marked the first step toward limiting offensive strategic nuclear arms. The ABM Treaty provided limits that could freeze an emerging massive buildup of multibillion-dollar strategic defensive arms. While codifying more constructive bilateral relations, the "Declaration of Principles" also muted competition and channeled all levels of U.S.-Soviet contacts to more productive ends.

Laboring on the bilateral agreements would turn out to be among the good accomplishments of my career. Today as I look back, I feel tremendous pride at having been there, at having contributed to the codification of opportunities for increased bilateral cooperation.

Nixon traveled a lot in 1972 for his diplomatic efforts. In addition to the Moscow summit, he made a breakthrough visit to Shanghai, Peking, and Hangzhou, to resume contact with the People's Republic of China; made a state visit to Ottawa, Canada; and met with Austria's chancellor Bruno Kreisky for an informal round of talks in Salzburg.

Between the 1972 and 1973 summits, additional agreements being negotiated covered trade, maritime affairs, and the USSR's repayment of its World War II Lend-Lease obligations. On the NSC staff, we monitored the new bilateral committees' initial deliberations at the same time that we helped with preparations for General Secretary Leonid Brezhnev's 1973 visit to the United States.

Of note, the Soviet tactics for negotiating consisted of holding out until almost beyond the last moment. We were very familiar with this, but I was still struck by its ruthlessness. For example, as the new U.S.-Soviet

Maritime Agreement was being implemented, a negotiating session in Moscow ended with the U.S. maritime administrator pushing away from the conference table. At issue was the hard-nosed, difficult business of cargo shares and cargo rates. There could be no agreement, the American said to his Soviet counterpart, since the Soviets insisted on holding to clearly unacceptable positions. The Soviet side did not budge, and the U.S. negotiator left, packed up at his hotel, and went to the airport. As he was climbing the stairs to his plane, the Soviet negotiator arrived with an offer of acceptable terms.

Nixon traveled abroad only once in 1973, for the talks with Pompidou in Iceland. With the Year of Europe still being organized, summitry's main focus was détente and Brezhnev's visit to the United States, June 18–26, 1973.

Kissinger flew to the Soviet Union in early May for four days of preparatory talks with Foreign Minister Gromyko. The Soviet advance party arrived in Washington in mid-May, having studied its U.S. counterparts the previous year. For Brezhnev's arrival, Pennsylvania Avenue was closed between his guest residence, Blair House, and the White House. An enormous Soviet flag festooned the side of the Old Executive Office Building facing Blair House.

In a crowded week of summitry, the two leaders built on the foundations of détente previously established. On June 21, Nixon and Brezhnev expanded on the 1972 interim accord by signing the "Agreement Relating to Basic Principles of Negotiations on the Further Limitation of Strategic Offensive Arms." This set a target date of 1974 to complete a more permanent agreement, while also opening the negotiating trail toward further reductions thereafter.

The next day, the two leaders signed an "Agreement between the United States of America and the Union of Soviet Socialist Republics on the Prevention of Nuclear War," which built on the 1972 "Declaration of Principles." As the framework of détente grew, the atmosphere between the two nations was no longer fraught solely due to struggles to eliminate ship collisions. Now, the talk was about establishing an overall code to avoid nuclear war.

The summit included the signing of many other new agreements on which I and my colleagues had labored in Washington and Moscow for months—cooperation on studies of the world's oceans, agriculture, transportation, peaceful uses of atomic energy, and more.

I was not yet forty years old, but since finishing college I'd been immersed in international affairs, issues that affected the entire globe. I was so preoccupied with work and the next steps that I didn't often pause to consider how much had been packed into these years. Gretchen was more and more involved. Our sons and their school were the primary focus. I remember their leaving classes early one day to come to the White House South Lawn for the high-tech pageantry of President Nixon's helicopter return following summit travel. We were still young, and family and professional events continued to blossom together in our lives.

And, speaking of age, General Secretary Brezhnev noticed mine. During the Soviet leader's 1973 talks in Washington, Secretary of the Treasury George Shultz hosted an informal meeting at Blair House so that Brezhnev and U.S. business and industry leaders could discuss trade. As I came through the receiving line and Shultz introduced me, Brezhnev kept a firm grip on my hand, his watering eyes studying my face as Viktor Sukhodrev translated the introduction. Then he smiled and said, "I envy you your youth."

Even though the Watergate scandal was deepening, the summit went well, capped off for me with a still-treasured inscribed silver dish from Kissinger, commemorating our diplomatic accomplishment of June 18–25, 1973. I see it to this day as a graduation gift symbolizing the completion of my behind-the-scenes apprenticeship.

But the world would continue to raise new challenges. By March 1974, the Arab-Israeli War of 1973 and a global energy crisis had created a pileup of disruption, death, and reshuffling. I had become the NSC's senior staff member for Eastern and Western Europe, meaning I would be at the negotiations held in Moscow from March 24 to 28. I flew with Kissinger on board one of the special-mission U.S. Air Force jets. Our task was to address force reductions while also seeking broader understandings for enhanced security and cooperation in Europe.

In the midst of détente, expectations were high. SALT headed the agenda. Separately, the West insisted on freedom of immigration from the Soviet Union. As always, parallel talks would take place on critical issues and developments around the world, including in the Middle East. I was monitoring the new bilateral negotiations.

On this 1974 visit, Foreign Minister Gromyko met us at Vnukovo-2 Airport. It was still winter in Moscow, albeit late winter, with city soot darkening the snow. Speeding past gray high-rise apartments, we continued on into the hills beyond Moscow University.

I had long ago internalized the knowledge that every motorcade is geared to the precision movement of one person: the summit principal. Motorcades do not wait for staff. This means it is essential to keep track of the principal's schedule, to gauge descent times in crowded foreign hotel elevators, and to know exactly how long it will take to get to the staff car or bus in the standing procession. After a motorcade sweeps away under police escort, local traffic closes in, and regaining the summit party is not easy. I can now say, looking back, that not once did I miss a motorcade.

However, I did get some good bruises from leaping into moving cars. Over the years, I also learned various nations' techniques for providing motorcade security. In Nigeria, soldiers stood in escort jeeps and trucks and used their rifle butts to bang on car roofs to clear a path. In the Netherlands, police in fluorescent orange and white Porsches darted ahead of the convoy. Here in Moscow, the KGB's security cars swerved into oncoming traffic lanes at the sight of an approaching car, heading straight for it until the motorist dodged.

We stayed in the Lenin Hills guest complex (renamed back to its original Sparrow Hills, Vorobyovy Gory, in 1999), renowned for its parklands, Moscow State University, and the view of the city and Moskva River.

Every day the breakfast table was laden with cucumbers, tomatoes, cold meats, and fish, in addition to breads and traditional Western fare. As always, my time was spent preparing for negotiations, drafting records of the day's talks, and attending the formal social events that are part of these important visits.

Inside the Kremlin conference room, mineral water and soft drinks kept us fueled while periodic banter between Brezhnev and Kissinger lightened the weight of the deliberations. The talks were heavy going, with neither side prepared to make the concessions needed for a permanent strategic arms agreement. Kissinger had initially touted this summit as an almost certain "conceptual breakthrough"—which it was not. Businesslike and constructive, it was neither a breakthrough nor a failure. It was agreed that negotiations would continue from the respective capitals.

And we were off. We stopped in London on March 28 for lunch and talks with Foreign Secretary James "Sunny Jim" Callaghan, who listened carefully and probed professionally in his cheerful, informal, engaging manner. This was the first of several meetings I would have with Callaghan during his years first as foreign secretary and then as prime minister.

We were back in Washington that night.

Five days after our return from the Moscow summit, Pompidou died. The newswire was brought to my desk in the Old Executive Office Building within seconds of its receipt in the White House Situation Room on April 2, 1974. I had been working down through a stack of NSC staff papers, having just made the return from Moscow—while also fighting the remnants of a nasty flu that had attacked half of the traveling party.

President Nixon issued a statement of profound personal regret, and shortly thereafter, the White House press office announced that he would fly to France for the memorial service. By that time an advance team was already airborne, en route to Paris to arrange the myriad details for the president's visit. I would travel with the president on that somber mission.

On April 5, 1974, I boarded Air Force One armed with my pocket-sized detailed staff schedule. As previously mentioned, these bibles of American summitry are central to the staffer's kit. They provide details not readily available elsewhere for the fast-paced events of overseas travel, including weather, time, location, security instructions, and transportation instructions. For this trip we were to arrive at Orly airport at 10:30 p.m., and I had my own debarkation arrangements, as did all the other members of our party. The French reception committee was identified, and I learned that the U.S. president would pass the French Honor Guard to a Pavillon d'Honneur. There he would make brief remarks after standing for a moment in respectful silence before Pompidou's portrait.

There were many other details, as many as could be covered. I always looked for anything pertaining to the first day and night, knowing that there would be plenty of time to study the rest of the bible during the flight.

President Nixon's problems were well underway at this time. It had just been reported that he had to pay nearly $500,000 in back taxes—there was a chilly atmosphere on board the jet that morning. Among those flying with us were Chief of Staff Alexander Haig, Deputy Assistant to the President for National Security Affairs Lieutenant General Brent Scowcroft, and Deputy Director of Central Intelligence Lieutenant General Vernon Walters. Walters, a phenomenal linguist who was fluent in at least eight languages, served as Nixon's personal interpreter. The two had already traveled extensively together, during both the vice presidential and presidential years.

No bilateral meetings with foreign leaders had been planned, but we expected that Nixon would call on Alain Poher, president of the French Senate, who would serve as interim president of France until Giscard d'Estaing was elected in May. We also prepared for possible meetings with other presidents, monarchs, and heads of state who would attend the service.

As we flew toward Paris, a message came in saying that most important Western Alliance leaders would welcome a meeting with Nixon after the service. This was followed by more requests. Now, while in flight, we had to work on staffing an entirely new schedule of informal, bilateral summit tête-à-têtes for the afternoon of April 6, the same day as Pompidou's memorial.

The president would meet with not only Poher but also Italian President Giovanni Leone, British Prime Minister Harold Wilson, German Chancellor Willy Brandt, Danish Prime Minister Poul Hartling, the USSR Chairman of the Presidium of the Supreme Soviet Nicolay Podgorny, and Japanese Prime Minister Kakuei Tanaka.

Nixon would need background for each meeting. In his preferred NSC / White House format we had to distill priority issues, likely specific interests of the other leader, and possible talking points for the president.

Usually I had months to prepare for U.S.-Soviet summits. Now I had hours, then minutes. We sent messages to Washington requesting additional information from State and other departments on key political and economic issues. All information was to be cabled to the U.S. embassy in Paris for availability upon our arrival. As Air Force One neared landing, I was dictating introductory pages for each meeting to the NSC staff secretary, while she built up a set of meeting folders that we would continue to fill in Paris.

Lesson learned: If you are a summit staffer, do not count on having ample time. There will be scrambles such as this.

All the talks went smoothly. Pompidou's memorial service took place at Notre Dame Cathedral on April 6. That evening, a diplomatic reception was held at the Quai d'Orsay for visiting foreign leaders.

On April 7, after Nixon's breakfast with Chairman Podgorny and meeting with Prime Minister Tanaka, the U.S. delegation departed for

Washington. General Walters sat across from me on Air Force One, appearing to read book after book. When I noticed what the books were—foreign dictionaries—I could only admire him. Walters relaxed during the long flight home by studying dictionaries.

Exactly one month later, on May 6–7, 1974, international wires carried a new flash: Chancellor Willy Brandt of West Germany had resigned. Günter Guillaume, Brandt's personal aide for years, had been arrested and had confessed to being a spy for the East German Ministry of State Security and an officer in the East German Army. Brandt had taken responsibility and resigned.

So now, within weeks, the leadership of France and the Federal Republic of Germany had changed. Giscard d'Estaing, former minister of finance, was now president of France. Helmut Schmidt, also former minister of finance, was the new chancellor of West Germany.

In mid-1974, the East-West swing from Cold War to détente reached its most pronounced, if short-lived, phase. Nixon captured and conveyed this reality in his address to the NATO Council in Brussels on June 26: NATO needed to accept, he said, that anticommunism no longer sufficed to hold the alliance together. New motivations were necessary.

We had just completed a productive tour in the Middle East, and after this we would fly on to the Soviet Union for the third of the summits of détente with Brezhnev.

In Brussels, the president promised close consultation with NATO members about the results of his upcoming meetings with Brezhnev. He held bilateral talks with Prime Minister Leo Tindemans of Belgium, Chancellor Schmidt of West Germany, Prime Minister Wilson of Great Britain, and Prime Minister Mariano Rumor of Italy.

The Moscow summit was held from June 27 through July 3, 1974. To my mind, it marked the grand finale of 1970s détente. The relationship had never been one of deep friendship or an enduring bond, but a comfortable, professional familiarity emerged from intensive negotiations and face-to-face contacts over several years.

The first day was spent moving from one event to the next in the Kremlin. I was struck by how, not surprisingly, the Soviets treasured the same items as the czars—luxurious oriental carpets, elegant lace curtains, brass and crystal oil-lamp wall sconces, chandeliers, and more displays of opulence. That evening, Nixon spoke of the transformation of relations from confrontation to coexistence to ever-expanding bilateral cooperation.

He and Brezhnev met twice the next day for difficult talks on core issues of strategic importance. These moved slowly. On the afternoon of June 28, the two delegations assembled in St. Catherine's Hall to sign bilateral agreements that had involved my staffing efforts: the U.S.-USSR Agreements on Cooperation in the Field of Energy, Cooperation in the Field of Housing and Other Construction, and Cooperation in Artificial Heart Research and Development.

There were now some fifteen bilateral agreements, together forming a new web—barring the unforeseen, as always—of cooperative ties between central elements of U.S. and Soviet society. These agreements were thoroughly thought through, designed to draw the two nations into increasingly productive cooperation. With the agreement on housing, given the inferior quality of Soviet efforts in that area, we neared the limit of these undertakings. The very technical Artificial Heart Agreement had been negotiated between the U.S. Department of Health, Education and Welfare and the USSR Ministry of Health. As Nixon prepared to sign it, Secretary Kissinger turned to those of us watching and quipped, "My most difficult negotiation."

Over the first days in Moscow, Nixon, Brezhnev, and their delegations continued to address SALT, including measures to limit further antiballistic missile deployments and to further narrow the scope of permissible nuclear weapons tests. On June 29, 1974, Nixon and Podgorny signed a

"Long-Term Agreement between the United States of America and the Union of Soviet Socialist Republics to Facilitate Economic, Industrial, and Technical Cooperation."

After that accomplishment, we all left for a weekend at Brezhnev's Crimean vacation complex on the Black Sea, at Oreanda, Yalta. The Nixons were housed in a seaside villa, while most of the U.S. delegation stayed in two sanatoriums. These facilities, built on the Crimean Peninsula and elsewhere in the USSR, provided vacations mixed with medical care, both mandatory for Soviet workers annually. My room was in the Parus Sanatorium, a high-rise on a cliff. From my balcony I looked out over the water and beach, where tiny figures sunbathed. To the right below me, perched on another promontory, was the magnificent castle Swallows Nest, which businessman Baron von Steingel had built around an original nineteenth-century wooden house in 1911–12.

With little work to do that weekend, I welcomed the company of a rather senior Soviet diplomat with well-established KGB connections. Bright and cheerful, he appeared at the bar for evening cocktails, then at my table for dinner, and finally at breakfast the next morning. I understood this man had been assigned to keep an eye on me. Every member of high-level U.S. delegations is of interest to a foreign government. The Soviets would observe and learn whatever they could. This "friend" would file a personality report, adding to information on the United States that could later be drawn on as needed.

I knew as a summit sherpa that I was never really off-duty or on vacation, however pleasant my surroundings and company were at times.

On the morning of June 31, I decided to start the day with a swim. The Parus Sanatorium had a private beach, which I reached by an elevator descending through a shaft cut in the granite cliff. From there I walked out to the beach—and faced a U.S. telephone. It had been placed on a stand at the edge of the beach's granite rocks, emblazoned on the dial with the words "Oreanda White House." The distinctive White House Communications Agency symbol completed the décor. To reach almost anyone anywhere in the world, all I had to do was pick up that receiver and identify myself. The connection was invariably made in seconds.

Another reminder of the amazing technical support that travels with U.S. presidents.

Later that day, I conveyed to the director of White House Communications my disappointment at not finding another phone floating on a rubber seahorse during my swim in the Black Sea.

Nixon and Brezhnev continued with their arms control discussions, and possible progress began to take shape. A three-hour Black Sea cruise capped the weekend. Two nearly identical 115-foot yachts awaited us, tied to a pier off the Soviet leader's villa with engines running. Nixon and Brezhnev sat on the poolside terrace when I arrived, with the surf breaking on the rocks just beyond. The pool was a long rounded rectangle, with a roof holding tracks for sliding glass walls that could be drawn in bad weather. My mind flashed to scenes from James Bond.

The two nations' leaders took their places in *Boat One*, in upholstered seats around a table on an open upper deck. I and my colleagues, accompanied by several Soviets including the deputy chief of protocol, boarded the *Back-Up Boat*. *Boat One* led the way, slowly at first off Yalta to permit the media in a chartered tour boat to capture our departure. U.S. and Soviet flags flew from the yardarms of *Boat One*. Both yachts flew the naval ensign of the KGB Frontier Forces from their fantails—green and blue, with the red hammer and sickle in a block of white.

Varnished bridgework and fine blue trim set off the white hulls, the large windows of the curved main deck saloons forward, and the upper decks. Oriental carpets ran the length of both the open passenger decks and the interiors. The wood-paneled interiors held crystal and mirrors engraved with contemporary Soviet art, their tables laden with a late afternoon lunch.

Brezhnev's love for big, fast cars had been well reported in the course of the summitry of détente, and his pleasure for speed was as true on the water. Throttles were opened, and the two yachts, charging against white-capped waters, were soon tearing across the Black Sea at thirty knots. Far in the distance, the faint gray shapes of Soviet warships on station for the summit visit broke the southern horizon. To my mind, that cruise marked the high point in friendship and ease between the U.S. and Soviet leaders of détente in the early 1970s.

On July 1, the president flew to Minsk for a ceremonial visit to the Belorussian Soviet Socialist Republic, where he honored those massacred by Nazis at Khatyn during World War II by laying a wreath.

Back in Moscow, I walked along the Kremlin's long halls of the czars' apartments to the U.S. staff's office to resume my share of the work drafting the president's speeches, toasts, and the culminating Joint U.S.-Soviet Communiqué of the summit. The permanent SALT agreement on offensive strategic arms was not reached at the 1974 Moscow summit. Nixon and Brezhnev did agree to a communiqué underscoring the importance of such an agreement, that it should hold until 1985, and that the U.S. and Soviet SALT delegations should reconvene in Geneva to resume negotiations.

The summit marked limited strategic arms control progress despite this pronounced stall. A protocol now limited both nations to a single deployment area for antiballistic missile systems (the 1972 treaty had specified two). An agreement limited underground nuclear explosions; a Threshold Test Ban prohibited explosions above 150 kilotons. Critical international political discussions had continued during the summit, taking on points of friction and contention including the Middle East and East-West relations more generally.

When Nixon again addressed the Soviet people on July 2, 1974, his tone echoed awareness of a closing chapter. He reflected on progress over the past two years in the context of his own career-long experience with the Soviets, pointing to the web of new bilateral agreements. While recognizing that he would no longer be able to help guide the work yet to be done, Nixon celebrated what had been accomplished and the diplomatic seeds that had been planted. A formal reception beneath the massive chandeliers of the Kremlin's St. George Hall brought the 1974 Moscow summit to a close.

Just over one month later, Nixon announced his resignation following the Watergate scandal. I was in the East Room of the White House when he bade farewell to his cabinet and staff, midmorning on August 9, 1974. Gretchen had driven in from Annapolis to join me. Nixon wept as he spoke and recalled his mother. At 11:35 a.m., he had a one-sentence letter delivered to the secretary of state: "Dear Mr. Secretary: I hereby resign the office of President of the United States. Sincerely, Richard M. Nixon." This development completed a stunningly fast change in much of the West's leadership: Pompidou, Brandt, and Nixon were all gone.

Their replacements—Giscard d'Estaing, Helmut Schmidt, and Gerald R. Ford—along with Harold Wilson of Great Britain, seemed likeminded and dedicated to cooperation.

CHAPTER 8

Ford's Continuity, 1974

Less than three hours after Nixon's farewell, I listened to Ford in the Roosevelt Room as he held his first meeting with NATO nations' ambassadors to the United States on August 9, 1974. His theme of continuity made great sense to me, given my labors since 1971. This had, of course, been developed by Secretary Kissinger, also in the room that first day.

As he acknowledged the shock of the sudden change, Ford would echo his theme three days later in a joint session of Congress. He planned to continue collaborating with U.S. allies in the Atlantic and Pacific; to work on improving relationships in Central and South America; and, in the wake of Vietnam, in Asia. Ford wished to build on the achievements of Nixon's summitry with the Soviet Union, to follow through on progress with China, and to continue negotiating for a lasting peace in the Middle East, with a stable structure of trade and finance among all nations.

Ford also embraced continuity with Kissinger, announcing before he took the oath of office that he would ask the assistant to the president for national security affairs and secretary of state to continue in his dual role. In seeking this guidance even before beginning his presidency, Ford was off to a running start in his own summitry.

With the coming of September and the opening of the UN General Assembly, the annual surge of high-level foreign visitors—ministers, heads of government, and chiefs of state—kicked off, with intense diplomatic pressure for calls on President Ford before or after each leader's UN address in New York. Every one of these encounters was planned meticulously, including proposed toasts.

The drafting of toasts is among the summit staffer's responsibilities. Anecdotes, gentle humor, historical vignettes, and specific goals of the summit should all be included, with reference to the significance of the event not only for the participating nations but also for international relations in the broader sense. The toast should enhance the spirit of the occasion and seamless flow of the summit, from the media's coverage to the public's appreciation of the event. Of course, the toast needs to seem natural. It has to capture the summit leader's cadence and manner of speech. The order in which topics are raised should be such that a quick scan allows the leader to internalize the themes and outline for a smooth read—or, even better, to depart from the prepared text for spontaneity based on prior study of the text.

Toasts are part of the substance and record of a summit, and presidents—particularly while flying to several nations in quick succession—rely on their staffs for carefully drafted remarks. Last-minute flurries among a delegation's speechwriters are not uncommon. Even en route, a president may request that NSC and foreign policy advisers produce new or revised language to better capture the dynamics of a summit in progress.

True to Ford's foreign policy commitment, he kept up an extremely fast pace of summit-level consultations for the rest of 1974 and into early

1975. From October 8 to 13, 1974, First Secretary of the Central Committee of the Polish United Workers Party Edward Gierek paid an official visit. For at least four months before then—while Nixon was still president—representatives of the Polish embassy in Washington had been discreetly, nervously taking soundings of me and my U.S. government colleagues on the prospects for this visit, given Nixon's mounting domestic problems. My counsel had not been complex: Whatever the outcome of Nixon's problems, Poland should expect the United States to continue on a steady course. The nation would honor its international commitments, and Poland should assume that the first secretary's visit would proceed as planned.

Which it did, reflecting the interests of both nations in extending the benefits of détente beyond U.S.-USSR bilateral relations. This productive encounter yielded several agreements in the finest tradition of the 1972–74 summits. There was one major variation from that tradition, however. During his lengthy, formal reply to President Ford's toast at the White House dinner on October 8, Gierek stated unequivocally that Poland had "consciously chosen" to ally itself with the USSR. All the more reason to proceed with the groundbreaking Soviet visit that was planned for the end of November.

The schedule for November included a White House meeting with Chancellor Bruno Kreisky of Austria, a visit to the Republic of Korea and Japan, and a meeting with General Secretary Leonid Brezhnev in the port city of Vladivostok, on the Sea of Japan. President Ford cautiously planned a get-acquainted visit with the Soviets, one that would include the opportunity to discuss bilateral relations, nothing more.

This did not make staff-level preparations any less intensive. We prepared background papers, personality studies, and position papers on every issue the president might address. President Ford devoured the information in the months preceding the trip, while receiving visitors in Washington. The schedule was extremely crowded, domestically as well as with foreign visitors, to reinforce continuing U.S. strength and leadership.

On October 10, 1974, the White House and the Élysée Palace simultaneously announced that President Ford and President Giscard d'Estaing would meet on the island of Martinique, the French West Indies, that December.

But President Ford's summit travel began with a trip to Mexico on October 21, 1974, for a day's talks and ceremony with President Luis Echeverría. A month later, the president was in Tokyo on a state visit that included a ceremonial call on Japan's Emperor Hirohito. In an important caveat to all summit sherpas, here I emphasize an omission in planning: The president was incorrectly advised about what to wear. The visit was entirely cordial, but this oversight highlights that appropriate diplomatic attire should be on every summit sherpa's checklist.

Ford also met for talks with Japan's Prime Minister Kakuei Tanaka, focusing on the international energy crisis of 1973–74 and the need for consumer nations to cooperate more closely. Air Force One then carried the president on to Seoul, South Korea. A crowd of 2 million welcomed him on a twelve-mile motorcade from Gimpo International Airport to the Blue House for talks with President Park Chung-hee, the highly effective, if controversial, leader of the country from 1961 until his assassination in 1979. Here Ford assumed the role of commander in chief as well as president, pledging further U.S. cooperation in the development of South Korea's defense industries. Ford pledged that U.S. troops would remain on the peninsula in shared defense of the nation. Next he helicoptered to meet with soldiers of the U.S. Army's Second Division, just a few miles from the demilitarized zone separating North and South Korea. Having firmly recommitted to allies in the Pacific, the president was again airborne, this time for Vladivostok.

Summit sherpas should enjoy travel, whatever the form, the mode, and the pace. In November 1974, cold air stung my face as I stood informally with General Secretary Brezhnev, Foreign Minister Andrei Gromyko, Ambassador Anatoly Dobrynin, and other members of the Soviet and

U.S. delegations on a snow-covered taxiway at Vozdvizhenka fighter base. We waited for President Ford to disembark from Air Force One.

Brezhnev was in high spirits. A reporter in the traveling press corps pointed to closed-door hangars for interceptor aircraft, asking, "What's in those, Mr. General Secretary?" Brezhnev absorbed the translation and immediately shot back, "Tomatoes! Vegetable cellars where we store tomatoes." Everyone laughed.

He stepped forward to greet the new U.S. president. A long motorcade rolled into position to take us one thousand feet or so to the luxury train that would carry us to the summit site, on the outskirts of Vladivostok.

The Soviets brought the best train in the entire USSR across the nation for the ninety-minute run. It was a beauty, replete with the same rich paneling, mirrors, carpeting, and crystal I had last admired on the Black Sea. The staff cars were windowed compartments with sliding doors that opened onto a corridor running the length of each car.

The president and general secretary occupied the dining car, where they engaged in preliminary—and essential—small talk and banter. A couple of cars behind them, I leaned against a window chrome rail and studied the passing landscape: small rural houses, chimney smoke wisps, outhouses, an occasional person. Keeping pace with the train, several black cars sped along a parallel road. This was our VIP motorcade on a breakneck race that would bring it to the train platform at our destination just seconds before we arrived.

Also catching my attention were several heavy cables that ran underfoot along the train's corridor. I followed them the length of my car, past the ajar door of the toilet compartment—where they plunged through the open flap at the base of the toilet bowl to the exterior of the train.

Once again, the White House Communications Agency had preceded us. As he rumbled through the far-Pacific reaches of the USSR, the president of the United States had secure communications leaping from the roof of the train to a global link of communications relays. Aside from regular telephone service at Vladivostok, the president and his party could also access secure voice communications, teletype service, a two-way staff radio net available to any member of the official party, and an individually tailored paging system. Such communications support is a feature for U.S. summit parties and other high-level delegations. The staffer must become familiar with the range of this support and how to use it most effectively. After a summit has begun, there is no time for on-the-job training.

Our destination for the summit was the Okeanskiy (Oceanside) Sanatorium, a hundred-acre health spa and recreation area ten miles north of Vladivostok. The two sides proceeded to the conference building and immediately convened the first session of SALT discussions. The conference room was a steamy greenhouse lounge, bordered with palms and flowing plants—an environment conducive to progress.

Ford and Brezhnev were workers. The first session ran officially from 6:15 to 8:15 p.m. on November 23, but they agreed to push ahead. An elaborate dinner planned for the first night was postponed until the second. The second session ran from 8:45 to 11:30 p.m.; then a third from midnight until 12:30 a.m., now on November 24. During breaks, Ford, Kissinger, and General Brent Scowcroft conferred while strolling the grounds, or behind closed doors in the president's own limousine, which had been flown ahead to USSR.

When I entered the talks on the morning of November 24, spirits ran high. The discussion had switched to East-West relations and prospects for the Conference on Security and Cooperation in Europe. Ford was euphoric; the talks had far exceeded his expectations. Now, as he and Brezhnev expanded their discussions, the delegations' SALT experts were closeted elsewhere at the conference site putting the final touches to the language of the new understanding.

The preceding March, Kissinger had suggested a conceptual breakthrough—which was now realized. The Vladivostok Accord of November 24, 1974, established the principle of strategic parity between the United States and the Soviet Union. A ceiling of 2,400 strategic delivery vehicles—ICBM launchers, SLBM launchers, and heavy bombers—was permitted for each side, with a subceiling of 1,320 ICBMs and SLBMs to be armed with multiple, independently targetable warheads, or reentry vehicles. It was further agreed that the new agreement should run until 1985, and that U.S. and Soviet delegations should reconvene in Geneva in January 1975, to negotiate the details of the formal permanent agreement text, guided by the Vladivostok Accord.

Next came the Soviet chefs' banquet, an abundant luncheon of delicacies including caviar and specialty seafoods, meats, and pies. With its closing words, Ford's toast marked the culmination of progress for détente summitry of the early 1970s: "Let us get on with the business of controlling arms, as I think we have in the last twenty-four hours." There would of course be challenges.

After the feast, we were offered a tour of Vladivostok (or "Ruler of the East," *vladet* plus *vostok*), the primary naval base for the Soviet Pacific Fleet. It was a handsome city, hilly like San Francisco, its harbor crowded with the gray hulls of Soviet warships. It had been closed to Americans since 1948.

At twilight, I reboarded the VIP train for the run north to Vozdvizhenka air base and the return flight to the United States on board Air Force One.

Less than two weeks after the return from Vladivostok, Ford hosted White House talks and dinner with Prime Minister Pierre Trudeau of Canada. Trudeau, who dealt with the United States as prime minister under Presidents Johnson, Nixon, Ford, Carter, and Reagan, combined the pursuit of distinct Canadian policies, variously merging and separating from those of the United States, with the underlying friendship and pleasure he took from America and Americans.

Canadian affairs were an important part of my NSC staff responsibilities, and December 4, 1974, was Trudeau's first visit to President Ford. Looking to the benefits to be expected from continuing close contacts, Trudeau said in his toast, "Mr. President, we hope . . . that you will find it convenient, as your predecessor did, to talk on a very informal basis even by phone or by quick visits which do away with all formalities, permitting us to come to the point right quickly and to solve whatever small problems we may have."

The papers we had staffed for these talks earlier in the day had included both small problems and the broader international subjects of shared interest on which the president wished to consult as part of his opening round of consultations with key allies—the results of the Vladivostok summit and their implications for East-West relations, the priority NATO agenda, the problems of Cyprus and the Middle East, and the West's efforts to extract itself from the global energy crisis, through both the work of the International Energy Agency and national efforts aimed at reducing dependence on imported oil.

Here, the broader international agenda merged with a very real bilateral problem of the moment. Canada wanted to cut back on its oil imports and to make greater use of domestic oil that traditionally had been sold to U.S. refineries along the northern tier of American states. This could not be solved in the course of an afternoon in the Oval Office, but the two leaders could and did agree to have their governments give closer attention to the issue, placing it in the low-keyed framework of neighborly respect and honorable obligations in which such small problems were best suited. And, despite occasional sparks in U.S.-Canadian summitry, cross-border relations saw continuing important progress.

As the 1974 toasts proceeded at the White House, behind the scenes at the staff level, we were bearing down on preparations for one of the most important summits of the new president's first months in office: meeting Giscard d'Estaing in Martinique.

The groundwork for this summit had been laid by Helmut Schmidt, the new chancellor of the Federal Republic of Germany (FRG), who on December 5–6, 1974, came to Washington for his first talks with President Ford. Intensely concerned about the impact on Western democracies of the energy crisis and economic problems, Schmidt first appeared at a NATO summit as chancellor in June 1974. He then remained in close touch with his friend Giscard d'Estaing. Schmidt fully grasped the need for oil-consuming nations to present a united front in dealing with oil producers. He knew France would have to abandon its previous positions and work more closely with the United States and other members of the International Energy Agency. For this to occur, both France and the United States would have to enlist skillful and flexible diplomacy.

With this background work accomplished, Schmidt spoke directly with Ford in Washington. Their two days together enabled Schmidt to advance his views on the range of economic and energy problems not only with the president but also with Secretary Kissinger, Secretary of the Treasury William Simon, the chairman of the president's Council of Economic Advisers, and the chairman of the Federal Reserve Board. The talks produced a detailed U.S.-FRG statement of agreed positions on political and economic issues, in language that helped set the stage for the talks to come in Martinique.

Great care was taken in all public statements relating to the U.S.-German talks to emphasize France's independence: France's decisions would be separate. Ford and Schmidt did not presume to speak for France. Schmidt's tone throughout the Washington meetings confirmed both his views on how critical the issues were and his satisfaction with the understandings reached.

Ford had a down-to-earth, congenial, forward-looking manner, which immediately made the chancellor comfortable. Schmidt liked the president's style, his willingness to depart from normal summit formality and stroll from the White House over to Blair House for a continuation of talks begun earlier that day in the Oval Office.

Ford, likewise, enjoyed his relationship with Schmidt, noting that after the first state dinner of December 5, the two continued talking in the White House residence until 2:00 a.m. "Relations between the U.S. and West Germany were excellent throughout my administration, primarily because Schmidt and I got along so well," Ford would later write in his autobiography, *A Time to Heal* (p. 221). "As we became better acquainted, we called each other by our first names, we joked with each other and we saw eye to eye on almost everything."

Ford would develop a similar bond and friendship with Giscard d'Estaing. As things would develop, the Martinique summit would mark a major step forward in U.S.-European relations, thanks in large part to Schmidt's tireless, carefully planned efforts.

On December 14, Ford flew to Martinique to meet d'Estaing for the first time. Two days of talks were planned. Our staff papers went into great detail on d'Estaing—his background, the policies of his new government, the interests at the heart of the enduring U.S.-French alliance, current differences and difficulties, and relations in the context of regional and global issues such as the Middle East, East-West relations, the ongoing energy crisis, and attendant economic difficulties for democracies. We had also prepared papers analyzing issues and where progress could be made.

With the Martinique summit having been announced simultaneously in Washington and Paris, the first, formal, public step had already been made toward a successful meeting. The prestige of each nation is committed when leaders meet at a summit, and it is critical that neither be seen as aiming for a political advantage by revealing unilaterally that such a meeting is planned. Summits announced or leaked in advance by one side may be postponed or even canceled by the other. No leader can afford the domestic political perception of having been treated as subordinate or inferior.

France, *évidemment*, was second to none in insisting on the correctness of this procedure—which was successfully carried out in December 1974. Given the splendid checks and balances of the U.S. democratic process and the need to engage several government departments in the careful preparation of a major summit, the business of managing simultaneous announcements is always nerve-racking.

"Un Grand Honneur pour Cette Terre Française des Antilles," the newspaper *France-Antilles* announced on December 15; "Le Monde Entier Regarde la Martinique." At 4:30 p.m. at Lamentin Airport, on the outskirts of Fort de France, Giscard d'Estaing alighted from his white Puma helicopter to receive formal military honors. Fifteen minutes later, at President Ford's scheduled arrival time, Air Force One rolled to a precision stop. The aircraft's forward door, from which the president would deplane, aligned precisely with the foot of the long red carpet that the French president traversed to greet his American counterpart. The "Star-Spangled Banner" and "La Marseillaise" were played. The island's tropical foliage shone in the fresh sunlight of a receding sea squall.

I enjoyed the colorful arrival ceremony as I savored the warm, thick Caribbean air, a most pleasant counterpoint to the recent snows of Vladivostok. It was a very special privilege to participate in America's summit diplomacy.

Giscard d'Estaing had signaled his desire for greater cooperation with the United States. His experience as finance minister had taught him that international monetary and energy problems were global, and that France could not afford Gaullist aloofness if her own interests were to be served. As Kissinger had noted, d'Estaing was far more pragmatic—and welcoming.

That evening, amid tropical flowers, torchlight, and Martinique rums at the prefect's residence, d'Estaing and Ford gave toasts reinforcing the positive tone of the alliance and summit. Both presidents seemed genuinely relaxed, enjoying each other's company thoroughly. As my colleagues and I reboarded a launch from the French aircraft carrier *Foch* for the return trip to our hotel across the harbor, the omens for the following day could not have been better.

On December 15, the two leaders and their foreign ministers retired by helicopter to a secluded mountainside villa, an informal setting where they could review the agenda of French-U.S. interests. In parallel, their financial experts, Secretary of the Treasury William Simon and Minister of Finance Jean-Pierre Fourcade, closeted themselves at the U.S. delegation's hotel. Both dialogues continued through the day—as did the president's other responsibilities.

Ford had nominated his chief of staff, General Alexander Haig, to serve as commander in chief U.S. Forces Europe and at the same time as NATO's supreme allied commander Europe. Haig was in Belgium already serving in the first role, and now NATO governments gave their formal approval for the second. Sitting on my hotel room balcony overlooking the Caribbean, I drafted Ford's message of congratulations, which was sent on to him for review and approval.

That evening we enjoyed another dinner just as relaxed and cordial as that of the first night, this time hosted by Ford. At 11:00 a.m. the next morning, December 16, the summit communiqué was released. As reported in the conservative French daily newspaper *Le Figaro*, this summit marked the end of an era of U.S.-French quarrels. *L'Aurore* concurred, and this was the general consensus.

Addressing the energy crisis, Ford and d'Estaing agreed on the need for an early conference of oil-exporting and -importing nations. As prices continued to leap, France had previously distanced itself from the newly formed International Energy Agency, but under d'Estaing the country was moving closer to an agreed-upon consumer position. On the finance front, the two leaders heeded their ministers and agreed that the time had come to move from a fixed price for gold to a market price, easing one of many international monetary strains and tensions.

The communiqué conveyed the essence of all the summit discussions, including developments in the Atlantic Alliance. In this area, the outcome exceeded the desirable to become hard, positive accomplishment. President Charles de Gaulle, wanting to establish France as an independent power, withdrew France from NATO, which meant that U.S. forces and bases were relocated in 1967. By agreeing to compensate the United States for this move, D'Estaing eased the resulting tension tremendously. France would not rejoin NATO until 2008, but in the meantime, bilateral relations and actions could and did now move forward.

Among those who had met with President Ford shortly after he took office was British Foreign Minister James Callaghan. That encounter had been followed up with an invitation to Prime Minister Harold Wilson to come to Washington in late January 1975, as part of Ford's plan to continue head-to-head talks with key allied leaders. Like Schmidt and d'Estaing before him, he connected with Ford quickly. They got along famously. While pressing ahead with the international agenda of energy shortages, inflation, balance-of-payment deficits, regional tensions around the world, and shared security interests, both enjoyed smoking their pipes.

President Ford clearly also enjoyed the risky diplomatic method of summitry—which now set the stage for more intensive summitry throughout 1975. He would grow tremendously and become a highly accomplished statesman during his presidency.

CHAPTER 9

Navigating the Mid–Cold War with President Ford, 1975

Having been embroiled in Vietnam for nearly twenty years, the United States withdrew its military forces after signing the Paris Peace Accords in 1973. This left South Vietnam to defend itself, resulting in the April 30, 1975, fall of Saigon to the invading regular North Vietnamese Army. On May 12, naval patrol boats of the Armed Forces of Cambodia (Khmer Rouge) seized the U.S. merchant ship SS *Mayaguez* and her crew of thirty-nine in international waters, thereby violating international law. President Gerald Ford faced a crisis that challenged U.S. prestige and tested the nation's resolve.

U.S. demands for the ship's return produced nothing. A U.S. Navy–Marine Task Force built around the aircraft carrier USS *Coral Sea* (CVA 43) was immediately ordered to the waters off Cambodia. On the afternoon of May 14, the president ordered the Marines to rescue the *Mayaguez*'s crew. That evening I sat in the White House's state dining room amid a highly unusual atmosphere of distraction. President Ford kept up a flow of small talk with his official guest, the Netherlands' new socialist prime minister, Johannes den Uyl. Meanwhile, his cabinet and staff—Secretary of State Kissinger, Secretary of Defense James R. Schlesinger, and National Security Adviser Scowcroft—periodically excused themselves and left the room, returning a few minutes later. Den Uyl and his Dutch delegation maintained a reserved politeness while exchanges among the Americans intensified. At 9:00 p.m. Washington time, as the White House dinner wore on, the Marine engagement half a world away completed its bloody mission, and the *Mayaguez* crew was safe. But trapped Marines would battle on for another day before most of them were evacuated—at a cost of eighteen Marine and airmen lives.

Back at the White House, the president said goodnight after the toasts, liqueurs, and a few final conversations. From there he hastened past the Rose Garden to the West Wing's Oval Office. A new chapter had opened in the diplomacy of the Ford presidency. The previous year, 1974, had brought fresh unity of purpose to the West's Big Four, but this had not stopped challenges from multiplying. Of deep concern, nowhere was this more evident than within the North Atlantic Alliance. Greece and Turkey, both members, had reached crisis level in their feud over Cyprus. Portugal, long little noticed, was in the throes of revolution, lurching from right to left with the looming possibility of communist domination. NATO's southern flank was further threatened by political problems in Italy, where communists threatened to replace Christian Democrats as the largest parliamentary party. Meanwhile, the smaller NATO nations wavered in their commitment to the alliance's common defense as they smarted from a fivefold increase in the price of oil. Beyond Europe and NATO, also demanding attention were the Middle East, relations between the industrialized global North and developing South, and a possible slowing in the momentum to build on a mutually beneficial détente between East and West.

Acutely aware of the need for action and the need to demonstrate fresh American global leadership, President Ford moved in spring 1975 to engage the dynamics of summit diplomacy on several international fronts. On April 18, the White House, coordinating with spokesmen in other NATO capitals, advised its press corps of an upcoming NATO summit. It was critical, as always, that announcements be made simultaneously. This was the summit staffer's responsibility, as well as ensuring that the spokesperson who made the announcement had the correct text and anticipated press questions, along with recommended answers. The objective was—and remains—to keep the initiative with the spokesperson, rather than leaving so much space for reporters' follow-on questions that press coverage was distracted from the intended message of the announcement.

For the 1975 NATO summit, all this meant that my office prepared a very brief, straightforward document to be forwarded by Secretary Kissinger's NSC front office to the White House press secretary. We envisioned probable press questions and provided suggested replies, including this one: "The leaders will review the full range of security issues of common concern [and] the new steps achieved in recent months in promoting cooperation to meet economic and energy problems. The pace of recent international developments suggests that the time is at hand for Western leaders to take stock and consult on this agenda of common concerns."

This consulting and stock-taking involved far more than the multilateral colloquy around the NATO conference table. In Brussels, tightly scheduled tours would permit the president not just to deliver his formal North Atlantic Council address but also to conduct separate bilateral talks—of equal importance—with most of the summit's participants. The mere presence of the U.S. president in Europe provided a springboard for additional summit stops—in Spain, Austria, Italy, and Vatican City.

I, as an NSC staffer, monitored preparations for this visit with a long checklist of every event to be staffed. These were numbered and listed in chronological order in a far-left column, leaving space for three more columns to be filled in as progress was made. The columns were headed, from the left, "Event," "Drafts received from State Dept. and others," "Cover memo drafted," and "Forwarded to HAK [Kissinger]." This level of detail allowed us to build into each cover memo the president's primary reason for holding the talks in question, all relevant background information he might need, and recommended talking points. We carefully crafted the drafts in language that the president might choose to use in the meetings, as he pursued U.S. and allied interests to the greatest advantage.

On May 28, I boarded Air Force One at Andrews Air Force Base in advance of the president, Mrs. Ford, and six of his staff members. The Secret Service had inspected my luggage. All of my directions had been included in the "trip bible." For each of the special-mission Air Force jets on which I flew, I made it a practice to learn the interior layout and where important equipment was stowed. I knew where backup supplies were in the staff work area, and any idiosyncrasies of the telephones located at various points in the aircraft, and if there were copier-machine glitches, I had been advised of them. I made a point of introducing myself and getting to know crew members in the passenger compartments and the communications center on board each aircraft. Even though these flights could be long, the drafting, revising, and communications required during a presidential flight were often carried out under extreme time pressure. I learned that any revisions made to the text of the president's arrival statement should be anticipated. Even the best seasoned summit secretary can type only so quickly when a jet is banking for its final approach to the summit destination. Even the best photocopier will not do its work when the aircraft is climbing or descending at a certain angle.

The presidential Air Force jets are handsome machines, their hulls white and lined with blue. In lieu of an airline name, "United States of America" distinguishes the "flying Oval Office." When I flew on Air Force One, a senior staff room covering the aircraft's full beam included two conference tables, telephones connecting to the communications center, and two L-shaped secretary's desks. On the flight to Brussels, I sat at one of the staff tables with General Scowcroft. The president's chief of staff, Donald Rumsfeld; press secretary Ron Nessen; presidential aide Terry O'Donnell; and advanceman Red Cavaney sat across the aisle. The flight was seven hours and ten minutes long—all of it filled with a steady flow of papers to and from the president's office. Periodically he and Mrs. Ford strolled through the jet, conversing with staff and the traveling press, in an atmosphere at once professional and relaxed.

In this friendly environment, which President Ford encouraged on board Air Force One, we made the final changes to the president's summit address. And from the moment of arrival at Zaventem Airport, Brussels, precisely at the scheduled hour of 8:00 p.m., the president launched into an extremely heavy schedule. Each event had been planned to contribute to his summit objectives. Following remarks at the airport arrival ceremony, he traveled by motorcade to the Royal Palace for a courtesy call on the king and queen and then the first of his NATO bilateral meetings with Prime Minister Leo Tindemans and the Belgian minister of foreign affairs.

This pace continued, all of it thought through meticulously ahead of time—a major part of summit staffers' responsibility. In the words of Louis Brownlow, chairman in 1936 of President Franklin D. Roosevelt's Committee on Administrative Management, "a passion for anonymity" is the marker of an effective White House staff member. A dedication to discretion is essential, as is good judgment about when and where to appear. A good staff member need not, and often should not, be present at various of the many events scheduled during a president's overseas travel.

That said, to participate can be exhilarating. At 4:15 p.m. the day after landing, I was in the presidential motorcade to NATO headquarters for the first of two days of multilateral summit sessions. Following the opening ceremony and the traditional "family portrait" of NATO leaders, the U.S. delegation proceeded to Conference Room Number One for a restricted session, not open to the press. The president, flanked by Secretary Kissinger and U.S. ambassador to NATO David Bruce, took his seat at the famous oval conference table surrounding an open floor space centered on the NATO sword and shield emblem. Here, with the United States placed between the NATO secretary-general and the U.K. delegation, the principals of fourteen nations faced one another as allies and peers. Their accompanying delegations were arrayed behind them in conference chairs fitted with translation headsets. I sat in one of these as I studied participants' faces, attempting to gauge their reactions to the U.S. president's address.

After two days of consultations, the NATO summit's final communiqué was issued. Within the rounded language of diplomacy, it addressed every critical point identified by the United States as essential for alliance-wide progress. The main U.S. goal had been to reaffirm solidarity, which was accomplished. As well, the alliance's central raison d'être of safeguarding members and creating lasting peace was restated. The summit's final communiqué provided a formal record of this bond. All the bilateral talks had been even more important in developing frank, constructive understandings among member nations' leaders—in terms far more explicit and operationally oriented than would have been either possible or desirable in any communiqué. These agreements would guide the work and cooperation of each nation's foreign policy and defense ministries after the summiteers left Brussels.

I loved my job and felt a deep sense of honor in being able to carry it out. While I was overseas, the family was thriving in Annapolis. Alex and Ty were moving up the line from Mrs. Hansel's Children's Workshop kindergarten to the Key School, which offered grades 1 through 12. St. John's College, also in Annapolis, had a Great Books program that produced several graduates who became Key School faculty members. This meant young learners had the opportunity to become familiar, from a very early age, with classic works of philosophy and the humanities. Gretchen also immersed herself in Key School activities, starting as a volunteer in the library, then moving to president of the parents' league, and finally to trustee. In the lovely Maryland 1975 springtime, my sons were learning the sport of lacrosse on the Rolling Knolls junior team. The family was busy, with Gretchen solidly at the helm.

In Brussels, after the NATO summit, most of the U.S. traveling party turned its attention to Madrid, where a U.S.-Spanish summit was scheduled for the following day. But President Ford focused on two more bilateral talks to maximize the opportunities afforded in Brussels—one with Norwegian Prime Minister Trygve Bratteli and the other with François-Xavier Ortoli, president of the Commission of the European Communities. I was note-taker during the president's talks with Bratteli. While scribbling away, I was struck by the depth of the friendship and ties of purpose. Clearly these were far more significant than any transitory alliance problems. The two leaders' conversation ranged easily over the events of the summit, and the white-haired Bratteli, a World War II member of Norway's Resistance and survivor of German concentration camps, also shared some of his personal story. Most of the Bratteli family had emigrated to the United States, and he had many relatives in Staten Island, New York. He himself could have emigrated, but a life of politics in Norway was his destiny.

On December 20, 1973, while Ford was vice president, the Basque terrorist wing Euskadi Ta Askatasuna (Basque Homeland and Liberty) assassinated the Spanish prime minister, Admiral Juan Carrero Blanco. His funeral was held the following day, attended by dignitaries including Ford. Now, a year and a half later in 1975, President Ford was determined to negotiate a new agreement for the U.S. use of Spanish military bases. Even more important, Ford saw Spain as a critical geopolitical crossroads for Western democracies. Generalissimo Francisco Franco was very ill, and upon his death (just a few months later, on November 20), Juan Carlos would be declared king of Spain. Ford believed Spain must receive credit for its contributions to Western security—and must be encouraged to transform itself into a democracy during the final quarter of the twentieth century.

At the NATO summit, he had pressed this case and been rebuffed. His visit to Madrid under these conditions highlighted both Ford's boldness and wisdom. The colorful Spanish welcome reflected Spain's appreciation. When the door of Air Force One swung open at 11:00 a.m. on May 31, at the foot of the ramp were Generalissimo and Mrs. Franco, Prime Minister and Mrs. Carlos Arias Navarro, and Minister of Foreign Affairs and Mrs. Pedro Cortina y Mauri. The summit motorcade was lined with a military guard of honor, while spectators packed the sidewalks. This marvelous pageantry reinforced my staffers' thinking about the key importance of thorough preparations for such a visit. Here we were, in this moment when an important new page was about to be turned between the United States and Spain. And we were playing a part in the high-flown action.

The limousines stopped at the Plaza de Cibeles, where Mayor Angel Garcia-Lomas presented Ford with a ceremonial Key to the City of Madrid. As the motorcade continued, the Royal Palace Guard dressed the parade. Guardsmen in golden spiked silver helmets and scarlet tunics rode tall chestnut horses, their ivory capes flowing down to the stirrups and covering the horses' rumps. From the heart of the city, the motorcade headed north toward Ciudad Universitaria and the Palace of Moncloa, where the Fords would reside for their visit. They greeted the palace staff, and in fifteen minutes they were again on the move.

Still not having seen my quarters, I joined the Fords when they returned to Moncloa for a working luncheon with Prime Minister Arias. About twenty of us sat at a single table, where at my end the conversation was tentative. We were all eager to pursue the positive goals we shared—yet remained formal, seeking the types of exchanges that would emerge only as the relationship developed.

The president and prime minister adjourned after lunch to a lounge where they could continue their exchanges. After the future king and Princess Sophia arrived at 5:00 p.m., Ford and Prince Juan Carlos spoke alone for more than a half hour. I still think back on this meeting as significant in Western history, because it confirmed the identical purposes on so many fronts of the United States and Spain, which in the years ahead would grow into a democracy.

It wasn't until after 6:00 p.m. that I left the staff offices at Moncloa Palace to visit my hotel room, which I first had to locate. The advance team had designated one for me, and it was, as always, stellar. My baggage and black-tie attire for the evening's state dinner were waiting, along with a note from the advance team cautioning me not to trip when entering or exiting the elevator; it did not always meet the floors at level.

Dinner was held at the royal palace, which transported three centuries back into Spain's rich history. We passed through halls and drawing rooms heavy in gold, tapestries, statues, and paintings to the palace's ceremonial dining room. One hundred fifty of us took our seats at a single table beneath sixteen chandeliers. The waiters wore livery of deep blue and orange. Spectacular courses were served in profusion—and quickly. As each one was whisked away after only a few minutes, I noticed many of my American colleagues and our Spanish hosts starting to eat faster. Eventually a spontaneous, very discreet grapevine carried the explanation: The courses were being timed to the pace of Franco's eating— and in his ailing state, the generalissimo cared very little for food. This challenge lasted for the entire banquet. But it was more than offset by the warmth and generosity of Spanish hospitality, which concluded with toasts of sparkling white wine poured from bottles that had been labeled with President Ford's signature.

The feasting was followed by coffee in the Salon de Gasparini, and finally the Salon de Conciertos for music. Selections from Borodin and Joaquín Turina were performed on an ornamented quartet of two violins, one viola, and one cello, all created for the Spanish court at the end of the seventeenth century by the Italian master Antonio Stradivari.

From Spain we flew to Salzburg, Austria; we had been traveling less than a week so far. I was oriented not by days of the week but by the trip bible, which pointed me toward the next summit location and event. With detailed, annotated diagrams of arrangements for each arrival ceremony, the bible provided all the answers and information I needed. For Austria, the Salzburg Airport terminal building was sketched in, with a welcoming band and local crowd in front of it. In the center of this drawing, a column listed all the vehicles in the motorcade. I scanned it for our staffers' ride, designated "VIP bus." The diagram showed where the Austrian honor guard and official party greeting the Fords would wait, where the press would be, and where staffers should stand for the arrival ceremony. We could see where the microphone would be placed in relation to the parked Air Force One, and which stairs from the plane the president and Mrs. Ford would use.

Everything had been considered in depth and was mapped—but surprises do not adhere to plans. As we debarked from the aircraft, it was drizzling. Having nearly reached the bottom of the stairs, the president fell, his arms held out to brace him as he tumbled onto the wet tarmac. His military aide and Chancellor Bruno Kreisky rushed to assist, but there was no damage, and Ford took the mishap in good humor. As I recall, while regaining his feet the president quipped to Kreisky, "Thanks for letting me drop in on you." The arrival ceremony proceeded, followed by the motorcade to Schloss Klessheim, a Baroque palace where the Fords would reside.

The main purpose of this visit was for the president to meet for the first time with Egypt's president, Anwar Sadat, to establish face-to-face contact and develop a summit-level dialogue essential for further progress in the Middle East. I and my Middle East colleagues on the NSC and at the State Department staffed these U.S.-Egyptian talks. The first round of the Ford-Sadat talks was held on June 1.

I found a vacant desk in the staff office at Schloss Klessheim, where I settled in to draft a lengthy report from the president to Vice President Nelson Rockefeller covering highlights of the NATO summit and the visit to Madrid. This message would be reviewed by General Scowcroft and transmitted later that afternoon. Back in Washington, both the executive and legislative branches were, as always, intensely interested in the latest developments during the president's summitry. Much of the day-to-day news had of course come from the international press, but an insider's view allowed the vice president to stay well informed and provide more authoritative status updates to members of Congress. For all these reasons, missives such as this are an important part of the business of summitry.

This was the pattern for all our visits—intensely focused work, luxurious lodgings, and wonderful entertainment, always with more to learn about history, diplomatic relations, and each country's art and music, in all a most welcome mix of hard work and summit adventure.

The work demanded 100 percent attention regardless of the circumstances. The summit staffer is always expected to be at the appointed place at the appointed time, a mandate that can involve strenuous maneuvering. In October 1974, for instance, during a visit to Rome with Secretary Kissinger, I learned two routes to the Italian prime minister's office in the Villa Madama, a sixteenth-century architectural masterpiece of vaulted ceilings, framed in gardens and surrounding parks, rich in frescoes and stucco work. One route is via a small elevator that ascends through the middle of a steep corkscrew staircase. The other is the staff route: walking up that steep corkscrew staircase. Or dashing, as I had to do. I thought of that earlier rush as Air Force One flew us to Rome on June 3, 1975.

Maybe it was a way of preparing myself for a repeat. A full summit's program had been packed into only a few hours. After the usual ceremonial welcomes, and punctuated by a lavish banquet at the Palazzo del Quirinale, President Ford was hustled from one place to the next for the talks. He met one-on-one with President Giovanni Leone, followed by an expanded Italian session, then a meeting with Prime Minister Aldo Moro and other ministers at the Villa Madama, and finally a private audience with Pope Paul VI at the Vatican. Throughout the day, the president repeated many of the same themes as during the NATO summit, emphasizing the importance of Italy's contributions as a NATO ally, and of our shared belief in democracy. While sensitive to the need not to interfere with Italy's internal political processes, President Ford also unequivocally voiced his preference for Italy's political direction, as an important Mediterranean ally of the United States.

As we sped from the Villa Madama toward Vatican City, General Scowcroft, anticipating the immediate future, asked if I had drafted remarks on which the president could draw after his meeting with the pope. So now I had to write the necessary sentences by hand with a briefcase on my knees, while the motorcade raced through twisting streets. As the limousine lurched and swayed, I braced and wrote, focusing my full attention on both the sense of the words and their legibility—there would no time to type this up. As a member of the NSC staff since 1971, I had a keen sense of the humanitarian and international issues that shaped the U.S.-Vatican agenda. I had had a hand in many drafts of President Nixon's correspondence with Pope Paul VI, a background that fueled my concentration in this intensive moment.

President Ford and the pope spoke by themselves for almost an hour, after which our official party was ushered into the pope's library to be introduced to His Holiness. We were seated in a large semicircle to hear the words of the pope and the U.S. president.

At 7:25 p.m. we were off again, in another motorcade speeding us to an improvised pad for three helicopters at Oratorio di San Pietro. From there we would be flown back to the airport at Ciampino. As we boarded our assigned craft, the main rotors of each started to turn, with the attendant noise and downwash. One of the president's most important immediate aides was among the last to leave the motorcade. He ran across the lawn to his helicopter—and his attaché case fell open. Strapped into my seat, I watched helpless from the window as papers flew into the air. The helicopters waited while as many as possible were retrieved.

Even the choice of briefcases is significant in the life of the summit sherpa. I preferred, then and now, a soft leather case. Unlike a rigid case, which must be laid on its side to open, the soft leather case opens at the top. It's secured by a band and clasp across the top, and its sides expand. My colleague's unfortunate episode in Rome sealed this preference for life.

We departed Ciampino at 8:00 p.m. After a ten-hour flight and a six-hour time difference, we arrived at Andrews Air Force Base precisely at midnight. Within a few hours the president was once again airborne, to deliver the June 4 commencement address at the United States Military Academy.

I called Gretchen shortly after landing. When I pulled into the family driveway with gifts in hand, she and the boys were bright with smiles. And then it was on to preparations for the next round of summitry, back in the Old Executive Office Building.

The Soviet Union had been advancing the notion of a conference to address European security since the 1950s, but the West had dismissed the idea as unrealistic because of Soviet policy and behavior. By the 1970s, however, progress in détente had resurfaced the proposal for a European security conference. With East-West negotiations expanding, the United States and its NATO partners set important preconditions for such a conference. We insisted on a new U.S.-U.K.-France-USSR Berlin Agreement that would put an end to Soviet harassment of West Berliners and ongoing challenges to Western rights in the divided city. Signed in September 1971, the Quadripartite Agreement on Berlin took effect in June 1972. The Soviet Union and its Warsaw Pact allies also agreed to the Mutual and Balanced Force Reduction (MBFR) talks.

Complicated, detailed, multistage preparations preceded talks that would draw to a close only in late spring 1975. Such is the life of the summit sherpa—learning, negotiating, organizing, and arranging that never ceases, all the while remaining flexible and sharp. To accomplish this, and thanks to my Navy and athletic background, I found that staying fit helped immeasurably, not only physically but also mentally and psychologically. In Annapolis I was up before dawn each workday morning, with the routine of calisthenics followed by rowing on the Severn River, just off our property. I did this religiously, feeling much fresher and healthier as a result.

The important work of the June 1975 NATO summit was behind us, along with the consultations in Spain, Austria, and Italy. President Ford's agenda for the second half of 1975 included three more overseas summits. But despite the August 1975 Helsinki Accords' commitment by the United States, Canada, and Soviet Union to recognize and respect human rights and post–World War II borders, domestic support for the agreement remained weak. Nor had Americans strongly favored the Conference on

Security and Cooperation in Europe (CSCE), the talks that preceded the Helsinki Accords. The U.S. president was once again reminded that for summitry to succeed, domestic public opinion had to be with him.

We worked intensively throughout June and July 1975 not just on summit preparations but also on helping the president to develop presentations for various groups of concerned Americans. He said that opportunities for progress were in the best interests of the United States, emphasizing that this was a chance to commit the Warsaw Pact nations to CSCE agreements regarding human rights and freedom of travel. His participation at Helsinki, he insisted, was going to bolster the U.S. policy of encouraging greater freedom for Eastern Europe, in no way recognizing Soviet incorporation of the Baltic States. Yet, in the meetings I attended, guests were polite but often not persuaded.

Nevertheless we proceeded, lifting off on July 26, 1975, from Andrews Air Force Base in Air Force One and landing at Bonn/Cologne airport. Both Ford and German Chancellor Helmut Schmidt were keenly aware that they must show solidarity on the eve of Helsinki. After another stop in Poland, including a wreath-laying at Auschwitz to honor victims, the president's next stop would be Helsinki.

My job throughout these travels was to help ensure that Ford was ready for every meeting and event. For the Auschwitz ceremony, a White House speechwriter and I collaborated on what he might choose to write in the special visitors' log, inscribing a possibility on an index card for him to carry in his pocket. In Helsinki, Ford would have several important bilateral meetings built around the schedule of the CSCE Conference. For all of these, the president needed background information and updates. For instance, for the meeting with Brezhnev, he would have to know the overall status of U.S.-Soviet trade relations. That meant I had to know it and find the concise, precise wording to convey it quickly and thoroughly.

In addition to the usual beautiful dinners and entertainments, this time the president also hosted a formal dinner, in Poland at Warsaw's Wilanów

Palace, the Fords' residence for that visit. The very special art of giving a formal White House dinner can be applied anywhere in the world, like the White House communications system. Top professional skills are of course essential to accomplish this, skills developed through extremely hard work and precision planning by the director and staff of the White House Mess. I had previously been the delighted beneficiary of this expertise, in Moscow and Martinique. In Warsaw on the evening of July 28, 1975, I once again sat in admiration of the U.S. team's culinary art and innovative presentation. Menu cards at each, bearing the president's seal in gold, detailed a dinner including wild rice.

But one of the Polish guests did not like the rice—and, to my astonishment, said so. Later in the meal, when finger bowls were placed, the same guest drank the water and pronounced, "Soup, very thin soup." None of this ruined the dinner. Everyone overlooked the faux pas and continued their conversations. Diplomatic skills are also an art form.

In Helsinki, the Conference on Security and Cooperation in Europe was held in the already renowned Finlandia Hall, designed by Alvar Aalto and completed in 1971. Streets had been cordoned off both for security and to assist in the meticulously timed movements of the convening thirty-five chiefs of state and heads of government and their delegations' motorcades. All of our careful prep work was quickly put to use as President Ford launched into an intensive program of formal CSCE meetings and associated bilateral talks.

Aside from the official proceedings, among those with whom the U.S. president met were U.K. Prime Minister Harold Wilson, Soviet General Secretary Brezhnev, Greece's Prime Minister Konstantinos Karamanlis, Finland's President Urho Kekkonen, Turkey's Prime Minister Süleyman Demirel, France's President d'Estaing, Germany's Chancellor Schmidt, and Italy's Prime Minister Moro. In Finlandia Hall, I listened to many of these leaders speak, heeding my duties as an official U.S. delegate not only to remain aware of developments but also to help meet all staffing requirements.

Meanwhile, any press that was admitted passed through extremely tight security before reaching the packed balcony. Anyone who participates in a summit of any type must always expect the press, everywhere, at all times.

As I watched everything unfold while remaining mindful that everything was being watched and reported on, I noticed Secretary of State Kissinger also multitasking, not just listening to the speeches but also acting on various foreign policy matters. Members of his staff would discreetly appear with papers for him to read, then depart armed with his instructions for further action. The system worked well—until one morning when portions of a classified U.S. paper on the Middle East were published. A crafty photographer in the balcony had kept his telephoto lens trained on Kissinger's reading material until he captured a document. Even secretaries of state must learn new tricks for ongoing security.

The signing of the Helsinki Final Act concluded the CSCE—and launched the process of monitoring implementation. Today, as defined on its website, the CSCE, "an independent commission of the U.S. Federal Government," has "for over 45 years . . . monitored compliance with the Helsinki Accords and advanced comprehensive security through promotion of human rights, democracy, and economic, environmental, and military cooperation in the 57-nation OSCE [Organization for Security and Cooperation in Europe] region."

This unequivocal, enduring success was counterbalanced by the difficulty of talks with Brezhnev. In the midst of the Cold War, the Strategic Arms Limitation Talks (SALT) had, dangerously, stalled. Challenges included the Soviets' deployment of the Tu-22M series of Backfire long-range aircraft, which could carry out nuclear strikes as well as conventional attack, antiship, and reconnaissance missions. Its actual purpose was debated fiercely in the NATO Intelligence Community, while on the U.S. side at the same time, new cruise missiles were being developed. All this made the Helsinki Accords even more of a remarkable accomplishment, taking place as they did, and then succeeding, in the middle of the Cold War's U.S.-Soviet arms race to stockpile nuclear weapons as a deterrent—or just in case.

Our next and final stops were Romania and Yugoslavia. Upon our arrival in Bucharest, we found trade to be foremost on President Nicolae Ceaușescu's agenda. Despite its precarious position—politically close to Europe yet still within reach of the Warsaw Pact's viselike grip—Romania was determined to develop at least a minimal amount of flexibility and quasi-independence in its dealings with the West.

Our sumptuous welcome featured marathon toasts by President Ceaușescu, banquets, and a Rhine River cruise on the MS *Drachenfels*. Then we rolled through northern Romania on a presidential train and climbed into the Transylvanian mountains of Vlad the Impaler fame, headed toward Peles Castle. In the mountain village of Sinaia, more than 2,500 feet above sea level, Ford and Ceaușescu resumed their formal talks and signed a document establishing Romania as a U.S. Most Favored Nation, in accordance with the U.S. Trade Act of 1974. It was a momentous accomplishment—made possible by many hours of staff work in both Washington and Bucharest before the summit.

But Ford had one more critical diplomatic mission to complete on this trip: meeting with Yugoslavia's President Josip Broz Tito. When he entered the Federal Executive Council Building in Belgrade at 7:00 p.m. on the same day we left the mountains, Ford was still going strong. Talks ranged across global political issues and possibilities for further trade—including military sales. At 8:15 p.m., the two chiefs of state joined their delegations for a banquet capped off by the Abrašević Company of Folk Dancers and Singers. With performers from the Island of Susak, Serbia, Macedonia, Croatia, and Vojvodina, it was a celebration of Yugoslav culture as well as a reminder of Tito's extraordinary success in harnessing—for the time being—these competing nationalities.

After further talks the next morning, a working lunch, and departure ceremonies, Tito bade farewell at Surčin Airport. Air Force One did its transatlantic work, and we were back in Washington at 6:00 p.m. As the plane headed for its hangar, I reflected on the success of our trip and my happiness to be home, soon to be reunited with Gretchen, Alex, and Ty. Much as the summit sherpa's thoughts may wander back to the States during multicountry passages through time zones, it is of the utmost importance to remain focused. Each ceremony held in the U.S. president's honor is of great significance. These events are covered in the national media and officially recorded in the history of international relations. Starting at the earliest stage of preplanning and throughout the process, the summit sherpa must keep in perspective, at all times, the importance attached to each and every event.

President Ford's intensive European summitry gave credibility to the words he spoke. In the few months of his presidency, he had proceeded from the bonding of relations among key allies to progress on a far broader agenda. As the year 1975 drew to a close, President Ford prepared to host summits while U.S. democracy entered its two hundredth year.

CHAPTER 10

The United States Turns Two Hundred, 1976

With the approach of the two hundredth year since the signing of the Declaration of Independence, U.S. government preparations were in full swing. For us, this meant far more than preparing for most diplomatic events. The entire Western world planned to celebrate with the leading democratic nation, as commemorative medals were designed, various commissions took shape, and schedules were drawn for ship visits. In my office, in addition to the usual heavy workflow, we now also had to handle a geometric increase in staffing requirements for the Bicentennial. At the top of the list, President Giscard d'Estaing would pay a state visit from May 17 to 20, 1976. Queen Elizabeth II and the Duke of Edinburgh would come from July 7 to 11. With every new announcement, interest intensified domestically. The White House was flooded with inquiries and offers from across the nation. On top of all that, 1976 was an election year.

Meanwhile, routine responsibilities for us included monitoring the NATO consortium of nations that were implementing the F-16 fighter production program; staffing Canadian, West European, East European, and Soviet issues; and shepherding NSC-system policy deliberations—which involved more than fourteen U.S. departmental, agency, and executive office entities—for negotiations on the UN law of the sea.

Very early in the Bicentennial planning, Mrs. Ford requested that General Scowcroft take charge of arrangements for state visitors from abroad. Scowcroft was now assistant to the president for national security affairs, while Secretary Kissinger continued to serve as secretary of state. To help assure that the planning and implementation of each European visit proceeded smoothly, Brent Scowcroft turned to me.

The first step was to hold our own internal U.S. consultations for each visit, and to sort out all the proposals, nationwide, that were pouring in. We needed to confirm the Fords' scheduling preferences and establish a network of working-level contacts to assist foreign pre-advance teams in every aspect of each visit, from arrival to departure. This included protocol, travel inside the United States, communications, security, and all the details involved in each visit.

Next, we set up bilateral planning sessions for visits that would involve on the U.S. side protocol, the White House's advance office and social secretary, and the NSC staff; and on the visiting sides ambassadors, embassy representatives, and pre-advance teams from each leader's nation. We held these sessions in the elegant Blair House guest quarters, a comfortable atmosphere where we could produce event-by-event detailed schedules for every visit.

Aside from France and Britain, nations joining us in celebration included Ireland, Sweden, Denmark, Canada, Spain, Germany, Finland, and more. Events that were arranged with meticulous care reflected an outpouring of international friendship. Nations offered generous official gifts, and the greatest number possible of Americans met royalty and heads of state, not only in Washington but also in special celebrations around the country.

The Department of State's detailed schedule for Giscard d'Estaing's visit ran to more than one hundred pages. Included would be two substantive rounds of Oval Office discussions with President Ford, each of which required careful NSC staffing for the two presidents to build on progress realized, along with other Atlantic Alliance members, since 1974. D'Estaing's presence carried special significance because of France's critical role during the American Revolution—although, despite his last name, he was not a descendant of Count Charles-Hector d'Estaing, commander of the first French fleet sent to support the American Revolution, who was guillotined during the Reign of Terror after outliving his wife and only child.

For planning these international state visits, I worked closely with the imperturbable, tireless, and charming presidential social secretary, Maria Downs. I also maintained a working channel for months with Minister of the British Embassy John O. Moreton, CMG MC, in addition to communications between the embassy and the U.S. State Department Office of Protocol. This direct contact enabled us to move proposals and time-sensitive issues more quickly between the White House and Buckingham Palace for consideration and guidance.

Pomp and circumstance in all the events was de rigueur, including for Britain's observance of this landmark anniversary of its former colonies' independence. Following the French model, British participation would feature months of exhibitions, touring performances, and programs in both countries. Parliament would loan Congress one of two original copies of the Magna Carta dated 1215. After being on display for a year, it would be replaced by the permanent gift of a gold and silver replica of the document. In this and many other ways, the Bicentennial was a splendid opportunity for Americans to more fully understand their country's origins.

In my personal life, aside from throwing my full energies wholeheartedly into all these preparations, I was excited about the opportunity for Gretchen and me to meet Queen Elizabeth II. In the White House receiving line, we stood between former Secretary of the Treasury and Mrs. John

Connally and TV star Telly Savalas. Gretchen, a gifted artist, designer, and tailor, had created and sewn her own long, ivory silk gown.

In our wonderful historic home in West Annapolis, we were continually making improvements. Here again, I had Gretchen in charge. When we purchased it in 1971, the house had been divided in half and rented out by an absentee landlord. In dire need of updates and repairs, its interior had not received gentle treatment. Original plaster covering the large rooms' high walls was cracked and crumbling. My job was to scrape it off, down to the wood lath, then put in place new four-by-eight-foot sheetrock. Other walls had been painted a dull light brown; that had to be replaced by white. My best challenge on this front was the beautiful, towering front hall, with its three-story central staircase. I, alone, got the exterior forty-foot extension ladder inside and scraped, spackled, and painted the staircase ceiling and walls. Gretchen, sometimes with recruited lady friends, sanded and painted the staircase's three flights of spindles.

On the third floor, she had set aside a room for her sewing headquarters, and here her creations came together. In the days following the White House reception for the queen and prince, Gretchen received half a dozen calls from all over the country from friends who had seen her on TV wearing the flowing gown.

For the queen's visit, the royal yacht *Britannia* served as a principal focal point. Sailing between several ports of call along the U.S. East Coast, the yacht gave the royal couple an appropriately impressive venue where they could invite their many American hosts and guests. On the morning of July 6, the *Britannia* would arrive at Penn's Landing, Philadelphia, and the next morning, a Royal Air Force VC-10 would fly the royal couple to Washington, DC. After several other events, that evening there would be a white tie banquet at the White House in their honor, and this is where Gretchen would wear her gown.

That morning, I arrived at my office in high spirits. All the time and effort I'd devoted to shaping and refining the schedule for this visit was behind me. Now I could just look forward to participating in the White House arrival ceremony and the day's activities, culminating in that evening's banquet with Gretchen.

Things would, of course, not be that simple. At about 9:00 a.m., Maria Downs called me. In all the planning, amid all the arrangements, gifts had been acquired for the Fords to present to the royal couple—but there was nothing for the children. Princess Anne and the princes Charles and Andrew should also receive gifts, and their arrival was now less than three hours away. Maria's message was brief: Help!

Mrs. Ford did not want to select from the normal range of gifts available from Protocol. She wanted distinctive items worthy of the occasion. Did I have any ideas?

Happily, I did. I had long admired the turquoise and silver jewelry on display at the American Indian Gift Shop at the Department of the Interior. The earrings, necklaces, belt buckles, and rings were not only beautiful; they were also distinctly American. This meant I had to trot four blocks in the DC early July heat, find appropriate items, call Maria on the shop's phone for approvals that would make their way through the chain to Secretary of the Interior Stanley Hathaway, wait for the call back, and trot back to the White House West Wing bearing the treasures. There I made my way along the ground floor, through the residence to the East Wing, and finally into Maria's office.

I received a personal note from Mrs. Ford on August 6: "Dear Denis, Please know how very much I appreciated your kind assistance in obtaining gifts for the Royal Family. This was a most thoughtful gesture on your part. With warm best wishes, sincerely, Betty Ford."

From this experience I internalized the importance to summit diplomacy of appropriate gifts.

Their quality and character, the aspect of the United States they symbolize, and their meaning to the recipients are all critical considerations not to be taken lightly. But, as this anecdote illustrates, in some cases there is no choice but to carry out the job in haste.

That evening, Gretchen and I attended the white tie banquet at the White House. Gretchen's long, hand-sewn ivory silk gown shone as we passed through the receiving line on the south grounds. The entire Rose Garden was covered by a white tent sheltering twenty-four circular tables adorned with at least a dozen types of flowers. The beauty of that evening was reflected in my wife's stunning, happy face. I soaked it all in, grateful at having been able to play a role in making this happen.

I was treated to another royal encounter the following evening, having been invited to Blair House for a personal meeting, the royal thank-you to a few of us who had contributed to the success of their visit. After accepting the queen's gracious gifts of a framed royal photo and a Battersea enamel pill box, I thanked them and said I also had a gift for them. This was not on the agenda, but they seemed pleased with my copy of a 1968 article I'd published about the *Queen Elizabeth 2* while she was still under construction on the building ways in Scotland. As Philip thumbed the pages, he murmured, "I say, I say!"

And with that, my brief encounter with royalty was over. It was time to focus on the next Bicentennial visit: that of Germany's Chancellor Helmut Schmidt.

Ford and Schmidt had established a highly successful bilateral working relationship. As they celebrated Germany's vital role in the American War for Independence, they also forged ahead on the work front. Two rounds of Oval Office talks produced the Federal Republic of Germany's agreement to contribute almost $70 million to the cost of relocating a U.S. combat brigade to the north near Bremen, highlighting thereby the shared Allied contribution to NATO defenses. Among the numerous festive activities during Schmidt's visit, on July 16, 1976, the Smithsonian Air and Space Museum opened its new Albert Einstein Spacearium. For this state-of-the-art space-viewing facility, Germany had gifted a Zeiss planetarium projector in honor of the Bicentennial.

August brought Finland's long-serving President Urho Kekkonen to close the parade of European heads of state Bicentennial visits. For Ford, the rest of 1976 was of necessity devoted to his reelection campaign, outside of necessary and ongoing working meetings with foreign ministers. After the election denied him a second term, Ford found time at the end of his administration to write me this letter of gratitude:

The White House, Washington

January 19, 1977

Dear Denis:
I want to thank you for your outstanding and dedicated performance as NSC Senior Staff Member for Europe during the two and a half years of my Presidency.

In strengthening our ties with our friends and allies in Europe, in our progress toward more constructive relations with the Soviet Union and Eastern Europe, in our oceans policy and negotiations on law of the sea, and in the conduct of our diplomacy at a time of economic difficulty and political change in Europe, your role has been central.

I know of the enormous contribution you made in preparing for my meetings with foreign leaders and my visits abroad. Of my 124 meetings with foreign chiefs of state and heads of government, you were responsible for the substantive preparation for well over half. You accompanied me to Vladivostok for my meetings with General Secretary Brezhnev, and to Martinique for my talks with President Giscard d'Estaing; in 1975, you were a valued member of the delegations which I led to both the NATO Summit in Brussels and the Conference on Security and Cooperation in Europe at Helsinki. And in our Bicentennial year, during which so many European leaders visited the United States, you took personal responsibility to ensure that their visits went smoothly in every respect, and you can take personal pride in the success of this deeply symbolic dimension of our Bicentennial celebration.

Denis, for my entire term of office, you have devoted yourself to the Presidency and to your country in the finest tradition of public service. I am in debt to you for your wisdom, professionalism, and skill. You have my admiration and lasting gratitude for a job very well done.

Sincerely,
s/ Gerald R. Ford

r. A. Denis Clift, National Security Council, Washington, D.C. 20506

The ability and opportunity to serve one's country is a high honor. Acknowledgment such as this is a summit sherpa's high reward.

Denis' mother, Ann Brewer Clift, holds him in Washington Square Park, New York, with daughter Jean in the background. *Author's collection*

Commissioning day for Ensign Clift, October 1958, Officer Candidate School, Newport, Rhode Island, with mother Ann and father Arthur Henry Clift *Author's collection*

Working on the foredeck of the icebreaker USS *Staten Island* (AGB 5) in 1961, the author sketched the USS *Glacier* (AGB 4) in the icy Bellingshausen Sea. *Author's collection*

Lieutenant (jg) Clift serving at Fleet Intelligence Center Pacific, 1960 *U.S. Navy photo*

Late autumn 1960, with Adélie penguins in Antarctica *U.S. Navy photo*

On March 1, 1961, the *Glacier* broke free of the ice and headed north to the Antarctic Peninsula. From the *Staten Island*'s foredeck, the author sketched it. *Author's collection*

In September 1966, Denis (*front*) and Gretchen (*front right*) sailed from New York to the United Kingdom on the SS *United States*. The ship's commodore, Rear Admiral L. J. Alexanderson, USNR (*back right*), invited them to this cocktail party. *U.S. Lines*

In preparation for the 1974 Brezhnev-Nixon summit, Clift (*front left*) flew to Moscow with Henry Kissinger (*center left*). In the Kremlin, they met with Soviet leader Leonid Brezhnev (*across from Kissinger*). *Kremlin photo*

Airborne on board Air Force One, en route to the 1975 NATO summit. *From right:* White House Chief of Staff Donald Rumsfeld, First Lady Betty Ford, President Ford, Clift, and National Security Adviser Brent Scowcroft. *White House photo*

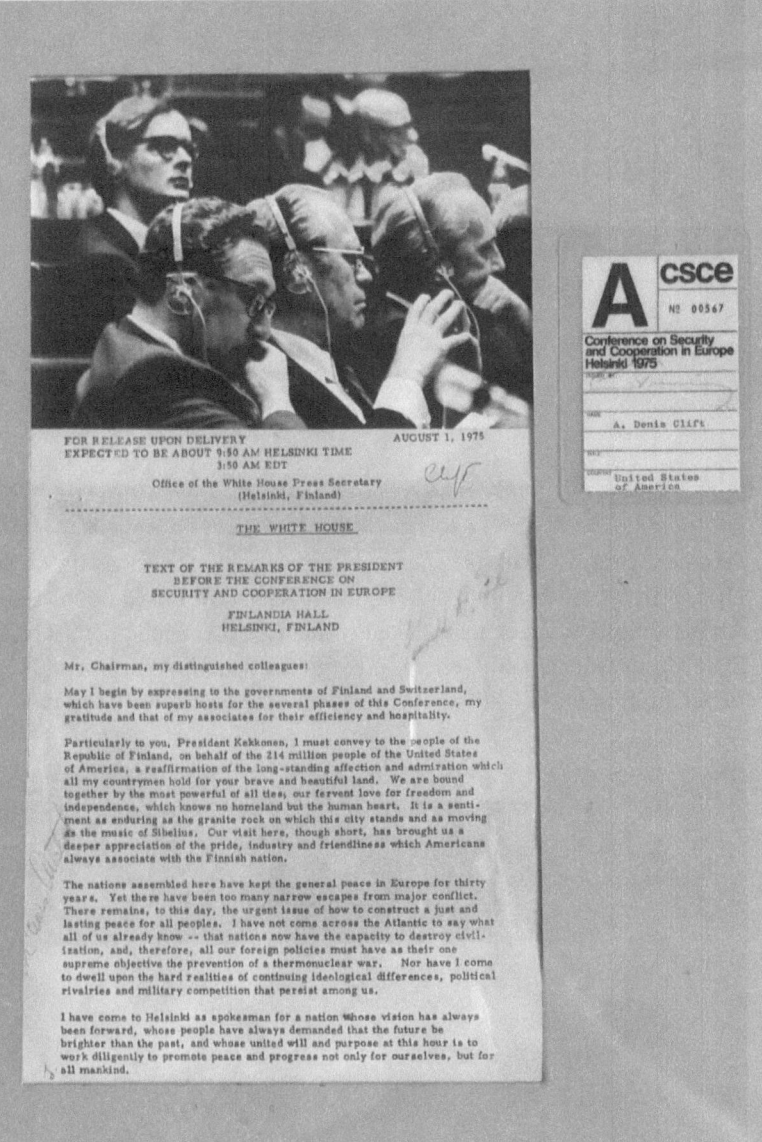

At the 1975 Conference of Security and Cooperation in Europe, Clift sits behind Henry Kissinger and President Ford in Helsinki. *White House photo*

President Jimmy Carter (*head of table, right*), holds a meeting in the White House Situation Room. To his right sit Assistant for National Security Affairs Zbigniew Brzezinski; Vice President Walter Mondale; Secretary of State Cyrus Vance; and General George Brown, USAF, chairman of the Joint Chiefs of Staff. Clift sits behind Mondale. *White House photo*

In 1980, the Clift family visited New Zealand. *From left:* Denis, son Tyrone, wife Gretchen, and son Alexander *Author's collection*

In the Oval Office, President Ronald Reagan receives the 1983 edition of *Soviet Military Power* from Secretary of Defense Caspar Weinberger. *White House photo*

In April 1995 the author and General Lieutenant Demitri Volkogonov initialed the first draft report of the U.S.-Russia Joint Commission on Prisoners of War / Missing in Action. *Author's collection*

Gretchen and Denis's firstborn was, like his parents, an artist. Alex acted, wrote, painted, and earned a master's in the classics from St. John's College. *Author's collection*

In 1992, Gretchen and Denis celebrated their thirtieth anniversary with a road trip across America that took them to eighteen states. Here, they relax in the Grand Tetons. *Author's Collection*

Denis Clift and son Ty continue to enjoy the house in Annapolis. *Tyrone Clift*

CHAPTER 11

First Year as Assistant to Vice President Mondale for National Security Affairs, 1977

Gratifying though it was to have my hard work acknowledged, I had realized since late 1976 that the in-depth knowledge I had developed about Bicentennial affairs was not going to lead to a lasting position in the future. In one capacity or another, including time in the Navy, I had now served under the Eisenhower, Kennedy, Johnson, Nixon, and Ford administrations. I had developed an understanding more broadly of how the U.S. government functioned. It was time once again to extend my professional feelers.

I arranged a meeting with the head of President-Elect James Earl "Jimmy" Carter's NSC transition team, David Aaron. Soon Aaron would become deputy assistant to the president for national security affairs. Having worked with him previously on President Nixon's NSC staff, I said that I hoped to continue in government service and would be especially interested in the position of assistant to the vice president for national security affairs. I offered a solid background for this work, having provided considerable NSC staff support to Vice President Nelson Rockefeller.

But David explained that the transition team envisioned a different system going forward. Unlike any former vice president, Walter F. Mondale would be closely linked to the president on all foreign policy and NSC issues, and thus there would not likely be a need for a full-time professional on the vice president's staff. NSC staff members could provide support when needed.

Among the skills of diplomacy I had acquired and refined over the years was a keen sense of when to withdraw and regroup. I wrote down all my thoughts and ideas and crafted them into a proposal based on thorough knowledge and conveying deep respect. In early 1977, I sent this off to Aaron, outlining the situation of a vice president who would be very busy and the proposed solution of a full-time staff member to assist in meeting his myriad domestic and foreign responsibilities. Only this could ensure that Mondale would have top-quality, fast-response assistance on his own staff. The specific examples I offered included NSC meetings, for which background information would not necessarily be identical for the president and vice president. Preparing the in-depth papers sometimes ran late, with tight deadlines. What if the vice president asked for further information—who could provide that quickly?

I listed staffing requirements in every category that I knew was going to be involved: meetings with ambassadors and foreign visitors in Washington; social invitations from those visitors; correspondence from U.S. citizens, foreigners, and foreign leaders regarding national security and foreign policy; press guidance; daily intelligence; commissions; meetings in Washington; and official missions abroad. Background papers would be necessary for some of these activities, but immediate and unforeseen needs would arise in every category. For all these reasons, I recommended that the vice president have one full-time staff member in the foreign policy/NSC field in addition to his military aide or aides.

Meanwhile, in discussions with the transition team, I offered my observations on the incoming president's communications with foreign leaders. Having worked under several administrations and become accustomed to the individual styles of three presidents, I could identify the methods and results of their communications as a characteristic that distinguished each administration. The frequency of communications had been dictated in some cases by the pace of events and the input of advisers for drafts, while in others, the president had been far more involved.

In the latter case, the president takes personal initiative by regularly staying in touch with selected foreign leaders, working closely with staff members who draft letters and messages, discussing significant domestic and foreign events, and developing a relationship with the foreign leader. Such an approach can ultimately result in greater understanding, personal friendship, and the ability to deal with major issues and crises with more flexibility. A change in administrations presents an opportunity for the incoming president to open lines of direct communication. By taking the initiative, the president ensures that the timing, style, and substance of contacts with selected leaders abroad become established procedure, rather than communicating as part of standard bureaucratic activities, or when, as inevitably happens, events arise that demand responses.

Because foreign leaders need the best possible understanding of the new administration's policy and program directions, they aim for a relationship of frankness, trust, and confidence. Discretion is paramount, because the issues involved may be sensitive not only internationally but also domestically. I closed my arguments by reviewing the essential steps involved in successfully accomplishing these goals. A president's supporting staff needs to consider all available channels of communication, I emphasized, from direct visits and phone calls to ambassadors and press releases. And the president's personal style must be adhered to consistently, because this tone governs how the messages are crafted, delivered, and ultimately received.

As I presented my case to the head of the NSC transition team, Jimmy Carter was selecting the members of his administration—a process that was shaping the principal policies of his foreign and national security programs. With the inauguration still weeks away, Carter decided that Vice President–elect Mondale should be sent abroad to convey personally and discuss the new president's thinking and proposed directions on key issues. Mondale would travel to NATO headquarters, the capitals of the main NATO allies, and Japan. While still on President Ford's staff, I was tapped, another job assigned, to be a member of the team that would organize, draft, and assemble all the documents and background information the incoming vice president would need for his first assignment in global summitry.

In mid-January 1977, to establish direct contact on the eve of his presidency, Carter placed personal telephone calls from his transitional Washington headquarters at Blair House to Prime Minister Callaghan, President d'Estaing, Chancellor Schmidt, Italy's Prime Minister Giulio Andreotti, and Japan's Prime Minister Takeo Fukuda. He also wanted to invite their approval of his proposed upcoming visit by Vice President Mondale. They gave the green light.

Fritz Mondale now set an intense pace in preparing for his trip. Background papers, briefers, and experts flowed steadily to his Senate office and Lowell Street residence. In four weeks, we had to cover international finance, trade, and economic issues; North-South issues; key NATO concerns; nonproliferation; U.S. relations with Japan and the other Pacific nations; southern Africa; Greece, Turkey, and Cyprus; the Middle East; and, of course, strategic arms issues, the Soviet Union, and the Warsaw Pact. January was busy.

It was also freezing. Usually Route 50 had been cleared enough for my commute between Annapolis and DC, but sometimes the roads were impassable or we had to work through most of the night. Downtown DC was a remarkable mess, with snows not well plowed turning into ridges of ice—cars sliding, running into each other. Thankfully, I had a big couch in my office. Gretchen knew the importance of a new job in the new administration. She was providing me with all her support.

Late one afternoon, as I was getting ready to leave Mondale's Senate office with the team, Mondale wanted to talk for a minute. Mentioning that I had been recommended because of my NSC background in summitry, he added that he was depending on me to oversee the overall arrangements for this trip. "If you do well," he concluded, smiling, "you'll go far." I was already giving my best to the job, but this propelled me to new depths of effort and focus. Clearly the newly elected vice president was a leader with a sense of humor. He knew he was leaving me to contemplate and internalize the "what if you don't do well" alternative.

In short, my busy, cold January 1977 was filled with putting the finishing touches on Ford's farewell-letter drafts to his European colleagues, helping guide all the papers for Mondale's mission, and getting back home to the family when I could.

We organized Mondale's trip into several categories, each with its own background papers, detailed schedule, and trip bible: predeparture; flight from Andrews AFB; Brussels, January 23–24; Berlin, January 26; Rome, January 26–27; London, January 27; Paris, January 28; Iceland, stopover; Tokyo, January 30–31; and postreturn, when Mondale would present his work to Carter. The press covered this whirlwind "getting to know you" tour, as *Time* magazine called it, and photos in *Newsweek*'s January 31 edition included one of Mondale engaged with me in predeparture discussions.

While I helped Mondale prepare for this critical trip, at the same time he was getting ready for Inauguration Day, January 20, 1977, a Thursday. I could not attend, because I had to work. As the peaceful transfer of power took place on Capitol Hill, I toiled away in the Old Executive Office Building, drafting a detailed set of talking points on the foreign mission for Mondale's use at the Carter administration's first Cabinet meeting on the morning of January 21. I did take a break to step out onto the office's balcony, from which I could watch a helicopter carrying the Fords on their farewell tour of Washington. Hours later, with work almost finished, I had time to watch the new first family use a boardwalk over the ice and snow to access their designated seating for the inaugural parade, which followed their inaugural stroll down Pennsylvania Avenue.

Traveling with Vice President Mondale, at 8:00 a.m. on Sunday morning, January 23, 1977, I was at Andrews Air Force Base for our 9:00 a.m. departure for Brussels on board Air Force Two. As we crossed the Atlantic, Mondale read and talked about each leg of the trip with staff members. The next morning in Brussels, Mondale addressed NATO allies. Emphasizing the alliance's success to date in deterring war, he restated Carter's readiness to increase U.S. investment in NATO—with a comparable increase from each ally. His tone of unity could not have been stronger.

That first address was followed by a day in Brussels of back-to-back working visits with NATO leaders and heads of government. Night had fallen by the time we arrived in Germany, greeted at Cologne/Bonn Airport by Foreign Minister Hans-Dietrich Genscher. He expressed his nation's warm friendship and gratitude at being among the new administration's first foreign direct contacts. But my day was not over yet: Upon arrival at our hotel, those of us on the staff continued to work well into the night, reviewing and polishing the drafts we had prepared for Mondale's discussions with the German chancellor, the vice president's speech in Berlin, and his entire set of papers for Rome and the Vatican on January 26–27.

A hard, close-to-last-minute review of such papers is absolutely essential for good staffing. Substantive issues must be updated; toasts and addresses must be purged of the generalities and clichés that typically clutter early working drafts. On the summit trail, a staffer has to remain in close touch not only with the U.S. traveling party, advance team, and embassy staff but also, and simultaneously, with contacts in each host country for background information and updates. All this ongoing work results in sharper detail and greater relevance and color in the papers used during each visit.

Carter had entrusted Mondale not just with getting-to-know-you visiting but also, more seriously, with discussing difficult issues such as nuclear proliferation and the global economy. This confidence was important from the outset in establishing Mondale's role and credibility as international statesman. As an authoritative representative of the U.S. government, he presented its views officially and on the record. Mondale, who had studied hard, handled the issues well, establishing a cordial basis for future dealings between governments.

In West Berlin, Mondale's strong address restated U.S. commitment and the deeply rooted ties between the two nations. Until this January 1977 visit to the Berlin Wall, in all my years of travel with U.S. delegations across the Soviet Union and Warsaw Pact nations, I had not seen such a stark delineation of the differences between East and West. The no-man's-land strip of watchtowers, trenches, armed guards, razor wire, beds of nails, and other obstacles indeed together shaped a death strip. This barrier, methodically erected to prevent people from moving freely from East to West, lent fresh meaning to the importance of democracy and America's commitment to the people of Berlin.

Next stop was Ciampino Airport, Rome, where, after quickly checking in at our hotel, we entered Palazzo Chigi with the vice president for his meetings with Prime Minister Andreotti. Three and a half hours later, we sat at dinner at President Giovanni Leone's dinner of plump, luscious seafood, and the next day, His Holiness Paul VI received Mondale at the Vatican. A frail man, he greeted our delegation at the end and presented us each with a bronze medal struck to commemorate his visit to the United Nations. "I am a numismatic expert," he joked self-deprecatingly to the vice president.

In London, on January 27 Mondale met Prime Minister Callaghan at 10 Downing Street, for talks to be resumed over dinner. The two leaders held a press conference that day. Callaghan announced that he would visit the United States in March, in his capacity as both head of the British government and president of the European Community. Mondale was asked about the newly appointed Ambassador Andrew Young's invitation to visit South West Africa (renamed Namibia in 1968, and independent since 1990), referencing the 1974 military coup in Portugal that led to civil war in the soon-to-be-former Portuguese colony of Angola—which bordered South West Africa. The 1974–75 Angola crisis flared into a Cold War battleground that strained détente. Nations fighting or sending aid to different sides in the conflict included Portugal, the Soviet Union, Cuba, China, the United States, and South Africa. The newly elected Mondale navigated this extraordinarily complex question by expressing the administration's full confidence in Young, his knowledge of the region and issues, and his ability to help "bring about a responsible settlement within the context of majority rule."

There were no contentious issues to be hammered out between the United Kingdom and United States—which allowed all thirty-one of us to relax that evening around the mahogany table in the prime minister's Downing Street dining room. Spirits were high, and laughter flowed easily as we savored the sole, duck, and other delicacies. When Mondale recalled songs he had learned as a young man visiting Great Britain, the prime minister led the room in a round of lusty after-dinner singing. After cognac (from Churchill's cellars), the evening seemed to be winding down when I joked to Roger Stott, one of Callaghan's political advisers, that we hadn't sung William Blake's poem-become-anthem "Jerusalem."

"You know it?" he shot back. I nodded, and he yelled, "Prime Minister! Clift knows 'Jerusalem'!" Shortly thereafter Callaghan and I had given a full voice duet to both verses, in a fitting bilateral conclusion to a most delightful evening and diplomatically useful visit.

In Paris, on Friday afternoon Mondale met with Emile van Lennep, secretary general of the Organization for Economic Cooperation and Development, and the following morning with Giscard d'Estaing. As the vice president was getting ready for the short motorcade drive to the Élysée Palace and his appointment with Giscard, I turned to the staff member who kept copies of Carter's gift of bound inaugural addresses. "Is everything in order for the Élysée?" I asked, a standard question fully expecting an affirmative reply. He confidently produced a leather folder from his briefcase and offered me a look. The copy was addressed to Prime Minister Fukuda! This is the type of detail that can all too easily be overlooked, leading to great embarrassment for the leader at a critical international moment. We made the change at light speed, and from that moment on, I became the custodian of such documents.

Saturday afternoon marked the start of our second week on the road. Exchanging some of our European experts for new Asian hands, we flew overnight to Tokyo, with refueling stops in Iceland and Alaska. As we deplaned at Keflavik, near–gale force winds tore across the runway. There was an honor guard of Icelandic motorcycle police, and they all leaned forward against the blast like airborne ski jumpers. Prime Minister Geir Hallgrímsson greeted Mondale at the terminal building and escorted us to a lounge for fifteen minutes of conversation. Both leaders expressed their enthusiasm for U.S.-Icelandic relations.

With Air Force II flying 30,000 feet over the North Pole, our entire party draped wherever we could for a few welcome hours of sleep. I found a storage bench in the passageway outside the vice president's cabin. It couldn't have been more than fourteen inches wide, but it was enough. By the time we landed in Tokyo at 9:45 p.m. Sunday night, the vice president had been reading for hours to prepare for his talks with Prime Minister Fukuda. His delicately delivered message had to include the expression of serious U.S. concern about the $5 billion trade imbalance with Japan—and that December, Japan would announce its reduction in tariffs and other helpful measures. The Japanese hosted us splendidly, clearly honored that the U.S. leaders had gone the extra Pacific mile for this initial diplomatic mission of great importance, both substantively and symbolically.

We used our time on the flight back to Washington to work on drafts of the vice president's report to the president. There was no doubt that the mission had been successful, despite a very few inevitable glitches. Still, I did not know, as we flew east across the United States, whether or not I would be looking for a new job the next day. But then, as Air Force II banked for its final approach into Andrews, Vice President Mondale said he had been observing me throughout the trip and thought I would be a good member of his new staff. It was then that he invited me to become his assistant for national security affairs.

I called Gretchen, who drove into downtown Washington with Alex and Ty. We had a celebratory dinner at Trader Vic's.

At 6:30 the next morning, most of our global team was with the vice president in his new White House West Wing office, with a seasoned-oak fire crackling in the fireplace. We again reviewed his trip report before he left as the sun rose for his 7:30 meeting with the president in the Oval Office. Still dog-tired from our marathon trip, we pressed on in the same tempo for many, many months. Without my regular exercise routine and the habits I had developed to remain healthy, I would have been unable to carry out my duties. Staying power is essential to the sherpa's psychological and physiological kit. On top of that, the reforms that Jimmy Carter and Walter Mondale would make to the vice president's role would from the outset lead to greater political influence.

Going forward, the vice president participated in meetings between the National Security Council and Cabinet. He would be welcome in the president's meetings with every foreign official and leader, and in every meeting that might fall in my new field of responsibility: I was providing assistance to the vice president in the areas of foreign policy, intelligence, and defense.

Carter instituted a Friday morning working breakfast to discuss the national security agenda with the vice president and other senior members of the White House staff. The president and vice president also had a working lunch every Monday. Carter specified that Vice President Mondale and Secretary of Defense Harold Brown be fully involved in all matters pertaining to the possible use of nuclear weapons in the defense of the United States and its allies.

I had been on the National Security Council staff for the previous six years. Now I had to retrain myself to get off the elevator at the second, not the third, floor of the Old Executive Office Building. The senior staff team I joined worked well together from the start and remained intact for the next four years: Chief of Staff Richard Moe, Deputy Chief of Staff and Counsel Michael Berman, Assistant for Domestic Affairs Gail Harrison, and Press Secretary Al Eisele—who had pitched for the Cleveland Indians' farm club. All our offices were in close proximity. In the West Wing were housed the vice president, Executive Assistant Jim Johnson, and Secretary Penny Miller.

I was busier than ever before, and I had already been fully and consistently focused on my government work. The first few months included the need for a giant wave of draft policy papers for heated work and debate at the action officers' level, review at the assistant secretary's and undersecretary's levels, and finally decision at the formal sessions of the NSC, chaired by the president. As a senior member of Mondale's staff, it was essential to ensure that the times set aside for these meetings on his calendar were confirmed with those of my colleagues. We were all responsible for juggling the endless competing demands of his schedule. Further complicating Mondale's calendar, in order to keep the vice president fully informed, his staffing was dovetailed with the president's.

Until now I had started the morning drive from Annapolis at 6:00 a.m.—which now moved up to 4:00 a.m. This meant an early night at home whenever I could afford it, with some nights still spent in my office on the couch. Gretchen, ever the stalwart love warrior, was undaunted by all of it. She pressed in her own cherished sphere, with our sons growing up amid her gardens and close involvement in their sports and academic advancements.

I now often also had to work Saturdays, aside from the weekdays when my job was to ensure every early morning that Mondale had the latest updates on international developments. This meant screening messages, telegrams, and wires from the Departments of Defense and State and the CIA, along with any late-breaking wire stories and of course all the major newspapers. Carter's national security adviser, Zbigniew Brzezinski, brought him the Intelligence Community's Presidential Daily Brief (PDB) every morning in the Oval Office, after which it was hand-delivered to Mondale. I stood by for any directions or requests for follow-up information. I worked with the White House Situation

Room to provide subsequent updates at noon and 6:00 p.m. every working day—barring a crisis, in which case we all remained fully on board as needed.

My days also remained filled with preparing background papers and talking points as needed for Mondale's nonstop meetings, both within the government and with foreign leaders; handling his ongoing correspondence and meetings, domestically and abroad, pertaining to defense, intelligence, and foreign policy; helping with speeches, toasts, arrival and departure ceremonies, press remarks, and more. Press guidance had to be provided to the press secretary on the issues discussed with foreign leaders; questions and answers had to be drafted as contingency guidance. The speechwriters needed draft language for Mondale's heavy schedule of public addresses. And the twenty-four-hour-a-day operational support required for the vice president's national command responsibilities involved my office and Mondale's military aides.

But the most challenging part of the job may well have been preparing and accomplishing the vice president's summit missions on behalf of the president. In May 1977, Mondale would travel to Vienna for two days of talks with Prime Minister John Vorster of the Republic of South Africa. The process we followed to prepare the vice president for these extremely important talks would set the pattern for every subsequent summit mission.

Apartheid still existed at the time, but its days were numbered, and the United States and allies were working with the United Nations on self-determination and majority rule in Rhodesia and Namibia. Broader regional reverberations were an obvious critical concern. Vice President Mondale would be speaking with Prime Minister Vorster in this complicated atmosphere.

As soon as the decision was reached to schedule talks with South Africa, we engaged the best minds in the government to assist in preparations. My focus was on ensuring that Mondale received the same information and background papers as those available to the president, along with the same level of support from the NSC and Departments of State and Defense.

We used a pyramidal process to prepare, starting in early March with a flow of background reading that included histories, novels, political science essays, and other works by known authorities.

Next, Mondale wanted detailed background papers on key issues in each region and nation to be visited. Only then would he assemble the government's experts to discuss objectives and nuances in his reading. This step was followed by our preparation of specific issues papers, including the vice president's recommended position. He was rarely satisfied with this, leading to critical reviews, more thought, appropriate changes, and finally another round of talks with experts supporting the mission.

By now the pyramid was reaching its tip. I refined and redrafted a two-page summary of key points the vice president wished to bear in mind on each key issue. Then I further boiled down these points so they fit on one, no more than two index cards that Mondale carried in his pocket to meetings. The process worked so well that he seldom referred to backup papers—or the cards—during meetings.

Austria would not be our only stop; Mondale would also meet with President António Ramalho Eanes and Prime Minister Mario Soares on May 15–16 in Lisbon; King Juan Carlos I and Prime Minister Adolfo Suárez on May 17 in Madrid; President Josip Broz Tito on May 21 in Belgrade; and Prime Minister Callaghan on May 22, thirty miles northwest of London at Chequers. We returned to Washington on May 23.

The May 18–20 talks in Vienna were, however, the force propelling the trip and the part requiring the most sensitive diplomatic skills. The site selected was the beautiful, historic Hofburg Palace in central Vienna. We had a conference room above an inner courtyard. We in the two delegations introduced ourselves on a warm spring morning, with the windows thrown open. White Lipizzaner stallions trotted by in their daily training regimen. It was perhaps an ironic setting in which to grapple for more than eight hours with the political vestiges of Europe's African empire. Mondale had several rounds of talks with Vorster, and between them a working lunch with Austria's Chancellor Bruno Kreisky, a courtesy call on President Rudolf Kirchschläger, and a press conference. A dinner was held in honor of the U.S. and South African delegations.

Vorster and Mondale both remained civil and diplomatically correct—and were candid to the point of sharp language in presenting their opposing views on the internal situation in South Africa. On Namibia and Rhodesia, there was no agreement, but diplomatic formulations were accepted for further exploration. There could be no doubt that each nation, while not encouraged, knew clearly where the other stood by the end of the third round.

In 1979, I was with Mondale at the British embassy in Washington at a luncheon honoring the new prime minister, Margaret Thatcher, when Foreign Secretary Peter Carrington excused himself to take a call. He came back bearing the news of a successful breakthrough in the Rhodesian negotiations. And in 1980, I was with the president and vice president when Prime Minister Robert Mugabe of newly independent Zimbabwe paid his first official visit to the United States to offer his thanks for America's support.

All that would come later. For the moment, in 1977 in Austria, we did not see such progress. With this second major assignment behind us, Mondale's foreign policy involvement for the rest of 1977 focused on meetings in Washington. That gave me a chance to be at home a bit more regularly—watching the boys, both budding school lacrosse aces; teaching a bit of dinghy sailing; and gardening with dear Gretchen.

CHAPTER 12

Building Toward the Camp David Accords, 1978

I was with Vice President Mondale for the December 1977 flight that took one his most important guiding lights and friends, Hubert H. Humphrey—former mayor, senator, vice president, and senator again—back home to Minnesota for the final time. Humphrey spoke with us on that flight with the spark still in those eyes, reflecting a splendid spirit despite the ravages of illness to his body.

In January 1978 I was again flying with Mondale, this time to Canada and Mexico for two intensively prepared working visits—visits that coincided with Humphrey's loss. I also had had the pleasure of knowing him. It was to Humphrey that I had written in 1967, when he was vice president and chairman of the National Council on Marine Resources and Engineering Development during his vice presidency. I was applying, successfully it would turn out, for a staff position in international marine science affairs. Humphrey wrote in December 1968 to thank me for my contributions to the council. Now, after his demise, the vice president's hosts in Ottawa and Mexico City recognized this man's extraordinary value and offered impressive tributes to him.

The Carter administration was at its full foreign-policy stride. In the face of tremendous domestic controversy, the president had pushed ahead in September 1977 to terminate prior treaties pertaining to the Panama Canal, and to conclude a new treaty with the government of Panama safeguarding America's strategic interests. This would provide for the permanent neutrality and operation of the canal, while ensuring Panama's rights as a territorial sovereign. Early in 1978, Carter and Mondale shaped a complementary schedule of summit travels for the first half of the year that would take the president to Venezuela, Brazil, Nigeria, and Liberia in late March and early April, and to Panama City in mid-June to confirm the exchange of documents ratifying the Panama Canal Treaties. As these plans would develop, Carter would also meet with the presidents of Venezuela, Colombia, and Mexico and the prime minister of Jamaica; and in mid-July he traveled to Bonn in the Federal Republic of Germany, for the 1978 Economic Summit of Industrialized Democracies.

Meanwhile, Mondale would travel to Canada, Mexico, and the Pacific region.

On January 17, 1978, we visited Prime Minister Trudeau's official residence at 24 Sussex Drive for a dinner honoring Vice President Mondale. As a former border state senator, Mondale was very knowledgeable about key U.S.-Canadian issues and had made it clear he supported doing everything possible in favor of the relationship. To understand this unique relationship, one must grasp the limited authority of Canada's federal government over certain actions of each of the provinces. It is more limited on some matters than that of the U.S. government over each of the states. At the time of our visit, for example, the United States had an interest in a greater flow of natural gas from the gas fields of Alberta to the American Midwest. The Albertans, in turn, wanted greater access to American markets for their beef. It was not an issue that could be quickly resolved in Ottawa by a meeting of U.S. and Canadian leaders. Talks in Ottawa could only help set the tone for more detailed discussions with premiers of the provinces, but the quest for improved understandings on the arrangements for the sale of gas and beef meant we would also visit Edmonton on this trip, including a working session with Albertan Premier Peter Lougheed.

Such was the nature of the discussions over cocktails at 24 Sussex, when the prime minister's young sons, including seven-year-old Justin wearing his Doctor Denton pajamas, appeared for a moment to say goodnight to their father. Trudeau then escorted our party to dinner—the vice president, Senator William Dodd Hathaway of Maine, Senator Robert Stafford of Vermont, Senator Wendell Anderson of Minnesota, Ambassador Tom Enders, Assistant Secretary of State George Vest, David Aaron, and me, together with members of his cabinet and other Canadian leaders. Trudeau casually set the pace of conversation. In turn, he asked each minister to touch on subjects of primary concern to him at the moment. The process opened a high-spirited, colorful exchange—but honors for the evening went to Ambassador Marcel Cadieux, Canadian chairman of the Maritime Boundary Talks with the United States, and former ambassador to the United States.

As he recounted details of talks and impasses with the United States, Cadieux, in his lively French Canadian accent, painted a canvas of the absurd, the improbable, and the hilarious. By the time he finished, everyone at the table was doubled over in laughter. Cadieux captured the essence of the frustrations and barriers encountered in trying to deal with any number of bilateral "small problems" at the federal level. He received a rousing round of applause for his effort. And Canada and the United States successfully negotiated a maritime boundary agreement.

Early the next morning, we left for Edmonton. One of the conveniences—and challenges—of official travel to foreign land is the baggage call process. All luggage destined for Air Force One and Air Force Two receives a careful security check at every stop. To facilitate this process and free delegation members from the task of hauling luggage while they move from one event to the next during tightly scheduled visits, the administrative members of each delegation slip notices under hotel room doors advising participants of the hour bags must be placed in the hallway. This hour is so early, and return to the room the previous night so late, that there is often the temptation just to lie out in the hall with your bags, to be scooped up and deposited on the plane in the morning.

Instead you must focus, regardless of the hour. Concentration, protocol, and survival all fold into the tedious process of setting aside everything you require in the morning, from shaving gear to rain gear. Only then can you consign your luggage to the hall and fall into bed. As a result of this process, colleagues have been known to appear in the morning wearing a suit and tie—and a pajama shirt.

It was snowing when Prime Minister Trudeau's dinner ended. The baggage call notice had been slipped under my door upon my return to the Chateau Laurier. I adjusted my packing slightly with this turn of the weather, and the faithful flight bag that had been my road companion for twenty years again took its post outside my door.

However important it is to meet the baggage call, catching the plane is essential. Tales abound of staff members arriving thirty seconds too late, watching the tail of their intended jet disappear into the skies. These are grim, career-chilling experiences. The snowfall had been heavy, and while the center of the storm had passed by the early morning of January 18, the flakes continued to fall, adding to three-foot shoulders of plowed snow en route to the airport.

While the wings of Air Force Two received a final sweep and deicing, we were shown into a reception room looking out on the airfield and offered a welcome cup of coffee. Within a few minutes, the Air Force jet started its engines and began to taxi slowly through the swirls of snow to its boarding chocks. And then we were treated to a moment of delightful drama.

A colleague had slept through his wakeup call and missed the motorcade. He came charging through the terminal and out onto the taxiway, furiously waving his arms at the cockpit as big jet wind fanned his hair. Desperately, he insisted that the plane stop and take him on board. Ground crew, concerned for his safety, intercepted him and led him inside. There, purple-faced, he received an unmerciful reception. But he did make the flight. Such is the sherpa's life.

In the wake of the U.S. withdrawal from Vietnam, regional allies expressed a sense of abandonment and uncertainty. The year 1978 was for me one of particularly intense diplomatic efforts leading to the opening of new vistas, the culminating experience of the Middle East summit at Camp David—and more, including the vice president's strategically important visit to the Pacific. Human rights were at the top of our agenda.

As a summit staffer, it's of the utmost importance to bear in mind that the person whose work is being supported—the principal—is a human being with concerns that must be understood and anticipated. This is what allows the professional calendar to be shaped in a way that contributes to the broader national objectives, shared by both the principal and the staffer.

I took the sherpa's initiative of assisting in the formal signing ceremonies, the staffing task under the eyes, lens, recording, and transmission equipment of international media, of ensuring that the right page was opened with the right spot identified for signing duplicate copies of the multiple agreements. In such events, instant, correct action is the only standard accepted by the media—and, because summit events move so quickly, it is unrealistic to expect more sophisticated coverage. Presidents command coverage by their very office, but vice presidents, Cabinet officers, and officials at sub-Cabinet rank compete in the news with other stories—which means reporters seek a fresh angle, often a "color angle" such as a mistake.

We traveled in May: May 3–4, the Philippines; May 4–5, Thailand; May 5–7, Indonesia; May 7–9, Australia; May 9–10, New Zealand. I had learned over the years that even in the close, airborne confines of Air Force Two, key papers could vanish at crucial times. So I now prepared two complete duplicate sets of all the classified and unclassified papers needed for each event in the mission, taking meticulous care to organize appropriate folders within individual large rectangular carrying cases. Every folder held the desired end result for each stage of the journey.

Mondale's fundamental message, publicly and privately throughout the mission, was that the United States was a nation of the Pacific. Freedom of the seas and prosperity of U.S. trade were essential to our interests, and regional alliances were central to stability and the global balance.

To underline the vital nature of these interests, the vice president succeeded in breaking an impasse with the Philippines, then under the martial law of dictator President Ferdinand Marcos. Mondale skillfully navigated the sensitive diplomatic space available to him between Marcos and his critics, insisting that human rights be respected while also offering financial aid and reaching an accord on the principles for renewal of U.S. base rights at Clark and Subic Bay, agreements that would be finalized in December. Mondale and Marcos signed agreements on rural road development aimed at expediting farm crops to market, on the development of farm cooperatives similar to those in the United States, on water purification for the people of the Barangay, and on a nonconventional energy project aimed at providing energy sources other than fossil fuels and nuclear power—energy from solar, wind, and biomass sources—for rural Philippine areas.

We helicoptered on May 4 with Marcos and Foreign Minister Carlos Romulo from Manila to Corregidor to pay tribute to those who had died thirty-six years earlier, in 1942. Romulo, now in his late seventies, had fought with General Jonathan Wainwright at Corregidor. He guided us through the main wing and laterals of the bombproof Malinta Tunnel, built by the U.S. Army Corps of Engineers and used as a hospital and General Douglas MacArthur's headquarters and, until the May 6, 1942, surrender of Corregidor to Japan, the seat of the Philippine government. Wainwright described this dark, damp, poorly ventilated maze in his 1946 memoir, *General Wainwright's Story*: "The place shook from the bombing and shelling outside. More than once the tunnel's shaky lighting system . . . failed and cast all of us into the most Stygian blackness imaginable—a fearful hardship on the hospital, where blood-stained doctors and nurses worked day and night" (Doubleday, p. 96).

Thirty-six years later, we emerged together from the tunnel to join the commemorative ceremony. It was marked by a historic event: For the first time since the battle, a representative of the government of Japan had been invited to participate, and was with us to honor the memory of all those who gave their lives.

In Thailand, Vice President Mondale assured Prime Minister Kriangsak Chamanan that the United States would continue to supply defense equipment, with plans to deliver more A-4 aircraft. The agenda included energy cooperation; Mondale and President Suharto signed a $30 million rural electrification loan. Additionally, the U.S. vice president offered $2 million to assist Thailand in the development of its longer-term plans for handling the flood of refugees still fleeing Vietnam and Cambodia—and said America was ready to expand its quota of Southeast Asian refugees by 25,000 a year.

Finally, in Canberra and Wellington, with his Australian and New Zealand hosts, Mondale reaffirmed the U.S. commitment to the Australia, New Zealand, and United States Security Treaty (ANZUS), calling attention to joint naval exercises soon to be held off the west coast of Australia.

But the visits to our ANZUS allies were more informal and collegial, a welcome change of gears in our swing through the Pacific. There were, as always, trade issues and other minor bilateral irritants to be pursued, but we could also discuss more freely broader international concerns, not just in Asia and the Pacific but also in the Middle East and the Warsaw Pact.

On Monday, May 8, talks were held in Canberra with Prime Minister Malcolm Fraser and members of his Cabinet, with a luncheon hosted by the U.S. ambassador, consultations with the leader of the opposition, a wreath-laying ceremony at the Australian War Memorial, and a dinner hosted by Prime Minister and Mrs. Fraser.

Tuesday morning, we had flown 1,200 miles across the Tasman Sea when Air Force Two began its descent into the Royal New Zealand Air Base at Ohakea. From his window seat, Mondale looked out on lush green countryside dotted with sheep. He had grown up in the bountiful farmlands of southern Minnesota and was impressed by what he saw. "The entire place looks like a grass factory," he mused.

At the air base to greet us was the delightfully bluff, if controversial, Prime Minister Robert Muldoon, who had earned his reputation of abrasiveness. I enjoyed his company. In Wellington on May 9, we received grim news from Rome: The militant leftist terrorist group Red Brigades had murdered the former premier, Aldo Moro, after kidnapping and holding him for nearly two months. As our agenda with Prime Minister Muldoon and his government moved forward, we also remained in close contact with the White House to determine whether we would proceed immediately to Italy. Finally it was decided that the vice president should complete the Pacific mission as planned.

At 6:00 p.m. on May 10, Air Force Two was wheels-up for a long night flight. Crossing the international dateline, we flew north to Hawaii for a refueling stop and Mondale's 10:00 a.m. address at the East-West Center. His speech reviewed the goals and accomplishments of the five-nation visit just completed. Fully aware of his audience—not just the packed auditorium, but also the Pacific nations that would carefully read his speech—Mondale reaffirmed the U.S. commitment to a leading role in the Pacific community.

Back home in Annapolis, Gretchen's spring garden was in full bloom. Alex and Ty, now eleven and nine, were finishing their club sport years, getting ready to try out for the Key School's varsities. Our saintly black Labrador, Cleo—Cleopatra, queen of the Severn—was a nonstop joy. She had joined us as a six-week-old, with unconditional love for all in the family. She used to come with me when I went on my very early morning rows and loved to stand on the rowboat's small, triangular bow seat.

Within days of my return from the Pacific, I was on the phone with Simcha Dinitz, Israel's ambassador to the United States. From June 30 to July 3, 1978, Vice President Mondale would lead the U.S. delegation to honor the thirtieth anniversary of Israel's independence. America's recognition of this milestone called for a national gift equal to the importance of the event, and I was probing the minds of as many experts as possible to develop some good recommendations for White House consideration.

Dinitz underlined the importance that the people of Israel attached to their history. He steered me in the direction of Daniel Boorstin, the Librarian of Congress. This, in turn, led to the recommendation of the gift of a copy of the first Hebrew-language edition of the Bible to be published in America, in the first decade of the 1800s. A copy of this extremely rare edition was located in Philadelphia, and the proposal was approved by the president and vice president, as well as the loan for a year to Israel from the National Archives of President Harry S. Truman's instruction to Secretary of State George C. Marshall directing formal U.S. recognition of the State of Israel.

President Carter, Egyptian President Anwar Sadat, and Israeli Prime Minister Menachem Begin would sign the Camp David Accords on September 17, 1978—but the process that resulted in the March 1979 peace treaty between Israel and Egypt had been launched as soon as Carter took office. He saw this as a core challenge and opportunity for his presidency. It was then that he and Secretary of State Cyrus Vance had begun negotiating with Arab and Israeli leaders.

On June 21, 1978, Vance sent messages to Tel Aviv and Cairo proposing that the Israeli and Egyptian foreign ministers meet with him in London in mid-July. As the time of the thirtieth anniversary visit neared, the president asked Mondale to carry letters to both Begin and Sadat that would place the Vance invitation on a personal, leader-to-leader basis.

From the outset, it was clear that this would not be solely a ceremonial trip for the vice president, with so much at stake in the Middle East. President Carter had worked hard, but with little to show by the spring of 1978, to further the peace process. Sadat's historic visit to Jerusalem in November 1977 had shown that direct talks between Egypt and Israel were possible, but the United States searched for the appropriate context, channels, and venue to make such talks a reality. And, given several controversial positions that President Carter had taken publicly on issues key to such talks, Prime Minister Menachem Begin was not as comfortable as Sadat with the prospect of a U.S. middleman.

In addition to the official staff party, the vice president would be accompanied by a special delegation of private U.S. citizens, further underscoring the importance attached to this independence anniversary. That meant additional staff members were needed to attend to the details of the private citizens' agenda. These were important guests of the U.S. government, and, thanks to thorough planning and preparation, they did receive the minute-to-minute attention they deserved. At the same time, having the extra staff members freed those of us who supported the vice president to carry out our duties for the mission without what would otherwise have been distractions. And there was much business to be conducted.

At the public level, in his July 2 Knesset address, Mondale restated America's commitment to UN Resolution 242, adopted in 1967 but never fully implemented, as the framework for peace in the Middle East. The vice president also devoted long hours to discussion with Prime Minister Menachem Begin, starting the moment our motorcade left Tel Aviv bound for Jerusalem. We wound through hills, past hulks of armored vehicles and transports dotting the route, preserved in red lead paint from the time of Israel's war of independence, past Bedouin camps. All the while, Mondale and Begin discussed America's commitment to working with Israel. Wolf Blitzer of the *Jerusalem Post* later reported that Begin said this car ride with the vice president turned everything around—that before it, he had seen no chance of progress. The official talks proceeded with Begin and his cabinet in the prime minister's office, and in tête-à-têtes at his residence. President Carter's letter of invitation to the London talks was delivered, and the vice president continued to exercise his personal diplomacy in a final private meeting just before our departure for Egypt.

While the private-citizen delegation returned to the United States, we proceeded to the military base in Egypt. President Sadat was at his expansive best when we helicoptered in to his Mediterranean seaside villa just east of Alexandria. After showing us to a lawn setting of armchairs and end tables for talks and refreshments, he escorted Vice President Mondale to a bank of microphones prepared for their joint press conference. Sadat confirmed that he had received a communication from Carter, and that he agreed to the proposed London talks. In mid-July, Foreign Minister Mohammed Ibrahim Kamel would meet with Israeli Foreign Minister Moshe Dayan and U.S. Secretary of State Vance. This would be followed by President Carter's invitation in August that Begin and Sadat meet with him at Camp David in September. Our thirtieth-anniversary mission had made a significant contribution to the launching of this summit process.

Pope Paul VI died on August 6, 1978, succeeded on August 26 by Pope John Paul I. Vice President Mondale headed the U.S. delegation that traveled to Rome and the Vatican for the celebration. A fascinating Air Force Two manifest included Senator Claiborne Pell of Rhode Island, Senator Thomas J. McIntyre of New Hampshire, Senator William Dodd Hathaway of Maine, Representative Silvio Conte of Massachusetts, Representative Clement Zablocki of Wisconsin, Representative Peter Rodino of New Jersey, Representative Eligio "Kika" de la Garza of Texas, Governor Brendan Byrne of New Jersey, Notre Dame University President Father Theodore Hesburgh, Mayor George Moscone of San Francisco, and more. For us the celebration would be quick, departing Saturday, September 2, and returning Monday, September 4.

As always, I guided the drafting, assembly, and final review of the background papers for each event, including the papal audience and talks with Prime Minister Giulio Andreotti and Chancellor Helmut Schmidt. I also had to come up with the best gift from the nation. When the former Cardinal Albino Luciani, patriarch of Venice, appeared for the first time as Pope John Paul I to greet the masses waiting in St. Peter's Square and raised his hands from the St. Peter's Basilica balcony, his signature welcoming smile illuminated his face. That special historic moment had been captured on the front page of every U.S. newspaper in each of the fifty states. On Air Force Two, we carried a custom-built mahogany portfolio containing those front pages, a spontaneous tribute from all of America.

Arriving at St. Peter's Square at 6:00 p.m. on September 3, our delegation was shown seats among heads of state and chiefs of government close to the platform erected for the inaugural mass. In the golden light of sunset, only one intrusion interrupted the spectacle of John Paul I's installation—a large balloon, beyond the square, protested the presence of Argentina's brutal dictator, President Jorge Videla. Few could know that I had been in touch with a member of his staff to confirm the details of a meeting with Mondale on September 4.

When Chancellor Schmidt joined the vice president for breakfast the next morning, the ease of conversation made it clear that the two administrations had come to know each other better and were now free of the protocol of formal diplomacy. Later, at the Palazzo Chigi for talks with Andreotti, I was reminded once again of the importance of such opportunities for informal contact on the fringe of international occasions. Because the positive chemistry of these meetings is unburdened by the heavy logistics of more formal state-to-state discussions, they represent an important dynamic in summit life. Not only do they contribute to continuing dialogue on matters of shared interest, but their face-to-face nature also enables advances on differences not susceptible to resolution by bureaucracies. Both benefits held true on this mission.

The military takeover of Argentina and subsequent human rights abuses, disappearances, and confirmed heavy loss of life in the government's "antiterrorist" campaign had compelled President Carter, reinforced by punitive action of the U.S. Congress, to chill U.S.-Argentine relations. Military sales were canceled, and the entire future of contacts between the two governments now depended on internationally credible evidence of respect for human rights.

The vice president had one of his most capable, experienced advance men, Mike Murray, in Rome to pave the way for the September 1978 mission. Upon our arrival, Murray buttonholed me: Videla's aide had been in touch and wanted me to call as soon as possible to confirm the time, place, and any other particulars of the meeting. Murray's ex-Marine voice dropped to a disparaging growl as he told me the U.S. ambassador thought the meeting was a bad idea, and that he specifically did not want it to take place at his official residence. I replied that the president, vice president, secretary of state, and assistant to the president for national security affairs thought the meeting was a good idea—that the ambassador was outvoted, both on this and on the venue. There was no other logical site, given the need for discretion and Mondale's tight schedule. In less than an hour, Mike was back in touch; all was in order.

Upon the vice president's return from the Palazzo Chigi, he joined Mrs. Mondale and the members of our presidential delegation to depart for the papal audience in the Sistine Chapel. John Paul I reached out in his greeting to the delegation. When Representative Conte mentioned that his family had come from Vicenza, the pope's roots in Italy, John Paul warmly expressed his pride.

Back at the ambassador's residence, a planned reception was underway in the gardens when Mondale and I proceeded to a second-floor drawing room, where President Videla joined us. Mondale's message was polite but to the point, much along the lines of his message to John Vorster of South Africa a year earlier. Argentina's internal affairs were for Argentina to decide, but America could not be indifferent to the outcome. The vice president told Videla that we wanted to return to our traditionally good relations, and to give favorable consideration to requests in this context from Buenos Aires. However, we needed evidence of Argentina's good faith on the issue of human rights. To launch this process, the vice president urged Videla to agree to a long-standing request by the Inter-American Human Rights Commission for a visit to Argentina. Videla, soft-spoken and polite throughout, listened carefully. Within a very brief time following his return to Buenos Aires, the commission's request for a visit was granted.

Characteristically, before leaving for the airport after that discussion, the vice president told members of the press about it, including its purpose and his hope for progress.

Thirty-four days later, the Vatican was jolted by the news of John Paul I's heart attack and death. As *Newsweek* reported Cardinal François Marty's reaction, "The Pope had a message to give our world. He gave us the smile of God. In the grayness of these days, this smile will remain like a beam of light" (October 9, 1978, p. 73).

Within twenty-four hours of our return from the Vatican, I was at Andrews Air Force Base to assist the vice president with the reception ceremonies first for Sadat, then for Begin. Marine Two, Mondale's helicopter, made a quick journey of the sixty-five miles from Washington to Camp David. We arrived on September 7, and I remained through September 17, participating in the summit's stunning success.

President Carter had invested his prestige and that of the United States; either he would break the stalemate in the Middle East, or he would be broken politically by his failure to do so. The very fact that I was at Camp David was testimony to the partnership between the president and vice president, and to the integrated working relationship between their staffs, a relationship unparalleled in U.S. history.

Carter had correctly predicted that the summit would take time, and he knew that if it were to succeed, drum-tight integrity would have to be maintained throughout the process. The president had asked Mondale to divide his time between Washington and the summit. This would help ensure that the routine business of government flowed smoothly in Carter's absence, while Mondale would also participate in the negotiations with Begin and Sadat. Because Mondale would have to be kept fully abreast of hour-by-hour developments at the summit, the president agreed that to make this possible, I should be admitted as a member of the very limited summit staff.

Franklin Delano Roosevelt was the first president to motor up to northern Maryland's Catoctin Mountains seeking a brief respite from the Depression and wartime pressures, and from Washington's humid summer heat. Navy stewards from the president's yacht had traveled with him to summer cottages that Roosevelt named Shangri-La. The retreat, which President Dwight D. Eisenhower renamed Camp David in honor of his grandson, became a favorite of every president who followed. By the time of the Carter presidency, Camp David had evolved into one of the world's most exclusive, secluded year-round resorts, which the Navy by tradition and expertise continued to manage for the White House.

Within its fenced, carefully guarded perimeter, the camp at one end had a fully equipped helicopter landing pad and hangar facility set in an open field that would be the site of the Marine Corps' silent drill performed in the evening of September 7, in honor of the summit leaders. A narrow service road led from the landing pad to the heart of Camp David. The president's lodge, Aspen, commanded a view of many miles out over the ridges to the south, with a terraced patio, swimming pool, and putt-and-pitch golf range at the foot of the lodge in a clearing of the forest.

Beneath the towering hardwood trees along the roads and foot paths curving from Aspen, more than a dozen separate guest lodges housed the members of the three delegations. Subtle variations distinguished them in their rustic, comfortable designs. Carved wood address plaques identified them: Maple, Elm, Red Oak, Walnut, Hemlock, Hickory, Hawthorn, and more. Laurel Lodge, a relatively recent addition, provided the main dining room and lounge for some participants. Tennis courts, a bowling alley, a horseshoe pitch, a swimming pool with bath house, the camp commander's quarters, a dispensary, and barracks for additional personnel were all placed discreetly among the trees. There could be no finer place to relax—or to work—free from distraction.

The Camp David Summit was a unique diplomatic experience. Normal schedules, calendars, and timetables were set aside. The hours of the day and night and the days of the week were far less relevant to the summit's participants than the nonstop dynamics of consultation, the drafting of new proposals, the analysis of Egyptian and Israeli proposals, and the informal, continuing mission-oriented dialogue between participants at all levels, all keyed to support the president's negotiations with Begin and Sadat. With very few exceptions, the U.S., Egyptian, and Israeli delegations remained within the confines of the presidential retreat from start to finish. Contact with the media was limited to briefings that the president's press secretary, Jody Powell, provided in the news center established miles away at Thurmont, Maryland. This "lid" on summit news was virtually absolute. The absence of thousands of conflicting, inevitably controversial news stories freed all three summit leaders from having to posture publicly or take irreversibly unbending stands driven by domestic politics. The press was kept in the waiting room during the summit's labor.

President Carter guided the Camp David process with a deep intensity and sense of purpose, twenty-four hours a day, from start to finish, a remarkable feat of both diplomacy and endurance. Early in the summit, I sat perhaps four feet from him at the large round conference table in Holly Lodge at a night strategy session. Carter sketched the wide differences between Begin and Sadat, clearly evident gulfs, that he had encountered in the opening rounds of their talks. He stressed his total trust in the integrity and skill of his American team, and his dedication to sharing his innermost thoughts and the most sensitive information with this team in pursuit of the summit's goal. His pale gray-blue gaze probed our faces as he spoke. Periodically he very briefly paused, holding his words until he had driven his mind to shape each of the precise thoughts he wished to convey. I remember wondering if anyone's health could stand up to such strain. Palpable tension hung in the air throughout the summit.

The president's principal summit lieutenant, Secretary of State Vance, played a U.S. role second only to the president's in achieving the Camp David accords. Vance worked day after day, with no more sleep than that of a destroyer skipper's in combat, at three different levels of the summit process: with the president, Begin, and Sadat; with the U.S. team reviewing tactics, revising draft texts, and shaping new formulations in light of each preceding day's discussions; and with the Israeli, Egyptian, and U.S. delegations at the ministerial and experts' levels. To mesh political intent with international law and the code of formal diplomacy, Vance worked late into the nights and early into each new morning. An electric golf cart, not an Air Force jet, became the vehicle for Vance's successful

Middle East shuttle diplomacy. A veritable demon of the cart, he whizzed along the asphalt footpaths connecting the cabins and delegations. Camp David lent itself to such travel.

But wide gaps between the Egyptian and Israeli positions were not easily bridged despite personal diplomacy, and the trilateral talks were adjourned after two sessions. Not until the final day would Carter, Sadat, and Begin all meet again. On Sunday, September 10, the United States offered the Israeli delegation the first of a score of compromise texts. Mondale met early into Monday morning with Begin and Carter and then left later in the day for Washington to attend to the other business of government. This pattern would be repeated all week.

Each time Mondale left, I remained glued to the evolving talks. I knew and worked easily with the experts in our delegation: Ambassador at Large Roy Atherton, Assistant Secretary of State Hal Saunders, Bill Quandt of the NSC staff, and our ambassadors to Israel and Egypt, Sam Lewis and Hermann Eilts. I also maintained a fairly detailed status report on developments by attending our delegation's meetings, working late nights during the preparation of new drafts, sitting in on talks between Secretary Vance and the Egyptians, receiving a summary of other talks from various participants, and dining with different members of the three delegations at Laurel. I presented all this information to the vice president each time he helicoptered back to reenter the talks.

Sadat, Begin, Dayan, and Ezer Weizman had fought for their countries' independence and very existence. Their beliefs on the issues of the Middle East ran in their deepest veins. They had many good stories to tell. Weizman, who had commanded the Israeli Air Force before becoming minister of defense, told us that he had been a truck driver for the Royal Air Force in Egypt during World War II. Weizman, with his military secretary Colonel Ilan Tehila, took the pressures of Camp David in stride.

Menachem Begin, invariably accompanied by his wife, strolled the camp's grounds and often dined with us at Laurel, always maintaining a courtly, old-world manner. It was hard to believe that he had been among the fiercest of guerrillas in Israel's war for independence.

Moshe Dayan was truly a grand, charismatic figure who delighted in discussing his real interest in life—the archaeology of Israel and the Middle East. He recounted the adventures and misadventures in his literary efforts, intended to augment his government salary. To me, Dayan exuded the spirit of Israel. His words were the words not of an individual but of a people.

President Sadat, throughout the summit, remained in relative seclusion; I caught a glimpse of him only from time to time during his morning strolls. Day after day, President Carter kept the process going. Israel's withdrawal from occupied territories—the Sinai foremost in terms of issues vital to Sadat—was clearly the most difficult issue confronting the negotiators. The status of Jerusalem was a close second. On Thursday, September 14, the tenth day of the summit, the Israelis agreed that they could withdraw their air bases from the Sinai provided the United States built new military bases in the Negev, but Begin insisted that the Jewish settlements would have to remain. When Sadat received this news, only Carter's personal intervention kept the Egyptian president from demanding a helicopter for his immediate departure.

On Friday, September 15, I accompanied the vice president on a mission as unique as the summit itself. The president had penned personal letters to Sadat and Begin setting a deadline of Sunday for the conclusion of the summit; this was done not out of optimism but as a last-ditch effort to produce concessions from Israel and Egypt. Mondale delivered these letters to each leader, discussing their contents and receiving comments, first to Sadat at Dogwood, then to Begin at Birch. Late on Saturday, Begin agreed that the question of the settlements could be put to a vote by the Knesset, and if the Knesset approved, Israel would depart. The president somehow found time to dictate the following note to the American team: "There is one major issue on which agreement has not been reached. Egypt states that agreement to remove Israeli settlements from Egyptian territory is a prerequisite to a peace treaty. Israel states that the issue of the Israeli settlements should be resolved during the peace negotiations.

Within two weeks the Knesset will decide on the issue of the settlements." To which he added, in his own hand, "This is the only statement to be made by any of the U.S. delegation regarding the Sinai settlement issue—whether on or off the record. JC."

Sadat agreed to this formulation on Sunday morning, September 17. The status of Jerusalem could not be resolved, but all at Camp David knew that what had already been achieved was too important to let slip away. The parties agreed that the issue would remain unresolved. Both Egypt and Israel included side letters stating their positions as part of the summit's formal documents.

That same day, President Carter suddenly appeared at Holly Lodge and asked me where he could find Weizman. I pointed to Sycamore, and he was at the door in a second or two. Weizman urged him not to come in because his cabin was a mess. But the president was leaving nothing to chance. He had achieved his breakthrough to success but sought—and received—the minister of defense's word that he would do everything possible upon his return to Israel to have the summit's decisions approved by the Israeli Knesset.

In a Wagnerian finale, thunderstorms tore through the Catoctin skies Sunday evening as the delegations prepared to depart, at last, for Washington and the White House. The dash south by helicopter was as rough as the very worst I had endured during my Antarctic years; however, we were soon on the ground, and euphoria was on every face in the East Room of the White House late that evening when President Carter, President Sadat, and Prime Minister Begin entered to sign the Camp David Agreements.

The Framework for Peace in the Middle East pointed toward a comprehensive peace settlement. It established principles to guide the process, many of which have endured. The core conflict between Israel and Palestine, however, remains unresolved.

The Camp David Accords represented a towering achievement—one that hinged, even with the September 17 signing, on Knesset approval, including the dismantling and removal of all Israeli settlements from the Sinai.

On September 28, after many hours of impassioned debate, the Knesset would vote its approval.

President Carter had achieved the near-impossible, bringing great honor to the United States at home and abroad, and dramatically demonstrating anew the unique diplomatic opportunities afforded by negotiation at the summit.

I returned from that summit with a prized expedition jacket—the navy-blue windbreaker with the seal of the president, topped by the words "Camp David" framed in anchors. The president would send me another trophy, a photograph of Begin, Sadat, and Carter in front of Aspen, smiling broadly, inscribed by each leader. The experience of that summit has never faded from my mind.

One conversation in particular remains etched in my memory. On the final evening, just before our departure, I was in Laurel Lodge enjoying a cup of coffee with Ed Sanders, President Carter's principal staff liaison officer with the Jewish American community. Prime Minister Begin and an aide entered the dining room, and we invited them to join us. Begin shook our hands warmly; he was still absorbing the splendid meaning of his actions that day. "For years," he said, "all the time I was in the opposition, they said, 'Don't elect him; he will bring war.' Last year I was contemplating retirement, and now, I am bringing peace!"

CHAPTER 13

Shuttle Diplomacy with Mondale, 1979–1981

When you are at a conference table in Hong Kong at 2:00 p.m. local time, and you have just arrived from the U.S. East Coast, your mind and body silently but forcefully advise you that it is really 2:00 a.m. and that you should be asleep. Long flights affect the body's biological rhythm, which means summits can be impacted by jet lag. For me, understanding this phenomenon from the outset and adjusting to it helped tremendously. Formulas for contending with jet lag rival those for hangovers, but I found the best solution was to accept instantly the local time as my own. If my body said I was tired, I ignored those signals and went to sleep when it was nighttime locally and the correct bedtime. Then I slept hard until the alarm ordered me up and back into the traces. This personal formula stood me well—combined with my absolutely essential regular exercise routine.

By early 1979, the diplomacy involved in implementing the Camp David Accords had been intense and sustained. Hours after the

September 17 East Room signing ceremony, Secretary Vance had departed for the Middle East to enlist the support of moderate Arab states. Israelis and Egyptians set to work in their respective capitals, and then together at the negotiating table to come to grips with the vital language that would terminate the state of war and establish peace between their nations.

The United States kept a close eye on this process. At the first signs of deadlock, Carter persuaded Begin and Sadat to move the negotiating teams to Washington, where the United States could perform most effectively as middleman. The talks continued at an intense pace. Late in the fall, I had a call from the ambassador of Egypt asking if his delegation might have permission to stroll the grounds of the Naval Observatory from time to time to relieve the close, near-continuous confinement of hotel and negotiating rooms. The vice president was delighted to offer the hospitality not only of the Observatory grounds but also of his residence.

While the Camp David process moved carefully forward, the rest of the world's pressing issues—the Strategic Arms Limitation Talks negotiations, formal relations with the People's Republic of China, developments of international concern and importance in Europe, Africa, Asia, and the Western Hemisphere—demanded White House attention, including at the summit. President Carter launched his annual travels early in January 1979, joining Giscard d'Estaing, Helmut Schmidt, and James Callaghan at Guadeloupe for four-power consultations. In mid-February, he met again with José López Portillo and addressed the Mexican Congress.

The self-generating nature of summit diplomacy always makes the process a challenge. Because talks at the summit are a measure of international recognition, in each new U.S. administration, many nations not immediately included in the process steadily increase pressure for a summit with U.S. leadership. Informal talks with a good number of foreign leaders in New York or Washington on the fringe of each autumn's United Nations General Assembly session help to ease the pressure—but do not solve the problem. Further complicating the schedule of an American president, nations that have enjoyed a summit early in the days of an administration often press for further rounds of talks, citing not only the merits but also the perils to the bilateral relationship if another round should not occur. The foreign leader's domestic political standing will suffer, the White House is warned, if he or she is not seen as sustaining personal diplomatic contact with the U.S. president. Positive results flowing from a first meeting may seep away if a populace believes it is being ignored or taken for granted because of no follow-up face-to-face talks. And media commentaries fuel demands for further summit contact.

Such considerations were weighed, with President Carter's administration now in its third year, and for Mondale and me, the following months were heavy with global travel. As always, Carter ensured that the world understood the vice president carried his full authority. For instance, to maintain high visibility in bilateral relationships with Venezuela and Brazil, where Carter had already made summit visits, he named Mondale to lead the U.S. delegations attending the mid-March 1979 inaugurations of Presidents-elect Luis Herrera Campins in Caracas and João Baptista de Oliveira Figueiredo in Brasília.

But then, on March 6, the White House announced that Joan Mondale, second lady of the United States, and Labor Secretary Ray Marshall would lead the inaugural delegations, while the vice president remained in Washington. This would free the president to travel to the Middle East, where diplomatic disaster loomed high, with the Egyptian-Israeli peace negotiations deadlocked. All of the Camp David accomplishments the previous September were about to be destroyed. Carter again gambled the prestige of the U.S. presidency with the announcement that he would personally go to Jerusalem and Cairo to take charge of the peace process. For national security reasons, the United States carefully avoids having the president and vice president overseas at the same time.

I accompanied the South American delegation. The host governments fully appreciated the reasons for the change, and the U.S. advance teams had smoothly worked the triangular coordination of schedules. Mrs. Mondale, a sophisticated patron of the arts with a background in history and French, had often traveled with the vice president and was undaunted by this new foreign mission, as was Secretary Marshall. They carried out most ably their chief task of conveying to both new leaders America's respect, friendship, greetings, and best wishes. On the day of Herrera's inauguration, the vice president called for a status report, and I was pleased to advise him that his wife and son William had dominated front-page press coverage that morning. "Tell them I'm proud of them. And," he added with a laugh, "keep that delegation out of trouble."

The delegates, mostly Hispanic American leaders, enjoyed themselves thoroughly and added a very positive social dimension to America's representation. It was a happy company on board our Air Force jet, and I even won first prize, coveted by all—a mounted piranha with jaws spread, baring its needle-sharp triangular teeth—for the closest guess of the precise minute and second we passed over the equator on our flight from Caracas to Rio.

Early in the morning of March 14, I ran along the empty Copacabana Beach, keeping up my strength, as ever, for travels I could not otherwise have handled.

Only the sounds of the light lapping of waves and my feet hitting the moist, hard sand intruded on my thoughts as I reviewed my myriad responsibilities. On the return lap, the sun burned through the morning haze, and the Corcovado statue of Christ the Redeemer was clear on Rio de Janeiro's magnificent skyline. I carried in our traveling files a letter for each new president from President Carter. Mrs. Mondale would present them, adding that she had word of favorable Middle East developments, and that the vice president looked forward to following through with an official visit upon the president's return to Washington.

And this occurred. On March 16, the foreign ministries of Venezuela and Brazil announced that Vice President Mondale would be making a visit. I accompanied him to his talks with President Figueiredo, and on March 22, I again stepped from a motorcade at Planalto Palace in the new capital city of Brasília, laid out in 1960 in the shape of a giant flying bird. The benefit of this high-level U.S. visit so soon after the inaugurations was immediately clear. With the flush of excitement still fresh in both capitals, the vice president and the new presidents were free to devote all their time together to serious discussion. No longer did the vice president need to fulfill the time-consuming duty of spectator at the elaborate ceremonies of little more than a week before.

There was much to celebrate—and even more to accomplish, given the fact that the "new moral dimension" of the administration's foreign policy had included Brazil among its early targets. The press reported progress along these lines, recalling earlier strains prompted by human rights abuses and U.S. efforts to block a $4.8 billion nuclear fuel and reprocessing sale from the Federal Republic of Germany. With Mondale's visit, as the *Los Angeles Times* explained, "President Figueiredo's acceptance of an invitation to meet with President Carter in Washington suggests that U.S. relations with this important country may indeed be on the mend" (March 26, 1979). And in Venezuela, a key member of the Organization of Petroleum Exporting Countries, Mondale, and Herrera held forward-looking talks that could benefit both countries' plans for energy sources. Of course, in 1979, none of the sad yet-to-come developments could be foreseen, and relations with both Venezuela and Brazil appeared promising.

Meanwhile, Carter had indeed worked another Middle East miracle. Back in DC, in the bright spring sunshine of March 26, I watched Begin and Sadat sign the Egyptian-Israeli Peace Treaty in a ceremony on the White House lawn.

We pressed on with Mondale's international diplomacy. Norway, Iceland, Denmark, Finland, and Sweden had been angling for a visit from the vice president, a Scandinavian American, ever since his 1976 election. Dates had been explored and then evaporated in 1977 and 1978. Finally, the visit came to pass in April 1979. The Netherlands, a close ally, was included from the outset, as it had been too often bypassed because of its proximity to the international hub of Brussels. Between April 11 and 21, Air Force Two carried us to Iceland, Norway, Denmark, Sweden, Finland, and the Netherlands.

April 13 found us in a fast Norwegian coastal charter boat, pushing north through the gray coastal seas of Fedjefjorden. A cold mist drove across the bow, as I enjoyed the snap of the vice president's flag flying at the yardarm. We headed out briefly into the open waters of the North Atlantic, then made a starboard turn into majestic Sognefjord on our four-and-a-half-hour run to Fjaerlandsfjord and the vice president's ancestral home in the headwater village of Mundal. A sleek, gray-green 100-ton *Snøgg*-class fast-attack missile gunboat of the Royal Norwegian Navy rode shotgun.

At a packed local meeting hall, a speech was delivered in Mondale's honor, followed by a reception by the people of Fjaerlandsfjord. As festivities drew to a close, the vice president took the microphone to express his thanks and commemorate his visit—by presenting the flag that had flown on the boat that brought him to Mundal. This flag had been my responsibility. I had given personal attention to ensuring that one would be available, even overseeing the addition of two grommets to receive the clips of the coastal ferry's yard halyard. But I had overlooked the fact that the flag was a multicolored silkscreen, not multiple panels of different-colored cloth. When we retrieved the flag for its Mundal presentation, I was appalled to see that the brilliant seal had dissolved into an indistinguishable blur during the misty, windy voyage I had so enjoyed. Yet another reminder that the summit sherpa gets no rest from full attention to every detail.

The week was filled with tributes to the vice president, cordial meetings, receptions, and glittering banquets in the palaces, official residences, and halls of government kings, queens, presidents, and prime ministers. The Nordic countries and the Netherlands celebrated the national satisfaction they took from the U.S. administration's foreign policy, which emphasized fundamental respect for human rights, initiatives by industrialized nations to seek improved patterns of cooperation with poorer developing nations, improved relations with all of Central America, and continued dedication to the success of the Strategic Arms Limitation Talks with the USSR.

At Oslo city hall on the evening of April 17, the vice president likewise expressed deep U.S. appreciation for Norway's contribution to regional and East-West stability. With King Olav, members of the Norwegian royal family, the prime minister, and cabinet members in attendance, Mondale offered eloquent praise for Norway's steadfast perseverance against challenges, which had historically included efforts to stop the country from joining NATO. Mondale pledged continuing U.S. support and friendship—words that were reinforced from the vice president's first day of talks with Prime Minister Ólafur Jóhannesson in Reykjavik through his final session with Prime Minister Dries van Agt in the Hague. At the center of all these exchanges, Mondale and his interlocutors kept revisiting the defense objectives and requirements of the West, and the resulting steps being taken to enhance NATO security. U.S. and Soviet negotiators were finally gaining momentum for agreement on SALT II, but the alliance also faced the stark, growing presence of a new generation of highly capable Soviet mobile, five-thousand-kilometer-range SS-20 missiles, each with three independently targetable nuclear warheads. This fundamentally destabilizing act on the part of the Soviet Union, unconstrained by intercontinental strategic arms talks, would necessitate upgraded NATO deterrent forces.

In the NATO capitals, Mondale took stock with each ally of efforts to realize the alliance's goal of 3 percent real growth annually in defense budgets. He reviewed progress on NATO's "two-way street," which provided for better sharing among allies of increasingly expensive weapon systems production and purchasing.

With bonds of friendship and alliance reaffirmed and national defense strategies discussed in depth, this series of warm, informal, critically important visits came to an end.

Following Carter's urgent mission to the Middle East in March and the signing of the Israeli-Egyptian peace treaty, his administration turned top priority to the SALT II negotiations. In mid-June 1979 Carter flew to Vienna, Austria, to join Leonid Brezhnev at a U.S.-Soviet summit marked by the signing of the SALT II Treaty. Upon his return, I began many days of travel with the vice president as he crisscrossed the United States rallying domestic public opinion in support of SALT II, which still required ratification by the U.S. Senate.

Meanwhile, in now-communist Vietnam, a mass exodus of people had been underway since 1975, reaching crisis proportions by 1979. More than 3 million would flee the region by 1995, often in small, dangerously crowded, and unseaworthy boats. Those who survived arrived at their destinations sick and with nothing. Their numbers created deep political problems and a near-crushing imposition on the governments of Thailand, Hong Kong, Malaysia, and Singapore. The United States responded by doubling the total of permissible refugees from Indochina to 17,000 a month. Mondale announced this welcome development at the United Nations Conference on Indochinese Refugees, held in Geneva on July 20–21, 1979.

Detailed planning for this mission to Geneva had begun via telephone from the West Coast while I was with the vice president on a SALT II speaking tour. During a return stopover in Philadelphia, Air Force Two took on board new members of the party who would accompany us to Geneva.

In preparation for departure, I went through the cases of documents that had been developed by State, the NSC, and White House and vice presidential staffs, carefully checking each set of papers for the conference, and for accompanying bilateral talks that the vice president would hold in Geneva as he pressed for an international response sufficient to meet the refugee crisis. Shortly after takeoff, Mondale called me forward to brief the private citizens who had been invited to accompany the U.S. delegation.

The vice president delivered his address on July 21, in the great assembly hall of Geneva's Palais des Nations. Mondale laid fundamental blame for the boat-people crisis on Vietnam, calling for an immediate moratorium on expulsions. Urging countries of first asylum in the region to provide safe haven, he exhorted all other countries to assure the nations of Southeast Asia of a global long-term resettlement commitment, as the United States already had done. Mondale stressed the need for larger national contributions to the UN High Commissioner for Refugees, and for new transit centers in the Pacific to assist. He announced that the United States would request funding to help finance these new United Nations

Human Rights Council facilities, and that additional ships and aircraft would be ordered to intensify the search for refugee boats on the high seas. "History will not forgive us if we fail," he concluded, and "history will not forget us if we succeed."

Mondale's powerful address brought thunderous, prolonged applause.

Ambassador Zhang Wenjin, head of the delegation from the People's Republic of China, was particularly vociferous in his support of the vice president's condemnation of Vietnam. Zhang, a very refined sixty-four-year-old diplomat, served as the PRC's ambassador to Pakistan and Canada and was vice minister of foreign affairs. He was among several delegation heads who paid bilateral calls on Mondale in his hotel suite during the refugee conference. This also provided an excellent diplomatic opportunity to discuss U.S. objectives for Mondale's upcoming official visit to China in August.

It would be the first summit-level mission to the PRC since the commencement of formal relations and Vice Premier Deng Xiaoping's visit to the United States in January 1979, and we wanted the visit to highlight progress in the relationship. In Washington we had been working hard to this end; however, so far we had met with little response from the Chinese side.

Seizing this opportunity in Geneva, Deputy National Security Adviser David Aaron, Assistant Secretary of State Richard Holbrooke, and I waited patiently for Mondale and Zhang to complete their consultations. Then we took the Chinese vice minister of foreign affairs aside. This moment was key, and I zeroed in to isolate exact details in my memory, as invited by my colleagues. I sketched out precisely every proposal the United States had advanced to the Chinese for the vice president's visit, explaining the potential benefit to both sides. With an aide taking notes, Zhang listened attentively, seeking an occasional clarification or confirmation. Our time and efforts were rewarded. Within a very few days, the diplomatic logjam began to break in Beijing, in yet another illustration of the irreplaceable value of face-to-face meetings.

Chapter 13

Air Force Two departed Andrews Air Force Base at 8:45 a.m. on Friday, August 24, bound for China. The Mondales brought their daughter, Eleanor. It took seven hours and fifteen minutes to arrive at Elmendorf Air Force Base, Alaska. The next leg, to Yokota Air Base, took seven hours and ten minutes, and the third, to the PRC, four hours and twenty-five minutes. So after more than eighteen flight hours, we were greeted with full military honors at Beijing International Airport. It was now Saturday, August 25. The motorcade wound through a sunlit countryside to the villas, walks, ponds, streams, and gardens of the walled Diaoyutai Guest Compound. Following a welcome shower and change of clothes, we proceeded to the Li Guan restaurant on Kumming Lake at the Summer Palace for an informal dinner in honor of the vice president given by Foreign Minister Huang Hua.

By the time I got to sleep, I was beyond ready and slept soundly and long. The next formal event was Sunday evening, the welcoming banquet. This was held at the Great Hall of the People, a massive revolutionary-era urban labyrinth of conference halls, conference rooms, banquet halls, reception rooms, offices, and professional suites. By now my body clock had mostly adjusted. But in the midafternoons, reminding me that in Washington it was the middle of the night, my eyelids would grow heavy for a moment or two throughout our time in China.

We had worked hard to ensure that the vice president's mission would be fully productive, and now we were able to build on the trade agreement and joint economic, scientific, and technological commissions that had already been established. The vice president's first round of substantive talks with China's political leader, Vice Premier Deng Xiaoping, ran from 9:00 a.m. to noon in an airport-terminal-size conference room of the Great Hall of the People. Deng was a tough little chestnut of a man. It was quickly clear how his sharp mind had led to his role as "first among equals" in China's thousands of millions. Deng chain-smoked Panda cigarettes while benevolently overseeing the steady refilling of large cups of green tea at each place on the long, green-felt-covered table.

A pattern developed: He invited Mondale to offer his views on an issue, then quietly gauged whether to respond instantly or address the question later. After that he launched into fast-clipped deliveries of his own on the crucial points to be addressed in relations and the world more generally.

A formal luncheon back at the Diaoyutai Guest Compound was followed by the vice president's departure for Beijing University, where he became the first American leader to address the university and the people of China via radio and television. I sat behind him on the auditorium stage, feeling very much like a trustee as I watched Mondale make history. In what Secretary of State Vance would later characterize as a preeminently significant visit to China, the vice president delivered an eloquent review of the past, present, and future of the relationship; the fundamental difference between political systems; the congruence of views on issues of global strategic importance; milestones that his visit represented; and progress yet to come. "Normalization signals our understanding that American security in the years ahead will be attained not by maintaining the status quo," he said, "not by colluding for purposes of domination, but by fostering a world of independent nations with whom we can build positive relations" (August 27, 1979).

We celebrated Mondale's public address with an evening of music and dance presented by the Chinese Opera and Ballet Company and the Fourth Troupe of the Beijing Opera Company. The next morning, a Tuesday, a motorcade carried us along Beijing's broad avenues, our official cars standing out like an extinct species amid the swarm of bicycle traffic. Enormous outdoor portraits of Marx and Lenin peered down on us as we neared the Great Hall of the People once again, for the vice president's second three-hour round of consultations with Deng.

Back in the fascinating complex, in a drawing room we settled into heavily upholstered Victorian-era armchairs topped with antimacassars, comfortably installed for the vice president's tête-à-tête with Premier Hua Guofeng.

Mao Zedong, who led the Chinese Community Party from 1935 until his death in 1976, had personally selected Hua as his successor. But jockeying for the post-Mao reins of power continued in 1979, and Hua had many political opponents. In addition to his role as premier, he served as chairman of the Chinese Communist Party Central Committee and chairman of the Military Commission. His manner on the afternoon of August 28 was very much that of the chief of state, removed from the day-to-day detailed work of government—yet, judging by his questions, fully briefed on every minute of the vice president's six hours with Vice Premier Deng.

At the conclusion of this conversation, we adjourned to a larger conference room that had been readied for a formal signing ceremony, with PRC and U.S. flags decorating the ample felt-covered table and risers behind the table where everyone took their places. Given the political competition between Deng and Hua, our diplomatic colleagues whispered their amazement that the Chinese premier had joined the vice premier for this occasion. They could not recall an earlier instance during this period of internal Chinese political struggle when the two had permitted themselves to be photographed together, a reaffirmation of the significance attached to this visit.

With this ceremony, Mondale and Deng expanded the framework for cultural exchanges and reached formal agreement on a program for the development of hydroelectric energy in China. In effect, this agreement resumed pre–World War II efforts of the Army Corps of Engineers to assist the Chinese in harnessing the potential for tremendous energy—and the destruction of such great rivers as the Yangtze. There was a proviso: The PRC would not compensate the United States for the new program of assistance.

The combined events of the summit talks with both Deng and Hua, together with the substantial agreements just signed, made for good press coverage. In addition to developing a feel for the right times and places for successful distant summitry, arranging summit schedules to a pace that produces the best news coverage is an even finer art. By 1979, banquet toasts in the Great Hall of the People and visits to the Great Wall were no longer the newsworthy events they had been in U.S.-PRC relations five years earlier. Immediately following the August 28 signing ceremony, the vice president proceeded to a news conference in the Minzu Hotel, residence for our traveling party of correspondents, joined by a sizable gathering of the Chinese and international press corps.

I saw many wonders of the world as a summit sherpa, this time closer than ever to the Himalayas. In Beijing, the Forbidden City preserves twelve palaces dating from the Ming and Qing dynasties. Three palatial structures with golden tiled roofs and red exterior columns—the Hall of Preserving Harmony, the Hall of Middle Harmony, and the Hall of Supreme Harmony—form the nucleus of the palaces' ceremonial quarters. White structural and ornamental stones, dragged overland from distant quarries with great loss of life, shaped terraces and broad stairways. One massive slab of more than two hundred tons, its face transformed into clouds and dragons, adorned the center of the stairs of the Hall of Preserving Harmony.

These majestic stairways proved good training for my visit to the Great Wall of China. Despite the many, many times I had seen photos of this unique defensive barrier, I had never imagined how steep would be its journey, snaking up and down four thousand miles of China's mountains. I hiked along the top, a twenty-foot-wide stone-paved highway broad enough for ten foot soldiers marching abreast. And this was not even the steepest part of the wall. In some lengths, steps have been cut into the surface for an easier climb. But there was no time to see more. Our motorcade soon whisked us back to Diaoyutai, and shortly after 3:00 p.m. we were airborne on a Chinese government jet bound for Xian, capital of Shensi Province, one of the oldest cities in the world, region of Emperor Qin Shi Huang's famous terra-cotta army.

Our host, the chairman of the Revolutionary Committee of Lintong County, guided us onto the site of an archaeological dig revealing the army vault of the Qin tomb. Qin Shi Huang ascended to the throne in 246 BC, we learned, and the tomb he commissioned upon becoming emperor in 221 took eleven years to build. Its ceilings depicted the heavens' constellations in compositions of pearls. Its palaces were constructed on a floor designed as a physical map of China, with the rivers created from mercury. The mound of the tomb was three hundred feet high and a mile and a half in circumference. Emperor Qin ensured that he would not enter the hereafter unescorted. The vault, discovered in May 1974, contained an entire army of life-size terra-cotta warriors and their horses. Digging as of the summer of 1979 indicated that the force numbered at least six thousand, and today it is estimated at eight thousand.

Before reboarding our flight, the vice president returned to Xian city to tour the General Factory of Petroleum Exploration Instruments. Including Xian on the itinerary had involved an additional dimension of planning, staffing, and logistical support, for both our party and our hosts. As one major example, we had to ensure the same reliability of communications as in Beijing. But the visit was important. In summitry, side visits such as this serve the purpose of advancing the business of nations. They are far more than relaxed intervals in the midst of high-pressure diplomatic discussions. At a time when U.S. relations with the PRC were on the verge of considerable expansion, such a visit could make a substantial contribution to the goals both nations shared.

In this spirit, with even more specific objectives, we continued on to the commercial/industrial city of Guangzhou, formerly Canton on the Pearl River, seventy-five miles northwest of Hong Kong. Guangzhou was important not only for the potential of trade but also because the region is the place of origin for the ancestors of many Chinese Americans. Here we realized one of the important objectives that I had discussed with Ambassador Zhang in Geneva: a ribbon-cutting by the vice president marking the opening of the first U.S. consulate in the new era of relations. Following this ceremony, Mondale addressed a luncheon of American businessmen, many of the pioneers in the developing commercial relationship, outlining steps being taken by the U.S. government to encourage bilateral trade.

On Saturday, September 1, we boarded a special train, complete with a fringed white canopy on the open observation platform of the vice president's parlor car, for the quick run to Hong Kong. We had been joined by another American party making its own diplomatic success—Abe Pollin and his Washington Bullets basketball team.

From the traveling documents cases, I pulled background papers prepared for a series of meetings aimed at keeping full pressure on all concerned for the boat-people crisis. At 2:00 p.m. that same day, the vice president met with the American ambassadors to the Philippines, Malaysia, Singapore, Thailand, and Indonesia. An hour later he met with regional representatives of the International Organizations and Voluntary Agencies grappling with the refugee crisis. A message was drafted to be sent to the UN High Commissioner on Refugees.

The following morning, I traveled with Mondale by harbor launch to the Shamshuipo and Jubilee Transit Centers. He was met by thousands of faces, cheers, and outstretched hands. At noon, Mondale continued on for an assessment of Hong Kong's future role over lunch with Sir Murray MacLehose, governor of Hong Kong. At 1:30 p.m., U.S. Navy helicopters took us from the landing pad at the Royal Navy's Hong Kong Headquarters, HMS *Tamar*, for the fifteen-minute flight to the USS *Midway* (CVA 41), anchored in the Hong Kong roadstead. The vice president was escorted to flag quarters, where he was given a status report on the Seventh Fleet's at-sea record of refugee rescues. He returned to the flight deck to address the carrier's company. It was Labor Day weekend in the United States. Mondale praised them for their service to the nation, and for the success of their humanitarian refugee mission. He recognized the demands this superimposed on the ship's already crowded responsibilities as an attack carrier of the Seventh Fleet. The helicopters lifted off again.

At 5:00 p.m., the vice president held a wide-ranging press conference at the Hong Kong Hilton, reviewing the success of the mission to China and the great challenge still to be met if the refugees were to be saved and assisted to find decent lives in new homelands. We were up early on September 3, soon winging northward to Tokyo for consultations over lunch at Akasaka Palace with Japanese Prime Minister Masayoshi Ohira, en route back to Andrews Air Force Base and Washington. Even this final meeting of the swing through Asia drove home once again the mandate for close consultations with allies on issues of common interest and concern—an essential ingredient of successful summitry.

Among the many important diplomatic meetings and ceremonies in 1979, on October 1 we traveled to Panama to mark the entry into force of the 1977 Panama Canal Treaties. We toured the length of the canal by ship and helicopter, observing the passage of ocean traffic through the Miraflores Locks, a flawless engineering achievement drawing only the force of gravity to fill the locks from reservoirs at higher altitudes, then drain into the sea. In his address to President Aristides Royo, other heads of state, and the Panamanian people, the vice president reemphasized the political significance of the treaties, quoting President Carter's judgment that they "mark the commitment of the United States to the belief that fairness, and not force, should lie at the heart of our dealings with the nations of the world." These historic words remain true today.

But then, in the first week of November 1979, force replaced fairness in Tehran, when the U.S. embassy was invaded. On November 9, the White House issued an official statement: "The seizure of more than 60 Americans in our embassy in Tehran has provoked strong feelings here at home. There is outrage. There is frustration. And there is deep anger. . . . The President shares these feelings. He is pursuing every possible avenue in a situation that is extremely volatile and difficult. . . . He calls on all Americans, public officials and private citizens alike, to exercise restraint, and to keep the safety of their countrymen uppermost in their minds and hearts." But, as is all too well known today, frustration grew, and Carter's presidency would suffer from this blow.

Then the Soviet Union invaded Afghanistan on December 24, and the U.S. president responded by asking the Senate to set aside its consideration of the SALT II Agreement. Additional steps were considered. The Olympics were affected. In the midst of this international turmoil, the president and vice president began their quest for reelection. Overseas summitry paused. Not until mid-June 1980 would Carter again depart the United States, for the Economic Summit in Rome, an audience with Pope John Paul II, and official visits to Yugoslavia, Spain, and Portugal. In the final overseas summit mission of his administration, the president boarded Air Force One to fly again to Tokyo for the memorial services of the late Prime Minister Ohira.

As the complex international problems of late 1979–early 1980 continued to unfold, my responsibilities to ensure that the vice president was fully abreast of the very latest information on all critical issues were more important than ever. Staffing ranged from monitoring international wires and electronic media to the quality of current intelligence reporting in the Presidential Daily Brief (PDB). I offered several suggestions, well received by Director of Central Intelligence Stansfield Turner, to help improve and streamline the PDB. Gratifyingly, in late March 1980 the vice president shared with me a kind thank-you note from Turner.

We were nearing the end of our travels for diplomacy. When Yugoslav President Josip Broz Tito died on May 4, 1980, President Carter named Mondale to lead a U.S. delegation. Papers were prepared for Mondale's talks with Yugoslavia's new leaders. Our advance team departed immediately, and before we left, their messages via Embassy Belgrade advised us of the central elements of the ceremony. The people of Yugoslavia were grieving the passing of a leader who had towered among them for generations. Tito had led the partisans' struggle against the Nazis in World War II, and then had led Yugoslavia throughout the entire postwar era. U.S.-Yugoslav relations had been a vital part of my professional work ever since. Tito had bucked the Soviets following the war, resisted the Warsaw Pact nations, and, together with Nehru and Nasser, founded the "nonaligned movement" as an international/political force independent of both the United States and Soviet Union. And Yugoslavia's place on NATO's southern flank was critical to U.S. and allied strategic interests.

Following our arrival in Belgrade, before the vice president's wreath-laying at Tito's bier, I penned possible words for him to inscribe on behalf of the American people in the formal book of condolences. It is always critical for a staffer to keep in mind that her or his role is one not of presumption but of assistance. The words suggested for such a moment may not be chosen; that is not the point. It is the staffer's responsibility to correctly frame the event; it is the leader's responsibility to represent the nation fully advised on all key aspects of the issue.

Early on the day of the interment, the delegations were assembled for the procession that would take Tito's flag-draped coffin from the great hall where he had lain in state, through the black-draped streets of Belgrade lined on either side by the people of a mourning nation, to the hillside mausoleum erected as his final resting site. There were several hundred of us, including kings, queens, presidents, accompanying delegation members, military aides, bodyguards, and staff—all carefully shepherded by Yugoslav protocol officers into various reception rooms to await further marshaling for the start of the procession, all according to careful plan, all designed to permit the somber ceremony to proceed as scheduled.

As we entered the large sitting room assigned to the vice president and the U.S. delegation, to the consternation of our Yugoslav escort, we immediately turned as a body and departed for another chamber. One of my colleagues' eyes had been even quicker than my own, but our decision was instantaneous. Yasser Arafat and the PLO delegation had been ensconced in the first chamber. U.S. policy denied official contact with the PLO; to have permitted such an encounter would have been a serious diplomatic error. Such an encounter would have become world news almost instantly. Straightforward coverage of the funeral would have been intruded upon, magnifying any such error into an international blunder of considerable dimensions. But the error was neatly avoided, with few the wiser. At the vice president's request I returned to the first chamber, introduced myself to Prime Minister Margaret Thatcher, and extended the vice president's apologies for his sudden exit. With a glare across the room, she laughed. "I only wish my staff had told me."

We had one more overseas mission in 1980, to Africa—Senegal, Niger, Nigeria, and Cape Verde—in July.

Talks went well in Senegal and Niger. The focal point of this mission was Nigeria, the world's fourth-largest democracy, the second-largest oil exporter to the United States, and a powerful political voice in international issues of importance to the African nations. Mondale's program aimed at progress on both bilateral and broader issues.

The rusted hull of an ocean freighter driven onto the beach from the Gulf of Guinea broke the otherwise tranquil seascape view from our hotel in Lagos, capital of Nigeria. Lagos, a port city born of British and Portuguese empire trade, built on a cluster of coastal islands, had boomed with Nigeria's oil wealth—and with the boom had come incredible urban congestion manifested most vividly by the traffic jams on the city's web of bridges and elevated highways. This offered a new page of learning to the student of motorcades.

Truckloads of Nigerian soldiers accompanied us throughout the visit, plowing ahead to part the traffic, swooping in on cars whose drivers were not quick enough in their reactions. Using their rifle butts, they pounded on the roofs of such cars. I could only wonder how this behavior contributed to strengthening relations.

The United States continued to press South Africa on both majority rule and independence for Namibia. At a banquet in his honor, Mondale said, "We know there is no simple answer. . . . We see the need to resolve a problem, and we believe that only blacks and whites, talking and reasoning together, can find its solution." He again stressed the policies expressed by President Carter during his 1978 visit: respect for human rights, mutually beneficial economic progress, and freedom from war and foreign domination.

On July 21, we flew to Kano, Nigeria's third-largest city, set in cattle-grazing plains. It was an ancient Hausa city that had served for centuries as a principal terminus of trans-Saharan trade. With the governor of Kano State as with President Shagari in Lagos, Mondale reviewed opportunities for new fields of cooperation and Nigerian investment in American technology to help balance U.S. purchases of Nigeria oil. Both sides were enthusiastic. But my enthusiasm dissipated as we exited the conference hall at Kano.

The American flag flew next to the Nigerian flag on two tall poles. But the U.S. flag was upside down. The vice president had not yet emerged with the governor of Kano. We instantly passed the word to our lead advance man to have them linger for a few more moments inside. One of our military aides sped over to the Nigerian officer in charge with the request that he immediately correct the flag. I watched the officer look up at the flagpole, laugh, then indicate that there was no need to make the change; he wished to get on with the pomp of the departure ceremony. I offered a few choice words in response—which were promptly relayed to the officer. The flag was run down, turned right-side up, and run up again.

The vice president and governor appeared, and it was a splendid departure ceremony. The insult—in fairness, the error—had been inadvertent. With or without the presence of the press, there would have been no room for compromise. But with the press there, any resulting wire story photographs would have undone all that was being accomplished.

And the results of the mission to Nigeria were considerable. The joint communiqué ran three single-spaced, legal-size pages. The visit had elevated Nigeria above the status of oil supplier to a valued friend among nations with whom the United States wished to work more closely across the board, on science and technology, agriculture, education, energy, trade, and investment. The person-to-person dialogue of summitry had politely pushed past the barriers erected by the complex Nigerian bureaucracy, with candid appraisals of problems inhibiting greater trade and effective arrangements for U.S.-Nigerian business contacts. The dialogue had reaffirmed the strength of America's commitment on international political issues of vital importance to Nigeria.

The results of the visit went far beyond those already realized through day-to-day diplomatic channels. For me, this visit stood for the positive, forward-looking character of almost four years of official overseas travel with Mondale. On December 12, 1980, he wrote in a treasured thank-you note, "Your role in every aspect of my defense, intelligence and foreign policy responsibilities has been invaluable, outstanding. We have circled the globe together in behalf of the President. We have worked hard together in Washington in the development of policy, in time of international crisis and in time of historic achievements. Where history records the results as good and lasting, you should take great and deserved pride. You helped in your positive, professional way to shape that history. With thanks, with friendship and with best wishes for your future success, Fritz (Walter F. Mondale)."

As the year 1981 opened, I closed a full decade of summit staffing. But I was not quite finished with my government service.

CHAPTER 14

From the White House to the DIA and Joint Commission on POW/MIAs, 1981–2009

With the election of President Ronald Reagan, in January 1981 my four years as national security adviser to Vice President Walter F. Mondale came to a close, as did my thirteen straight years in the White House and Executive Office of the President under Presidents Johnson, Nixon, Ford, and Carter. I had been serving as a high-level political appointee without tenure and now had to make way for the new staff coming in to serve Vice President George H. W. Bush.

There had been little vacation time, little annual leave, over all those years. Our sons Alex and Ty were thirteen and eleven—old enough for a good overseas trip. Well prior to the 1980 election, I had received the vice president's permission to take a month off in December to visit Gretchen's New Zealand birthplace with the family. This would be during the postelection interregnum, before the inauguration. The focus of day-to-day events in the White House would not be on new, high-level diplomatic and national security initiatives. It was a good time to go.

The visit was spectacular. Gretchen's sisters, brother, and father opened their homes to us on the North and South Islands. In Wellington we discovered the icebreaker *Glacier*, on which I had sailed in 1960–61, now red-hulled with the U.S. Coast Guard diagonal stripe on her bows, heading back to Antarctica, and were invited on board. We called on our ambassador for a fine dinner. This was a very special time for our family, for which I had carefully set aside the challenge of plotting and making my next career step. It could all wait until we returned to the United States.

My colleagues on the vice president's senior staff were all leaving government and urged me to do the same. There was the early possibility of a good job in California. I had set my mind on staying in the government if at all possible, and keeping our residence and very nice life and school in Annapolis. I had an investment of eighteen years of government service, and only needed twelve more to become eligible to exercise the option, if I should so choose, for retirement with pension—too valuable an investment to throw away. However, in trying to make this next career transition come to pass, I was setting the bar very high.

In early January 1981, Vice President Mondale presented me with the Secretary of Defense's Medal for Distinguished Public Service in a ceremony in the Roosevelt Room of the White House. My mind was immediately elsewhere. A place, still unknown, somewhere in the vast reaches of the Pentagon looked to me like my best prospect for the next career step. In the Ford and Carter administrations, I had done some good professional work with Frank Carlucci when he was serving first as ambassador to Portugal and then deputy director of Central Intelligence. President-elect Reagan named Caspar Weinberger to be his secretary of defense, and Weinberger chose Carlucci to be the deputy secretary. With the vice president as my reference, we were soon in touch.

Carlucci could not have been more gracious. He flipped my résumé onto his desk and laughed. "Denis, your problem is that you have done too much and risen too high too early in your life."

While he was still awaiting confirmation, he put me in touch with Richard Armitage, who was heading the Defense Transition Office vetting individuals for possible positions in the Defense halls of the new Republican administration. Armitage was a sharp, powerfully built, colorful individual, a Naval Academy graduate with valorous service in Vietnam. With my résumé in hand, he waved me to a seat in his Pentagon office and greeted me with another laugh. "Clift, you've got a hell of a nerve coming here!" This to one who was still an appointee in the Democratic Carter White House. He switched gears immediately, had good words about my career, but added that, given my current position, there was no way I could be considered for a political appointment in the new administration. We closed the meeting with a handshake and his "Let me see what may be possible."

In early February 1981, the call came. An assistant to the director of the Defense Intelligence Agency (DIA), Lieutenant General Eugene Tighe, USAF, invited me to an interview at my earliest convenience with General Tighe and his deputy in the DIA headquarters office—on the third deck of the south side of the Pentagon. Tighe let me know that he had been contacted both by Armitage, now deputy assistant secretary of defense for Asia and Latin America, and by Deputy Secretary Carlucci, now in office. He said that with my background and record of publications, I would bring new blood and fresh, executive-level thinking and writing to DIA. Given my previous rank, he could offer me one of his very scarce, highest, super-grade pay assignments.

As ever, Gretchen fully supported the move. I was comfortable with the thought of joining DIA, given my earlier tours in naval intelligence and my continuing close work with the Intelligence Community during the NSC and White House years. We agreed that I would join immediately. I had kept my security clearances and federal service intact. He said I had to have a position title and proposed "defense intelligence officer-at-large." "This will give you the rank and the flexibility you need, as we shape your future role."

The chief of DIA administration received the necessary orders, and the various staff offices were directed to process my papers without delay.

Many bureaucratic records must have been broken. I was in place in the Pentagon in a week's time. Tighe asked me to begin by taking a careful look at the length and breadth of the work of DIA at its various locations throughout the greater Washington area: "Take your time; every door will be open to you. I want to have your impressions." So I traveled and observed—through the watch centers and labyrinth basement; the fifth-deck offices of the Pentagon; the science and technology offices in Rosslyn, Virginia; the Buildings A and B analytic and production facilities at Arlington Hall, Virginia; and the Defense Intelligence College and Attaché School in Anacostia, Maryland.

I drafted my positive and negative observations, constructive criticism, and many recommendations as I came to know more and more of DIA. At the end of six weeks, I sent an eight-page, single-spaced, top secret / codeword report to Tighe. Within days, I received a handwritten note back from him that began, "Invaluable—taking for action!" I would learn quickly that I had ruffled a good number of otherwise nesting DIA feathers. Who was this high-priced interloper presuming to disturb ingrained ways and comfortable practices?

I weathered the storm, while noticing a distinct lack of social invitations. The day I left the White House office, *bang*—no more luncheons, dinners, theater, or other invitations. Similarly, I weathered the cultural shift from the White House to the DIA and the new, more grueling commute between Annapolis and the Pentagon. Morning and evening rush hours into, across, and out of Washington across the Anacostia and Potomac Rivers had at least one nasty snarl every day. Rain, snow, ice, and road and bridge repairs compounded the challenge. Listening to the radio traffic reports was essential, with real-time, behind-the-wheel decisions whether to keep going straight, roll left or right, or slant diagonally, drawing on my growing playbook of different street and route options.

In late April 1981, my life at DIA took a great stride forward. As part of his new responsibilities, Secretary Weinberger attended the spring NATO Defense Ministers Meeting in Brussels. DIA's premier photo interpreter, John Hughes, accompanied him and presented a top secret photo satellite briefing of trends and capabilities in the strategic and conventional armed forces of the Soviet Union, tracking the breadth and rapidity of the USSR's military buildup. During a break following the briefing, Germany's Defense Minister Manfred Woerner told Weinberger, "Cap, this information is vitally important, but when it is classified, it is absolutely useless. We need to present it to our publics."

Following Weinberger's return to Washington, he called General Tighe to his office and tasked him with producing an unclassified report of Soviet strategic and conventional force capabilities, and doing so quickly. Tighe saluted, "Yes sir," returned to his office, and reported the tasking to his leadership. Heads around the DIA conference room shook in disbelief. My name was raised in that meeting, including that I had served as *Proceedings* editor. Tighe summoned me to his office and asked me what I thought. I said, "Give me a shot at it. I think it can be done."

I set to work with DIA's deputy director of production mapping out a basic chapter outline. He organized DIA's analysts to begin providing draft text, charts, and graphics. The drafts started coming my way, and as editor in chief I had the lead action in accepting some, rejecting some, and calling for revisions. We were on a fast track, and where I had acceptable drafts, I began writing the finished product. We worked initially at a highly classified level, with the plan of circulating the complete draft for review through the Intelligence Community, declassification as required, and clearance for open publication.

We settled quickly on the title *Soviet Military Power*. I faced one enormous challenge: how to illustrate the publication. We could not use the classified satellite photography that was so effective in the closed-door official briefings. Unclassified photography of the USSR's strategic and conventional armed forces—land, sea, air, and space—either was not available or was next to worthless.

This was 1981. The publication would be going across the nation and around the world. Our competition for readers' attention and interest would be slick, four-color glossy magazines and new full-color cable and network TV news coverage. If there were dramatic advances in the USSR's forces, we needed to be able to show them: the new Tupolev Backfire bomber, for example; the new 25,000-ton Typhoon-class nuclear-powered ballistic missile submarine; the equipment and weapon systems of the combined arms armies; one of the new intercontinental ballistic missiles with independently targetable nuclear warheads; the new T-80 main battle tank; the new jet transports; and the Soviet Navy's new *Kirov*-class nuclear-powered cruisers.

My earlier travels throughout DIA now paid off. I hopped a Pentagon bus out to DIA Arlington Hall, where I remembered having come across a remote set of rooms filled with rather elderly artists producing large, exquisitely detailed, all-source-intelligence, four-color depictions of these weapon systems and more. When I reentered the rooms and looked at the art, I knew I had my *Soviet Military Power* illustrations answer. Over protests that they were classified, I had a sizable selection of paintings packaged up for classified delivery to General Tighe's office. We spread them out, and he and other members of the leadership listened to my proposal. Most of the faces were straight; his was smiling. After some back-and-forth, the consensus was, "Do it"—the idea was brilliant. Indeed, it was the answer.

We made a tentative selection for the publication, and Tighe had me take the art out to CIA headquarters to run the proposal by the new deputy director of Central Intelligence, Admiral Bobby Ray Inman, whom I had come to know when he was director of the National Security Agency and I was the vice president's national security adviser. He looked at each painting carefully, requested minor modifications to only one to keep the Soviets from knowing the extent of our knowledge, and gave his approval for use of the art.

We had started work on the first edition in late April. Five months later, it was cleared, back from the printers—full-color, ninety-nine pages, a remarkably detailed, authoritative text, 30,000 copies—and ready for release by Secretary Weinberger in a globally televised Pentagon news conference. The decision was taken that I should go to NATO Headquarters in Brussels with 300 copies to have a background press briefing for European correspondents immediately preceding the secretary of defense's briefing. I was delighted. To be plucked out of my new obscurity in DIA for the assignment had me climbing again on a new career track.

The first edition received wide publicity in the United States and overseas. The Soviets were not happy. *Izvestia*'s October 7 edition labeled it "99 Pages of Lies." The *New York Times* October 4 edition opened a story datelined London: "The European allies of the United States have generally welcomed the publication this week of the Defense Department's comprehensive study of Soviet Military Power. . . . 'It will be very useful in countering the unilateralists,' a British diplomat said, reflecting a common view." The 30,000 copies went quickly, and a second printing was ordered. In January 1982, Secretary Weinberger awarded me the secretary of defense's meritorious service medal for my "exceptionally talented and skillful role as Editor in Chief." I was promoted to DIA deputy assistant director for external relations, reporting to Deputy Director John Hughes, and moved out of my windowless warren into a third-floor, E-ring office—complete with a window opening onto Virginia.

The decision to proceed with a second edition was taken in the late fall of 1982 and had me again moving fast, at one point snowed in by a blizzard as I worked and bunked at our Arlington Hall production facility for two nights. President Reagan and Secretary Weinberger released *Soviet Military Power* 1983 from the Oval Office of the White House in March 1983. They sent me a framed photo of the release, inscribed by both with their thanks.

In his public statement, the president reaffirmed the defensive character of U.S. strategy, explaining that we design our defense programs to counter threats, not to further ambitions. "Today, and for the foreseeable future," he said, "the greatest of these threats comes from the Soviet Union, the only nation with the military power to inflict mortal damage on the United States. This also means," he said, "that if the American people are asked to support our defense program, they must get the straight facts about this threat."

In the press briefing at the Pentagon, among the questions fielded by Assistant Secretary of Defense for Public Affairs Henry Catto was one about whether the work had been contracted out. "No," Catto replied, "it is written within the department."

"Is there an author?"

"Yes."
"Who is that?"
"Denis Clift."

It was official. With each new edition, I would be asked to continue the practice of briefing the European press corps in Brussels. *Soviet Military Power* became a remarkably successful annual report. It continued with this title through 1990. After that, with the collapse of the Soviet Union on the near horizon in 1991, the final edition was titled *Military Forces in Transition*. Because it was written at the classified level, drawing on the best intelligence-derived data, and then declassified, it was authoritative—as Secretary Weinberger informed the world in one of his press conferences.

It was also a striking "information operation" that totally confounded the Soviets. As a closed, authoritarian society, they were inherently unable to discuss even their armed forces in public. In 1991, when Secretary of Defense Dick Cheney was in Moscow paying a call on the Defense Committee of the Duma with his counterpart, Minister Dmitry Yazov, a Duma member waved a copy of *Soviet Military Power* in the air and shouted at Yazov, "Why do we have to depend on the Americans for information on our forces?"

Because it was comprehensive and authoritative, it became the "bible" for U.S. and NATO governments and their publics. In two successive years, 1986 and 1987, British Minister of State for the Armed Forces Sir John Stanley flew to Washington to meet privately with me to receive his embargoed advance copies—allowing him to prepare thoroughly for parliamentary debate as soon as the edition was formally released.

When Prime Minister Margaret Thatcher named Stanley to become minister of state for Northern Ireland, he sent me a long, handwritten letter stating, in part, "I want you to know how much I have enjoyed our meetings in Washington, and how much I have valued and admired the immense contribution made to the public's understanding of the defence realities through your publication of *Soviet Military Power*. I sincerely hope it will continue to be published annually. It is an indispensable document for the conduct of the public debate on defence throughout the free world."

President Reagan wrote me a glowing letter in 1984, thanking me for my role in producing the report and conducting the press conferences. Secretary Weinberger awarded me the Defense Distinguished Civilian Service Medal in 1985. The president followed with the award of the Presidential Rank of Meritorious Executive in 1986.

But my charmed existence had more surprises in store. As early as 1982, my new professional life at DIA extended well beyond *Soviet Military Power*. John Hughes, as deputy director of external relations, oversaw a number of DIA liaison divisions—working with the Office of the Secretary of Defense and the White House, Congress, foreign attachés, international arms control negotiations, public affairs, and cooperation with the intelligence services of other nations. We had high-level foreign visitors coming to the Pentagon for talks variously with the secretary of defense, the chairman of the Joint Chiefs of Staff, the director of DIA, and other officials. Hughes engaged me in these visits as he did in the work of his divisions. I would sit in on his classified imagery briefings to study his technique.

From my years on the NSC and White House staffs and from my participation in meetings in the Situation Room, I had an appreciation for the value officials at the highest levels attached to satellite photographs. With a photo, they could see the evidence firsthand and did not have to rely solely on the often-couched words of the analyst and briefer. Hughes had been trained as an imagery analyst, had worked with U-2 imagery from the late 1950s, and was an expert on interpreting and presenting satellite photography—truly, he was proof that a good image was worth a thousand words. He used the best imagery possible in his Soviet military trends and capability briefing. He would make sure that some of the satellite images he included in each presentation were current, taken no more than a day or two before. The date, unmentioned, would show up on the briefing screen. His audiences were "flying with him real-time over the USSR," seeing what was transpiring. The briefings were riveting.

In April 1982, conflict broke out between Great Britain and Argentina over the Falkland Islands. That June, Argentina surrendered and the United Kingdom retained ownership of the islands. DIA was intensely interested in following the conflict at the strategic and tactical levels. While we were deep in the East-West Cold War era, this was a conflict being fought entirely with Western weapon systems: missiles, radars, ships, submarines, and aircraft. With hostilities over, the armed services, Department of Defense, congressional committees, and the media were assessing what had happened and lessons to be learned.

At Defense, Secretary Weinberger grabbed the reins, giving Andy Marshall, director of the Office of Net Assessment, responsibility for guiding a Falklands Lessons Learned study in partnership with the Institute for Defense Analyses. DIA was given responsibility for the classified intelligence chapters of the study, and I was put in charge. While I guided the drafting of this interagency text by member agencies of the Intelligence Community, I gave myself an additional project. It was hard to get good, running pictures of the conflict thousands of miles away in the South Atlantic. I thought that if I could put together some sort of video, it would nicely complement written lessons learned.

In the Pentagon, the Joint Staff's video facility routinely made reference copies of relevant portions of TV news running on the networks. I screened the facility's video files for the period of the conflict and found that the U.S. networks had carried many pieces of coverage taken by British and Argentine news services. I had my Joint Staff badge credentials, and the facility agreed to help me. I went through the files again and gave each separate piece of video coverage a number, and arranged the numbers so as to have the best sequence of footage for visual presentation. A technician cut together this first-draft video. We gave it another edit, shifting some of the footage and reducing it to thirty minutes. I went to my typewriter and, drawing on the draft intelligence lessons-learned study, wrote a classified lessons-learned narrative to accompany the images. This done, I checked the running time against my text, did a few more edits, and personally narrated the video in a single take. It proved quite a success, with screenings in the Pentagon, the State Department, the NSC staff, and the White House.

In 1984, John Hughes' health was in such serious decline that he took the decision to retire. He had reached national prominence two decades earlier with his televised briefing to the nation on each phase of the Cuban Missile Crisis. At that time, Republicans were challenging President Kennedy's words that all Soviet nuclear weapons had been withdrawn from Cuba. On February 6, 1963, Hughes had accompanied Secretary of Defense Robert McNamara to brief a congressional committee on the subject. Following the briefing, the president had directed McNamara to have Hughes present the same information to the nation that afternoon—including the classified U-2 photography. Hughes presented the briefing live on television to correspondents in the State Department auditorium. He was masterful. Two days later, the president wrote him a warm letter of thanks.

As assistant deputy director for external relations, I was playing an increasingly larger role while Hughes' health failed. In late 1984, I drafted correspondence for the new DIA director, Lieutenant General Jim Williams, to Secretary Weinberger, and for Weinberger's signature to President Reagan, recommending the award of the National Security Medal to Hughes. I attached a recommended award citation. I would be in the Cabinet Room of the White House when the president presented the medal to Hughes. In making the presentation, Reagan looked at Hughes' tall, grown sons towering over him, and quipped, "Blocks off the old chip."

Early in 1985, General Williams told me that I would be a good replacement for Hughes and promoted me to deputy director for external relations, one of the most senior DIA leadership positions. Hosting foreign policymakers and military leaders, and directing the work of the directorates' different divisions, including all those with which John Hughes had worked, I moved ahead comfortably. While I did not presume to be Hughes, I stepped into his role of giving the classified Soviet trends and capabilities briefing to the secretary of defense's and DIA's high-level visitors. On reflection, my work in parallel on each new edition of *Soviet Military Power* kept me up to date and well prepared for this new responsibility.

In 1986, Lieutenant General Leonard "Lenny" Perroots, U.S. Air Force, replaced Jim Williams as DIA director. We hit it off well, and Perroots made me one of his right hands. I was once asked by a DIA historian if it was not a great challenge to report directly to such senior officers. "Hardly," I replied, asking her to bear in mind that I had already spent thirteen years working directly for presidents, vice presidents, and Cabinet officers. The year 1986 was an important one for DIA, the twenty-fifth anniversary. Much of DIA had moved in 1984 from various sites in Virginia and the District to the Defense Intelligence Analysis Center (DIAC), a gleaming new home base, with a façade of aluminum and glass, at Bolling Air Force Base on the east side of the Potomac in Southeast Washington. I kept my office and those of my directorate in the Pentagon. The twenty-fifth-anniversary celebrations would be at the DIAC. With Perroots cheering me on, I personally wrote all the major anniversary speeches to be given by Secretary Weinberger, Director of Central Intelligence William Casey, and General Perroots. Copies of each are in the DIA historian's files.

Early on in my work with Perroots, I had had occasion to be discussing some aspect of Executive Order 12333, the executive order on intelligence signed by President Reagan in 1981. I noted a sentence Reagan had used in introducing the order: "Let us never forget, good intelligence saves American lives and protects our freedom." Perroots had the words cast in bronze and placed on a four-foot-high granite base standing in the center of the DIAC's plaza.

I had stayed in touch with John Hughes in his retirement in suburban Virginia. Every three months or so I drove out to his home for a chat and a lunch provided by his dear wife, Paula. John was not very mobile. He enjoyed the updates on the goings-on in his old office, DIA, and across the broader screen. During these chats, I told him he should commit to writing the story of his role in the Cuban Missile Crisis. The national briefing had been the tip of the iceberg. He had been one of the lead photo-interpreters during the crisis and the personal daily briefer for Secretary McNamara, Deputy Secretary Roswell Gilpatrick, and Chairman of the Joint Chiefs General Maxwell Taylor.

John was hesitant. He was modest, did not want to write about himself. And, even though almost all of the classified details of the crisis were now in the public domain, he was the quintessential intelligence professional who felt the details might be too sensitive to share. I pressed him, saying that I would do the research and writing if he would talk me through the details of his role. I said I would write the account in his first person. I added that we would copyright the work in his name. He still had his doubts.

I pressed harder in 1989, noting that the thirtieth anniversary of the crisis was just three years away. He yielded, and we set to work on what would become one of my favorite evening and weekend projects for the next several months. We titled his story *The San Cristobal Trapezoid*, taken from the trapezoidal siting of the Soviet SA-2 missiles guarding one of the ballistic missile sites under construction in San Cristobal, Cuba.

With a second draft done, I sent the work to the Office of the Secretary of Defense and had it cleared for public release. Even with this done, John would not agree to have me submit it to a publisher. I thought it important to time publication with the 1992 anniversary, but by mid-1991 he still would not budge. I called him to say that I had done my best but was giving up. There were no hard feelings, but he would never hear me mention the subject again. About ten minutes after we hung up, Paula, an elementary school teacher, was on the line. "Denis, what did you say to John?" We chatted for a while, and she said, "I will call you back." A few minutes later she was on the line again, to say that John had agreed that I should look for a publisher.

The editorial board of CIA's scholarly professional journal, *Studies in Intelligence*, accepted the work and published it in vol. 36, no. 5 (1992), the first-ever unclassified edition. It would go on to win the Sherman Kent Award for the best intelligence writing of the year. John passed away about six weeks before its publication. Director of Central Intelligence Jim Woolsey presented me with two framed citations and two checks. One of each immediately went to Paula Hughes.

In 1991, the next major career step came. Lieutenant General Harry Ed Soyster, U.S. Army, who had taken over from Lenny Perroots in the late 1980s, was now director of DIA as the United States was preparing to evict Saddam Hussein and Iraq from Kuwait. DIA was switching from an active-duty deputy director to a civilian, and the DIA civilian chief of staff had just retired. The former head of DIA production, Dennis Nagy, was named deputy director, and Soyster promoted me to DIA chief of staff.

Obviously, I welcomed this continuing professional climb to the top. Drawing on my observations and experiences since joining DIA, I put my own stamp on the position, with the goals, in particular, of making the senior-level meetings and decisions on personnel—including promotions, bonuses, and awards—more professional, and of eliminating bureaucratic surprises coming from the top. Personnel issues were and are important in a federal bureaucracy several thousand strong.

With Soyster's approval, I kept the divisions of the External Relations Directorate under my control. Soyster's retirement from DIA and the Army took place in September 1991. Major General James R. Clapper Jr., U.S. Air Force, had been selected as his replacement. But Clapper's confirmation by the Senate was put on hold for several months by the Senate Armed Services Committee as part of the committee's displeasure with certain Air Force actions and its resulting broader hold on all Air Force general officer nominations. During these on-hold months, Dennis Nagy served as acting DIA director, and I switched back and forth between deputy director and chief of staff roles.

Of note, this gave me the opportunity to be DIA's representative at meetings chaired by the acting director of Central Intelligence and the director of the Intelligence Community staff. General Clapper was eventually confirmed, and in one of his first acts as director told me that he had been observing me while he was on hold and wanted me to continue as chief of staff during his tenure. In so advising, he laughed, saying that this might come as a surprise given his long-standing reputation as an obsessive reorganizer.

The years 1992 and 1993 were particularly difficult years for the Department of Defense and the Intelligence Community. Following the Gulf War, a peace dividend for the nation was declared, with both defense and intelligence directed to cut budgets by 15 percent. We went through hiring freezes, lost personnel and capabilities, and tested eventually unsuccessful reorganizations in the process.

Working with Jim Clapper was a pleasure. He valued our partnership, and in 1993 he guided my promotion to SES-6, the government's highest senior executive rank, through the Office of the Secretary of Defense confirmation process. A year earlier, in 1992, with his guiding hand, I had become a plank-owning presidential commissioner on the newly created U.S.-Russia Joint Commission on Prisoners of War / Missing in Action (POW/MIA).

In January 1992, the Russian Federation's new president, Boris Yeltsin, received the chairman and vice chairman of the U.S. Senate's Select Committee on POW/MIA. During their discussions in his Kremlin office, he suggested that Russia and the United States create a joint parliamentary committee to try to account for all of the servicemen missing in action and unaccounted for during the forty-six years of the Cold War freeze. The senators returned to Washington and relayed this suggestion to President George H. W. Bush, who said, "Let's do it, do it now."

It was agreed that a U.S.-Russian joint commission would be formed. There were no congressional hearings, no new legislation. Retired U.S. Ambassador Malcolm Toon was asked if he would chair the U.S. side, and he agreed. He was a great choice: a PT-boat skipper in the Pacific during World War II, a career diplomat, and a Russian speaker with three tours in Russia, including his years as the no-nonsense U.S. ambassador.

The charter creating the commission was a White House statement by the press secretary—a press release, nothing more—dated March 20, 1992, which read,

> The United States and Russia have established a joint commission to investigate unresolved cases of Prisoners of War and Missing in Action dating from the Second World War, including the Korean and Vietnam conflicts. The creation of this commission underscores the commitment of both the United States and Russia to work together in a spirit of friendship to uncover the fate of missing servicemen on both sides. This effort symbolizes the determination of the Administration to resolve outstanding issues from the Cold War period and is another step in developing our new cooperative relationship with Russia.
>
> Former Ambassador to the Soviet Union, Malcolm Toon, has been designated the President's representative and Chairman of the U.S. delegation to this commission. The commission also will include Senators John Kerry and Robert Smith and Congressmen Pete Peterson and John Miller. The Russian Delegation will be chaired by General Dmitri Volkogonov, a senior advisor to President Yeltsin. The first meeting of the joint commission will be held March 26–28 in Moscow.

On March 22, General Clapper was on the phone to advise that there had been consultations with Secretary of Defense Dick Cheney and Director of Central Intelligence Robert Gates, and that I had been recommended as a commissioner. Would I accept? Of course I would. This was announced in a Defense Memorandum for Correspondents on March 24. Other U.S. commissioners were selected: the deputy national archivist, the deputy assistant secretary of defense for POW/MIA, and two regional deputy assistant secretaries of state. We were wheels-up a day later for Moscow on board the Air Force 707 that had been LBJ's Air Force One. I felt like I was home again.

Retired Colonel General Dmitri Volkogonov received our delegation most cordially. His remarkable life spanned Stalin's reign of terror in the 1930s, when his father was shot and his mother banished to Siberia. Raised as a Communist youth, he entered the Soviet Army and fought as a tanker in World War II. He then shifted focus to psychological and ideological warfare. Volkogonov was also a historian, and his doubts about the Soviet past grew as he researched. Following the publication of his critical history of Stalin, he was dismissed from the army and denounced as a traitor. As the USSR was collapsing, he became one of Boris Yeltsin's closest advisers. When Yeltsin became president, Volkogonov became his defense adviser.

Seated across the conference table from us with General Volkogonov in Moscow on March 26, 1992, general officers, colonels, and civilian archivists represented the intelligence and security services, the Foreign Affairs Ministry, and the Ministry of Defense. Their enthusiasm was muted. If there was one shared expression on their faces, it was a look of wonderment and disbelief that this meeting was actually happening. "This is not possible," their faces read, "this ambassador, these congressmen, these Americans demanding a free run through our military and intelligence files."

At the first break in the talks that morning, Colonel Vyacheslav Mazurov of the former KGB, now the Foreign Intelligence Service (SVR), crossed to our side of the table, introduced himself, and asked, "Which one of you is with the CIA?" My colleagues and I advised that I was representing the entire Intelligence Community. He looked at me, smiled, and said, "No, I know you are DIA. Which one is CIA? CIA would not pass up this collection opportunity."

But we were not in Moscow, not in Russia, to collect intelligence. We were there for the sole humanitarian purpose of accounting for our missing and helping the Russians to account for theirs. Our first objective was to determine if any American was being held against his will anywhere in the former USSR; second, to determine the fates of unaccounted-for U.S. servicemen; and third, to help Russia and the other former Soviet republics determine the fates of their missing.

By the time of our return to Russia in September and again in December 1992, there was a growing flow of documents from U.S. and Russian archives. As a commission, we began our fact-finding trips across Russia and the other former Soviet republics—with a press conference at every stop advising of our humanitarian purpose, and a call to any and all with information to come forward to our embassy. As a joint commission, we agreed to manage our work in four standing working groups: World War II, Korea, Vietnam, and the Cold War, including reconnaissance flights and the USSR's conflict in Afghanistan. I was named U.S. cochairman of the Cold War Working Group.

In April 1995, with Ambassador Toon temporarily unable to travel because of family illness, I led the U.S. side and initialed the draft of the commission's first report with Volkogonov in Moscow. We exchanged White House and Russian embassy pens, and he chuckled, saying, "You like this job, don't you?" Toon and Volkogonov formally signed the first report in Washington later that year, just before Volkogonov's death in December 1995.

By the time of our first report, our work had taken us to all of the former republics. When Ambassador Toon, Representative Peterson, and I were in Tbilisi, Georgia, we had a long discussion with President Eduard Shevardnadze. The skin on his face and hands was a shiny pink, still healing from an assassination attempt allegedly by Russian hands. He made two major points. He told us that when he was Soviet foreign minister, Secretary of State Jim Baker had asked him to intercede with the Vietnamese to find out if Americans were still being held or had been held after the conflict. The Vietnamese, he said, were adamant that no POWs remained on their soil; they assured him that all had been returned at the end of the conflict. Shevardnadze gestured toward his face and hands. "Look at me," he said. "You should not doubt my word. I have no allegiance to those who just tried to kill me." He said that as foreign minister and a longtime, high-ranking Communist Party official, he had never once heard even a whisper or hint that Americans were being held on Soviet territory. He said that such a secret, however secret, would have leaked in the leadership of the Soviet Communist Party. The secretive Soviet leadership, he said, lived on gossip.

Our work as a joint commission produced valuable archival information on the movement and fates of both Americans and Soviets at the end of World War II. Our examination of the Korean conflict produced circumstantial information that Americans had been taken into the USSR, but we could not produce confirming documents. The Russian archives did allow us to determine the fates of more than 140 U.S. airmen shot down but previously unaccounted for in that conflict.

Working on Vietnam produced the driest hole. The Russians insisted that while they provided the North Vietnamese with weapons and technical assistance, the Vietnamese, with one or two exceptions, never gave them access to captured Americans. Throughout these early years of the commission's work, I was struck by the instructive words of a retired Soviet colonel who had served as an interrogator and whom we had interviewed in 1992: "It will take another generation," he said, "before much of the information you are still seeking will be taken from locked safes and become available."

In my role as cochair of the Cold War Working Group, I was focused on accounting for those Americans still missing and unaccounted for from reconnaissance flights, and for Soviet personnel still missing from the USSR's 1980s conflict in Afghanistan. For several years, I had the benefit of having retired Soviet Rear Admiral Boris Gavrilovich Novyy, a *Yankee*-class ballistic missile nuclear submarine skipper in his time, serving as a member of my team, carrying out research in Moscow and across the Russian Federation.

Our working group produced some important results. The Russians could not account for hundreds of their servicemen who were lost in Afghanistan. To assist, we conducted a very detailed review of the reporting from that theater in the 1980s, screening diplomatic messages from our embassies and consulates in Pakistan and Afghanistan, as well as attaché and intelligence reporting from the theater. We were looking for specific references to engagements between Soviet ground and air forces and the Mujahideen, specific reports, specific dates, specific locations of shootdowns, and losses of armor. When we found such reports, we deleted information that was not relevant to the actual losses of Soviet personnel, and we provided a great volume of material to the Russian side, enabling them to reduce the number of their unaccounted for from 350 to 287.

When we embarked on the commission's work in 1992, we asked our Armed Services and Joint Staff to identify which Cold War aerial reconnaissance missions we should raise with the Russians. There had been thousands of such flights, highly sensitive, over four and a half decades. There had been many losses, but with the exception of ten flights, the United States had been able to account for the fates of all crew members.

In our early meetings with our Russian counterparts, we acknowledged that these had been intelligence flights. Our goal now was humanitarian. Soon thereafter, the Russians started providing us with valuable archival documents relating to several of the shootdowns, including top secret reports to Stalin from fleet commanders and defense ministers. The first incident on our list was the shootdown of a U.S. Navy PB4Y-2 Privateer over the Baltic in April 1950. Early on, the Russians gave us a copy of a typescript news story on the shootdown written for *Pravda* showing Stalin's extensive, penciled hand-editing.

The fourth U.S. reconnaissance loss on our agenda was an Air Force RB-29 shot down over waters north of Japan on October 7, 1952. The crew of eight included Captain John Robertson Dunham, a 1950 Naval Academy graduate. In 1993, a retired KGB Maritime Border Guard sailor named Vasily Saiko, who had heard one of our television appeals for information from his home in Ukraine, was flown to Moscow to sit across from me in the offices of the former Central Committee of the Communist Party.

Saiko told us that he and his crewmates had seen the shootdown, and that his cutter had been ordered to the crash site. On scene, he had been the petty officer in charge of the small boat put over the side to investigate debris. The plane had gone under by then, with aviation gasoline still bubbling to the surface. There was a tangled parachute with a body inside. Saiko said he had fallen into the sea as they worked to bring the body into the boat.

Back on board the cutter, he had first gone below to wash off the aviation fuel and then come back on deck. As they were heading back into port, he had lifted the corner of the tarp covering the body and taken a ring from the dead American's hand. He then reached into his pocket, forty-one years later, and handed me a ring, a Naval Academy ring with the name John Robertson Dunham engraved on the inside.

Working with the Russian side, we were then able to find the report of two border guard officers who had witnessed the burial of Dunham on Yuri Island, a small, uninhabited island north of Japan. The report included a roughly drawn map with an X approximating the burial site. Members of the commission staff mounted two expeditions with the Russians, and on the second recovered a coffin with skeletal remains and fragments of cloth bearing a Stars and Stripes patch. DNA confirmed that the remains were those of Captain Dunham. On August 2, 1995, I would watch a B-52 fly low overhead in an extremely moving final tribute as Dunham was laid to rest in Arlington National Cemetery.

On September 2, 1958, a U.S. Air Force C-130 with a seventeen-man crew was shot down over Soviet Armenia. The aircraft crashed into a rocky hillside some fifty-five kilometers north of the capital of Yerevan. There was a furious fire. Six sets of remains were handed over to U.S. representatives at the Soviet-Turkish border. Eleven members of the crew remained unaccounted for, and there were rumors that at least one parachute had been seen at the time of the attack.

I interviewed the retired general major who had commanded the Air Defense regiment that had guided the attack. He said that his signals intelligence assets had picked up the C-130, as they often picked up U.S. intelligence missions flying along the Soviet-Turkish border down to the Iranian border and back. This aircraft, however, had crossed over into Soviet air space, and two pairs of MiG-17s had been sent up to challenge.

The C-130 did not respond to the warning shots. The first pair of MiGs attacked with machine-gun fire. Smoke started streaming from the U.S. aircraft. The second pair attacked. The large tail assembly was shot off, and the C-130 dove sharply into the ground.

I also interviewed one of the Soviet fighter pilots, First Lieutenant Viktor Lopatov, who had participated in the second wave of the attack. He said that he did not witness the crash, as he had been caught in the doomed C-130's slipstream and had been fighting to save his aircraft. The Russian side of the commission gave us copies of the MiG gun-camera photography they had discovered in the Podolsk Central Archives, which confirmed the air defense commander's description of the attack.

In August 1993, the commission traveled to Armenia. We were joined in Yerevan by Ms. Lorna Bourg, sister of Airman Archie Bourg, still unaccounted for from the lost crew. We drove up through the hills to the crash site near the village of Sasnashen. Villagers who had witnessed the event thirty-five years earlier had assembled to talk with us. Several ragged pieces of the C-130's wing skin had been collected and recycled as part of their livestock fences. Ms. Bourg, accompanied by a member of the U.S. embassy staff, was walking with us toward the crash site when she spotted something on the red, rocky ground. She paused to touch it with the toe of her shoe; it was a piece of gray metal. She picked it up and froze—she was holding one of her brother's dog tags.

The villagers described the shootdown, the plane's tail breaking off, the plunge into the rocky ground, and the fire that had lasted for hours. None had seen a parachute. They suggested that as the tail broke free, it may have been mistaken for a parachute. We had with us forensic experts, members of the Army's Central Identification Laboratory in Hawaii. With lines and stakes, they divided the crash site into a grid, and over the next two days painstakingly sifted surface rock, soil, and subsoil through the fine, meshed sifting trays they had brought with them.

They returned to Hawaii with some two thousand bone fragments, tooth fragments, life support equipment, personal effects, and aircraft wreckage. As a result of many months of DNA analysis that followed, it was determined that all the members of the crew still unaccounted for had perished in the crash. On September 2, 1998, these remains were interred in a single-casket ceremony at Arlington—this time with a C-130 flying in a final salute to lost comrades.

We continued to work the losses. In late 1997, I was in Kaliningrad to interview a number of the Soviet Navy's Baltic Sea veterans about the 1950 loss of the U.S. Navy PB4Y-2 Privateer off Latvia. My flight arrived in the heavy snowfall of an early afternoon. Two members of the staff had preceded me and were pleased to report that the naval base commander wished to honor me with a *banya* that evening, a Russian banquet with all the toasts, followed by a stripped-naked steam bath with birch-branch massages, and then a plunge into icy water.

I had earlier agreed to a proposal from Embassy Moscow to have an Associated Press correspondent and AP photographer cover our work throughout my visit. I looked at my staff brain trust standing before me in the airport lobby and said, "Guys, just what kind of story are you trying to produce here?" But they said the commander would be insulted if I turned down his *banya*.

I said, "We'll do the *banya*, but we will have a business meeting first, with our clothes on—talk through our plans for the following day's program." The AP covered that meeting and were invited to the festivities afterward. It was a good afternoon and evening. An equally good AP article on the commission's work appeared in papers across the country soon thereafter.

I would remain a commissioner until I finished my federal service in 2009, even though work slowed to a near-standstill after our second formal report in 2001. Over the years, it had produced some important answers and provided clarifying information, comfort, and closure to many families. The White House press release of March 20, 1992, remained its only documented charter.

CHAPTER 15

Serving as President, National Intelligence College, 1994–2009

Three years was the normal tour-of-duty length for those serving in the posts of DIA director, deputy director, and chief of staff posts. With the coming of 1994, I had hit full stride in my third year as chief of staff. The agency had weathered the worst of the DoD / Intelligence Community belt-tightening after the Desert Storm Gulf War. General Clapper had replaced Dennis Nagy as deputy director, and I knew it would not be long before I would be asked to make a recommendation on my next assignment.

I was at a real crossroads. At age fifty-seven with more than thirty years' federal service, active-duty and civilian, I was eligible to leave government with pension and benefits, and to start a new career on the outside. I was also in a position to request an assignment elsewhere in DIA, Defense, or the Intelligence Community, but I viewed each of the likely choices as a step down.

In 1992, my former NSC staff assistant and now Director of Central Intelligence Bob Gates had told me that the team of Clapper, Nagy, and Clift had brought DIA for the first time into the Intelligence Community's front ranks. I had been promoted to the government's highest Senior Executive Service rank. I was thriving on the challenges, responsibilities, and adventure that came with my role on the U.S.-Russia Joint Commission. All that said, it was time for a change.

Clapper knew of my quandary and was aware that I had begun to explore job prospects in the private sector. We had a chat in September, during which—much to my surprise—he asked if I would consider becoming the first president of the Joint Military Intelligence College. He noted that it was time to replace the then-commandant, that he wanted the college to move to a higher level of performance and academic stature. Replacing commandant with a president would be the first step in that ascendance. He said that having worked closely with me, he knew I was the right man for the college-building job.

I weighed the offer overnight. From what I had observed of the college and what I had dealt with as chief of staff, I knew it would be a challenge. However, with Annapolis as home, I liked the idea of a good new federal appointment. Our sons Alex and Ty had graduated from Syracuse and Tufts Universities. Alex was writing and painting at home, and would soon have his master's degree from St. John's College. Ty had parlayed a White House internship under President George H. W. Bush into a sharp, young professional network that led to a good position in the new computer age, shuttling between Maryland and Texas. Gretchen, with her sons grown, was heavily involved and being recognized for her work on different City of Annapolis committees and commissions.

And we all loved our house in West Annapolis, where the improvements continued. In 1993 we added a nine-pillared, sixty-six-foot veranda off the back of the house on the south side, accessed on the first floor through French doors. With the feel of an open deck on an ocean liner, it overlooks the backyard gardens. Staying in the government would allow a continuing good family home base. And it would permit me to carry on as commissioner in the nationally important U.S.-Russian POW/MIA work. The thought of being president of a regionally accredited college also had real appeal. The next day, Jim Clapper and I shook hands on the deal.

But just what was I taking on? At the end of World War II, Fleet Admiral Chester W. Nimitz, USN, returned from the Pacific to become Chief of Naval Operations. General of the Army Dwight D. Eisenhower, USA, returned from Europe to become Chief of the Army Staff. Both had observed the importance of the play of intelligence in the global conflict. Both were concerned over the inadequacy of training and preparation of American servicemen for their intelligence roles. Almost in parallel, Nimitz created the Navy Intelligence School and Eisenhower created the Army Strategic Intelligence School to provide months-long courses of training for those who would have intelligence responsibilities in the Cold War era.

In 1962, a Department of Defense directive merged the Navy and Army schools into the Defense Intelligence School, assigned to operate under the director of the newly created DIA, and attached to DIA for administrative support. A Board of Visitors, appointed by the secretary of defense, was established to provide findings and recommendations on the work of the institution. In 1980, Congress passed and the president signed a law authorizing the school to award a master of science of strategic intelligence (MSSI) degree. The school, with the new degree, was regionally accredited by the Middle States Commission on Higher Education in 1982 and was rechartered that year as the Defense Intelligence College, with the twofold mission of education and research. In 1992, in the new era of joint warfare, the college became the Joint Military Intelligence College.

The institution's first home was in a worn two-story wooden structure, a "temporary" World War II–era building, on the mudflat eastern shore of the Anacostia River in Southeast Washington. In 1984, the college moved to far better quarters just to the south, in DIA's newly built Defense Intelligence Analysis Center at Bolling Air Force Base. An alumnus of the last mudflat class, Rear Admiral Bob Murrett, who would go on to become director of Naval Intelligence and then director of the National Geospatial Intelligence Agency, recalled that after the college made the move, the old temporary building was made a shelter for the homeless. Within six months, the District of Columbia declared it unfit for human habitation.

I packed up as chief of staff and moved to the college in October 1994. My new official DIAC home left nothing to be desired. As president, I had a third-floor corner office with nine large windows looking out primarily to the north and northwest, offering a striking view out across the heliport for the president's helicopter squadron, across the Anacostia River, up to the Library of Congress, the Capitol, the Washington Monument, and, miles away, the District's northwest skyline. The new quarters came with an adjoining private conference room, a private bathroom and kitchenette, and an outer office for my secretary and executive officer. Additionally, with the move to the DIAC from the Pentagon, I was now on the east side of the District of Columbia, shortening each leg of the commute by at least twenty minutes.

If I had a rosy setting, I had no want for problems. Morale among the college faculty and staff was lousy. The college had been treated as something of an orphan and headache in DIA; it was seen as just another small, insignificant DIA element, rather than an accredited college, subordinated to the deputy director for operations. I vowed to change that. I did change that, and I had to keep a close watch on it with the arrival of seven new DIA directors over the following fourteen years. On my watch, the college would be recognized and treated as an accredited academic institution rising in programs, research, and stature, with its president reporting directly to the director of DIA and its administrative support coming from DIA. There would be challenges. The government loves nothing better than trying to roll backward. I would beat those challenges.

The just-departed commandant had taken, or had tried to take, a number of actions during his years, a few of which I had approved of as chief of staff, but most of which I had thought were terrible. He had cut the faculty and staff by half, sending the training courses to DIA's training branch. The mission was education and research, but the way the personnel actions had been handled did not pass the test of a college or university.

Relations with the Middle States regional accrediting body were also terrible. The college had done very poorly in its last reaffirmation-of-accreditation report, and was officially on warning of probation. Indeed, as the provost would inform me, the senior Middle States staff representative had been insulted the last time she had paid a visit. Additionally, in a mishandled attempt to gain congressional authority for a bachelor of science degree, officials at the Office of Management and Budget, the Department of Education, and Middle States had been bypassed. There had been an uproar as the attempt collapsed.

Within days of taking office, I received an earful on this from a Navy judge advocate general commander on the DIA general counsel's staff. As a final blow to morale, the former commandant had recommended moving the college from the DIAC to a remote, unused set of federal buildings about eight miles away in southern Maryland—but he had not succeeded.

The state of the college's research program, to the degree it existed, was a shambles. During my first month, a five-inch-thick three-ring binder of research grant proposals was thumped into my inbox with the request for formal approval. There was not a single request from a member of the faculty or graduate student body. People outside the college were seeking the college's money—apparently a practice of long standing. I disapproved the entire book and told the college leadership we would build our own good research program as a matter of top priority. Within days of taking office, I put down in writing my view of the college and its primary education role:

> The Joint Military Intelligence College is a center of excellence for the education of intelligence professionals who will be called upon to provide foreign military and military-related intelligence as part of

military operations in peacetime, crisis and combat; force planning and weapons systems acquisition; and defense policymaking.

Today's Joint Military Intelligence College graduate serves in an era of widespread geopolitical change. It is an era in which joint doctrine guides the roles and deployment of operating forces; timely two-way flow of accurate intelligence from the national level, through theater Joint Intelligence Centers and Joint Task Forces to deployed tactical-level forces, is central to mission accomplishment; intelligence requirements in joint and combined military operations extend beyond U.S. forces to support for allied, coalition, and United Nations forces.

More broadly, the Joint Military Intelligence College is educating future leaders of the intelligence and national security community; leaders able to anticipate and tailor the intelligence required at the national, theater, and tactical levels; leaders who constitute a unique asset to the nation.

I had strong support for my work from the college's Board of Visitors as I began charting this course at the same time that I was repairing—and building—the various fences. The board members were most distinguished. Harvard don Dr. Anthony Oettinger had just taken over from Dr. Ernest May as chairman at the time of my arrival. Former Supreme Commander of NATO Forces in the Atlantic Admiral Ike Kidd Jr., U.S. Navy (Ret.), was in their ranks. All were very concerned over the trouble with Middle States. Their advice and words of support were buoying.

I kept pressing the importance of the college's classified and unclassified research, and students' ability to turn their requirement to write a thesis into their opportunity to publish their applied research. I named a director of research to work with both faculty and students; several articles began appearing in intelligence periodicals and as college occasional papers. By 1997 we would publish our first substantial college work, *Intelligence for Multilateral Decision and Action*, a six-hundred-page volume with twenty-three distilled master's theses examining intelligence across the globe in the new era of coalition warfare.

The bachelor's degree and returning to good standing with our regional accreditor were also high among my early priorities. What the college needed from Congress was a law authorizing a senior-year baccalaureate degree completion program awarding the bachelor of science in intelligence (BSI) degree to noncommissioned officers in intelligence across the armed services who had earned at least three years of college credit, but had never had the funds or the opportunity to earn the degree. With the degree in hand, they would be able to move on to commissioned service or up into the highest senior noncommissioned intelligence ratings.

My challenge, first, was to have the college understand what we were seeking and why. We produced a good fact sheet to meet this need, and it was mandatory reading. Second, I had to engage with and obtain the approval of a large number of people and offices in and out of government in the right sequence if the proposed congressional bill was to move forward and be passed. This journey had me moving from inside the college walls to DIA, to the Office of the Secretary of Defense, to the Intelligence Community staff, to the Department of Education, the Office of Management and Budget, Middle States, and a visiting team of academic leaders, then back to the Department of Education and staff calls at the Senate Select Committee on Intelligence, with testimony before the House Permanent Select Committee on Intelligence. The law authorizing the college's BSI degree was passed in the 1997 Intelligence Authorization Act.

While I was working my priority college issues at flank speed, I received a surprise letter, request, and invitation in 1996 from a former Carter administration colleague now serving in Romania, the Honorable Alfred H. Moses, U.S. ambassador to Bucharest. Noting that he had observed my NSC/White House staff expertise, he invited me to come to Bucharest to meet with newly elected President of Romania Emil Constantinescu and his national security adviser, Dorin Marian. The new leader, a career academic, was intent on turning Romania into a true democracy, and he and his staff thought that establishing a national security council system would be an important, positive step. Would I please come to Bucharest to brief both on the origins, structure, and evolution of the U.S. NSC system since 1947?

I accepted, did my research, and had excellent talks in Bucharest. To my pleasure and surprise, there were other important audiences awaiting me there—the chairmen of the parliamentary committees working the intelligence, defense, and foreign policy issues. Having lived until recently in a harsh dictatorship, they were amazed by, and wanted to learn more about, the oversight powers of committees of the U.S. Congress.

Returning to the college, my goals with our Middle States regional accreditor started with being seen as a credible, rational, dedicated college president by the Middle States staff. After that, I had a target date. In 1998, the college would have its formal ten-year reaffirmation of accreditation visit by a Middle States team of educators from various colleges and universities in the region. Prior to that visit, we had to devote the better part of a year to the preparation of a self-study examining every important aspect of our present work and goals, and measuring that work and those goals against each of the Middle States standards.

The college faculty and staff turned to the task with talent and, indeed, enthusiasm. We thought we had a good self-study. We prepared for the team, following a preparatory meeting with the team chair, Dr. Margaret Fitzpatrick, president of St. Thomas Aquinas College. Following the team's visit, the April 1998 Commission on Higher Education Evaluation Team's report, which would lead to the college's ten-year reaffirmation of accreditation—with commendation and in good standing—opened with these words: "The Joint Military Intelligence College (JMIC) exhibits the principles and practices that the Middle States Association (MSA) considers characteristics of excellence in institutions of higher education. Particularly noteworthy is the clear sense of mission and purpose which permeates the college and the dedication of its faculty, administration, and staff. It has been recognized that 'the Joint Military Intelligence College is a national asset performing a national service.' The team concurs."

This stunning accomplishment held singular importance in the history of the college. We drew applause from the Board of Visitors, DIA, the

Intelligence Community, and our alumni. Morale surged. The ship had been righted, was underway at speed, and was on course. Chairman of the Board Tony Oettinger and I had several discussions on how to further strengthen our ties with Middle States—with the result that, after his own consultations, he placed my name in nomination to become a commissioner.

On October 6, 1999, I received a letter from Jean Avnet Morse, executive director of the Middle States Commission on Higher Education, which opened, "Dear Mr. Clift, We are delighted that the membership of the Commission on Higher Education of the Middle States Association of Colleges and Schools has voted to elect you as a Commissioner on the Commission on Higher Education for a three-year term." Four paragraphs of administrative detail followed, with a "Sincerely yours" closing and the hand-penned "I am so glad that you can join us! Jean." While I did not have the same sense of levitation that I had felt when I received my surprise orders to Antarctic duty thirty-nine years earlier, Jean Morse's letter was splendid news.

As someone in the college noted, I was now not only a president but a commissioner twice over—and I jumped headlong into my new Middle States responsibilities. With some 530 universities and colleges accredited by Middle States in the New York, New Jersey, Pennsylvania, Delaware, District of Columbia, Puerto Rico, and the Virgin Islands regional area of responsibility, the work of the commission and commissioners, assisted by a very capable staff, was highly organized. There were meetings twice a year at Middle States headquarters in Philadelphia, and another meeting at a select spot in the region. Institutions' five-year and ten-year reports had to be read and evaluated. Decisions had to be taken on reaffirmation of accreditation, with or without conditions. Institutions had to be judged on proposals for expansion, as they had to be judged for admission, probation, and expulsion.

I enjoyed serving as a reader and committee chairman. I thrived on the interaction with the staff, the commissioners—including some of the nation's top academic leaders—and the region's colleges and universities. I grew considerably in knowledge as a college leader based on the peer-review education I was receiving. I focused on the academic side of the work. As a member of the federal government, I was careful to recuse myself on financial issues, the commission's interactions with the government, and any other issues that might involve a conflict of interest. I was impressed by how much the institutions being evaluated and accredited, from the loftiest Ivy League universities to the most remote junior colleges, benefited from the self-study/team-visit process. If an institution did good work on the self-study, including identifying strengths, weaknesses, and areas for improvement, it could expect a good evaluation by the team. But if the institution did not take the self-study seriously, it could expect a more critical team report, including the requirement for one or more date-certain follow-up actions and reports back to the commission. There was no getting off the hook.

In 2002, I was elected to a second three-year term as commissioner. Among the many professional highlights during these years was being named, first, to lead a team advising the century-old, highly respected U.S. Army War College on the issues that its leadership, faculty, and staff would have to address as it prepared to seek initial accreditation by Middle States. The college succeeded, and in 2005, I was selected to chair the Middle States team evaluating Carlisle for its first reaffirmation of accreditation. My team did thorough work, and with two requests for follow-up reports, we recommended and the commission acted to reaffirm.

Meanwhile, there had been additional recognition and greater stature for the college on the academic front. In 2002, the Consortium of Universities of the Washington Metropolitan Area voted to elect the Joint Military Intelligence College to membership. We joined, and I became a member of the consortium's board of trustees. For the first time, we were now on a peer relationship with American University, the Catholic University of America, the Corcoran College of Art and Design, Gallaudet University, George Mason University, The George Washington University, Georgetown University, Howard University, Marymount University, National Defense University, Trinity Washington University, the University of the District of Columbia, and the University of Maryland at College

Park. Among the presidents, there were some extremely sharp, world-wise, witty leaders. I found the meetings of the board a new delight, and would invariably return to my office with fresh ideas.

The turn of the century brought the September 9, 2011, terrorist attacks. With this being followed by U.S. military action against terrorists and the Taliban in Afghanistan and the 2003 invasion of Iraq, the increasingly important role of intelligence and the corresponding need for better intelligence gave the work of the college even greater purpose. Each new class now included men and women fresh from or bound for combat missions. With new monies, we added new faculty, expanded course offerings, and focused more intently on value-added applied research products contributing to U.S. intelligence strength.

I knew that if the college was to succeed in this new, extremely challenging national security setting, we needed as an institution to have a greater critical mass—beyond teaching at the baccalaureate and master's levels—to broader, even more relevant service to the nation. I had three primary goals: adding an international dimension, a research center, and an additional focus on science and technology intelligence. Each had one or more strong advocates on the Board of Visitors, and each had the usual "because it's new I don't like it" bureaucratic obstacles to overcome.

Since its founding, the college had been for U.S. students only, because of the high national security classification of the readings, lectures, and courses. That was a policy set at the highest levels of government, and while on the one hand I saw no reason to challenge it, I also felt that we were the proverbial ostrich with our head in the sand. Since the early 1990s and the coalitions formed first in the ouster of Iraq from Kuwait and then in the Balkans, we were fighting side by side and sharing intelligence with our allies and coalition partners.

As DIA chief of staff during Desert Storm, I had guided the work of our foreign disclosure division, directing defense intelligence analysts to share as much intelligence as possible with our partners. We printed large full-color posters after the fashion of World War II posters, and we placed them in the analysts' workspaces. Instead of "Protect Information," they now said, "Share Information." We created tear-sheet intelligence reports for the coalition wars, with the fundamentally important substance of the intelligence in the first paragraphs for all partners, and with more highly classified, compartmented intelligence, for U.S. Eyes Only, that could be stripped away below the tear-sheet line.

In this era of coalition warfare, it was unacceptable to have the college isolated, with no give-and-take between our students, faculty, and foreigners. As a member of our board, former Supreme Allied Commander Europe General George Joulwan, U.S. Army (Ret.), strongly supported us. In 2001, we finally received approval from the director of DIA to launch an International Intelligence Fellows Program, a two-week course for foreign flag and general officers and their civilian equivalents, providing a forum for the sharing of ideas, the exploration of pressing issues, and debate on international intelligence challenges. Our students participated in this forum. It was an immediate success and would be repeated in the years that followed.

Building on the fellows' program, we next created an international visiting scholars program offering international intelligence professionals the opportunity to come to the college to conduct research, lecture, and serve as mentors. The positive evolution continued. General Sergiu Medar, former chief of Romanian Military Intelligence and now, retired, the new national security adviser to the president, asked me if the college would consider hosting a conference of Black Sea and Caspian Sea Military intelligence chiefs. He noted that the countries of the region were still locked in the Cold War era, with many not talking and exchanging important information. His intelligence service, for example, did not speak to neighboring Moldavian counterparts and had no formal contacts with the Turks.

But the problem ran far deeper, an unacceptable situation in an era of illegal international trafficking in weapons, drugs, and human beings. Cooperative efforts were needed on the Black and Caspian Seas. Having been one of our first fellows, Medar thought that the college would provide a credible academic setting for a conference aimed at shaping new relationships.

My college leadership and I agreed and rolled up our sleeves. The first conference was hosted in 2006, with an excellent international turnout and only Iran not invited. A broad spectrum of international intelligence issues was addressed. All agreed that it was a valuable forum and should be continued. In 2007, the site of the conference was Constanta, Romania; in 2008, Batumi, Georgia; and in 2009, Sofia, Bulgaria. During these years, the college continued to serve as cohost. We created the Center for International Engagement and Outreach to guide the expanding programs. In less than a decade, we had moved from the fight to add an international dimension to having the college recognized as a valuable international intelligence player.

The institution's role as a change agent in the intelligence world was also growing in terms of the value of applied research, contributed by the faculty and by master's students through their theses. Earlier on, I had created the position of director of research. Good manuscripts, possibly worthy of publication, were now receiving peer review by experts inside and outside the Intelligence Community—and, thanks to the professional capabilities of the DIA print plant, we were now publishing the best.

With our international intelligence fellows, we were ready to create a U.S. Intelligence Research Fellows program. The Coast Guard's former commandant, Admiral Robert Kramek (Ret.), took the lead as a member of our Board of Visitors in promoting the value of the new program. He cited the example of the Chief of Naval Operations' CNO Fellows Program, and their valuable thinking and writing on issues of key importance to the Navy and the sea services. Our proposal was greeted positively by the departments and agencies across the community, and top thinkers, active-duty and civilian, were soon being nominated for the year-long fellowships to embark on book-length projects. All would work in an environment of academic freedom, with research ranging from unclassified to projects requiring the highest national security classifications. The research programs now had a new college focal point: the Center for Strategic Intelligence Research.

But Dr. Oettinger, as chairman of the Board of Visitors, reminded me politely and firmly that we were not done with opening new dimensions of college contributions and service. We needed to strengthen our ability to address science and technology intelligence. In this crucially important field, the United States had once been the global leader, but now, because of more than a decade of tightened budgets and resulting neglect, we were falling behind.

It was time for a third new focal point, a Center for Science and Technology Intelligence, addressing threats to national security arising from the globalization of science and technology, identifying the disruptive consequences of adversarial technology adaptations, and providing a framework for effective intelligence collection, warning, and dissemination. The center's director and participating faculty members would shape a science and technology intelligence curriculum as part of their work—and there was plenty of work, starting with a better understanding of threats from weapons of mass destruction, cyber warfare threats, and threats relating to U.S. and foreign energy and power systems.

As the new centers took shape and moved into action, another of our board members, Admiral Bill Studeman, USN (Ret.), former director of Naval Intelligence, director of the National Security Agency, and deputy director / acting director of Central Intelligence, commented to the board, "The college has really become an elegant academic institution." I concurred, but if we were elegant, we were not operating in a vacuum. Important U.S. intelligence changes were underway.

Following the 9/11 terrorist strikes, a 9/11 Commission and a Commission on the Intelligence Capabilities of the United States Regarding Weapons of Mass Destruction (the WMD Commission) were created, and as they went about their hearings and drafting, Congress set about hearings and crafting legislation to strengthen the Intelligence Community. The charge was levied that evidence had been present, here and there, that the attacks would take place, but that the community had not connected the here-to-there dots.

To strengthen coordination and results, Congress passed the Intelligence Reform and Terrorism Prevention Act (IRTPA) of 2004, in part creating a new Cabinet-level position: the director of national intelligence (DNI). My former NSC staff assistant Bob Gates, who was now serving as president of Texas A&M University, was offered the position by President George W. Bush. Gates declined, saying that too much power still remained with the intelligence departments and agencies, that he would not have hiring and firing authority. The first DNI would be Ambassador John Negroponte, one of the nation's most distinguished senior diplomats, who was serving as our ambassador to Iraq.

This pleased me. John and I had first met when we were at Phillips Exeter Academy, and then had developed a good friendship when we were together on the Nixon NSC staff, and in the years that followed as he rose in his foreign service career.

In early 2005, I called a meeting of the entire college faculty and staff to address the implications of the new era, including the implications of the new law, IRTPA. I said, "We can take great pride in what we have accomplished and are accomplishing. We are positioned exactly where we want to be, and if we want to stay there, we have to move ahead as fast as possible." If only I had known, I would have delivered those words with even greater emphasis. John Negroponte and I were soon in contact, but he was only one person and could not be aware of some of the dangerous mischief regarding the college that would emerge from his new large, high-powered staff, and from congressional staff.

In its final report, the WMD Commission had written, "The Joint Military Intelligence College, for example, currently operates a very successful program—a structured intermediate/advanced curriculum for Intelligence Community officers across the Community." The commission recommended adding an additional, modestly funded academic layer with the creation of a coordinating body, a National Intelligence University, to improve community-wide training at the entry and senior levels. The executive branch agreed, and an interim chancellor of the nonexistent NIU was appointed. In his first major speech, to my pleasure, he said that the college was the community's flagship, accredited, degree-granting institution.

Others at the staff level, as well as retired intelligence officers in the private sector, were not so well informed—or so generous. They saw money to be made in an NIU, with new positions to be had, and they saw the college as a rival standing in the way of this perceived progress. But here, fortunately and somewhat ironically, being in the business of intelligence worked to my advantage.

As the plotters against us began their moves, I encouraged the cultivation of an undisclosed contact on the Office of the Director of National Intelligence (ODNI) staff—who let us know that unpublicized, behind-the-scenes steps were being taken in the ODNI budget process to eliminate funding for the college. Without disclosing my source, I sounded the alarm to the director and deputy director of DIA, who represented the college at such higher levels of budget formulation. I also informed friends and admirers of the college, senior officials on the DNI staff, and others in the community. They promptly raised hell, and the college's funding was, for a few months at least, protected.

Next, I learned from our source that a young staff member on one of the key committees in the House of Representatives was in cahoots with those seeking to do us harm. That committee, I was told, was now planning at the staff level to eliminate the college's funding line in the following year's budget. Again, the alarm was sounded; hell was raised; and our funding continued. Such are the ways in the nation's capital, bringing to mind President Truman's famous words: "If you want a friend in Washington, get a dog."

In the midst of this skullduggery, we kept the college moving forward. New tough issues of our own identification had to be tackled. The nation and those serving in intelligence had moved from the decades of the Cold War to the post–Cold War to coalition warfare, and now into a newer era of globalization, radical extremists, terrorists, and asymmetric warfare.

We were now facing transnational challenges—health, climate, the environment, severe economic stress, failed and failing nation-states, religious and cultural conflicts, illegal international trafficking in drugs and humans, growing international gang activity, piracy, and the proliferation of conventional weapons and weapons of mass destruction.

In this new era, the computer, the internet, cell phones, handheld electronic devices, and global positioning satellites with global coordinates were available to all, and fiber-optic cabling had collectively caused the former balance to shift. With these new cyber technologies, individuals and groups large and small had command and control strengths, improvised weapons capabilities, global communications, and propaganda reach that until just a few years earlier had been beyond the reach of all but a relatively few nation-states.

In the face of this daunting, sweeping change, as college president I had the task of keeping us not only relevant but on the cutting edge in our graduate and undergraduate curricula—with stout opposition from many faculty who, in the best of faculty tradition, were determined to keep the status quo. My new provost and two of the best minds on the faculty did the initial brainstorming. As their ideas came forward and were circulated, the tumult grew.

What was being proposed, the critics charged, was heresy and destruction of all things valuable. They were wrong. We were no longer dealing with intelligence related only to tanks-on-tanks combat or the capabilities of a single satellite collection system. What was coming meant that a good number of such existing courses would have to be scrapped, and that faculty who wished to continue at the college had to move ahead in their own education to prepare to teach the new courses (at the same time they taught the existing curricula). Both the MSSI and BSI degree teachings were under close examination.

The master's curriculum that emerged flowed from globalization, the analyzing of worldwide social, economic, and political change leading to conflict. The curriculum set in place rigorous analytic methodologies aimed at present and future adversary capabilities assessments. The required courses in the new curriculum addressed argumentation, logic, and reasoning; intelligence and national security policy; intelligence collection planning; and the intelligence/operations partnership.

Growing out from this new core, the new elective courses included seven in the field of military strategy using intelligence in combat and peacetime; ten addressing different dimensions of Intelligence Community issues and management; twelve on different transnational threats; and eight on the geostrategic environment, closing the intelligence gaps in Africa, North Asia, South Asia, China, Europe, Latin America, the Middle East, Central Asia, and Russia. The new graduate and undergraduate curricula represented a remarkable achievement for any accredited academic institution. Truly, we were now in the business of educating the next generation of intelligence leaders. All vestiges of the semi-training courses I had inherited in 1994 were gone, as were faculty members unwilling or unable to take on the new mandate. New faculty, all with earned doctorates, were recruited. The tensions dissipated rapidly; it was an exciting time.

In December 2006, the Office of the Secretary of Defense recognized this positive transformation. The undersecretary of defense for intelligence signed a new Department of Defense Directive retitling the college the National Defense Intelligence College. The language of the directive captured the new national mission, stating in part that the college would

> Prepare intelligence professionals, both military and civilian, through education and research, to work with skill and dedication in identifying and effectively integrating foreign, military, and domestic intelligence in defense of the homeland and of U.S. interests abroad.
> Place high priority on education and research to meet the combat and peacetime intelligence needs of the Department of Defense.
> Enhance the competence of intelligence professionals attending the College, through a variety of academic and educational programs, which include granting intelligence undergraduate and graduate degrees and undertaking and disseminating intelligence research

- in the furtherance of those programs, and establishing and enforcing appropriate learning standards.
- Act as the Department of Defense primary point of contact for academic outreach regarding intelligence matters.
- Contribute to the education and professional career development of military and Federal civilian personnel who are pursuing careers in intelligence, defense policy and programs, homeland defense, or homeland security.
- Continue the expansion of degree-program offerings, international programs, research, and academic outreach to Federal, public, and private colleges and universities as part of a continuing advancement toward university status.

Those last four words shaped the goal ever in my mind. What a nice leap forward! The anonymous budget snipers had been stilled, and the Department of Defense was now backing us formally to become the National Intelligence University in name as well as fact.

In 2007, we reached agreement with the ODNI to create several joint National Defense Intelligence College (NDIC) / DNI Intelligence Research fellowships. At much the same time, we formally established the National Defense Intelligence College Press. The press's first title was *Shooting the Front: Allied Aerial Reconnaissance and Photographic Interpretation on the Western Front, World War I*, by former faculty member Lieutenant Colonel Terrence Finnegan, USAFR (Ret.). This dazzling 9-by-12-inch, 508-page, glossy-paper, cloth-covered study of U.S., French, and British aerial reconnaissance represented prime research with extraordinary photographs, maps, and other illustrations. As a book lover from a lineage of book lovers, I believed and unabashedly stated it was one of the finest volumes I had ever seen. Others agreed. Terry would find a British publisher for his expanded second edition.

More new titles in paperback by our fellows, students, and faculty began flowing from the press: pathfinding applied intelligence research on interrogation, the polygraph, cooperation between intelligence and the U.S. law enforcement community, cooperation between intelligence and the international law enforcement community, an intelligence assessment of underground tunneling programs by various adversaries, the intelligence environments of past empires, and the preparation of future U.S. intelligence leaders.

The college had an impressive, fact-laden past, present, and future self-study to offer the Middle States Commission on Higher Education when our next, formal decennial reaffirmation-of-accreditation visit took place in 2008. Webb Institute's president, Rear Admiral Bob Olsen, USCG (Ret.), chaired the team. Our accreditation was reaffirmed with commendation by the commission. I was now in my fourteenth year as president, and it was a pleasure to have length of tenure that enabled me to appreciate how far the college had come from the "on warning of probation" days at the time of my arrival.

In 2007, as part of the continuing growth of our international cooperation, I welcomed a visit by the chief of military intelligence of the Mongolian armed forces. Landlocked and sandwiched between the behemoths China and Russia, Mongolia struggled to make its way as a new democracy. It placed top priority on the emerging, constructive partnership with the United States, "its third neighbor." Could we, the general asked, help them break free from their decades-old Soviet General Staff / Cyrillic-language intelligence training model? Yes, I replied. We will give you textbooks, and we will send members of our faculty to work with your faculty.

In promising textbooks, I was aware that with the change in our curricula we had many copies of many books used in earlier years that were now gathering dust on the back shelves of our bookstore and storage areas and were destined for the trash bins and the maws of the recyclers. It would be far better to send them to Ulaanbaatar to contribute to the new bilateral cooperation. Needless to say, our bureaucracy saw a splendid new opportunity to impede such progress. "It is illegal to give away federal property," we were lectured by the DIA lawyers. Not illegal to heave them into the trash, I thought, but illegal to give them to a friend of importance to the United States. I worked the problem and found that if we sold the books to Mongolia, all would be fine. We settled with the embassy of Mongolia on an extremely modest selling price.

During this international finance period, I became good professional friends with His Excellency Ravdan Bold, Mongolia's ambassador to the United States. Over lunch one day, he asked if I would help Mongolia persuade the government of the United States to allow the erection of a statue to Genghis Kahn in Washington, DC. I allowed that that was beyond even the greatest of my powers. Our friendship survived, and as he was preparing to return to Ulaanbaatar to become director of Mongolia's General Intelligence Agency, he extended a formal invitation to me to visit, to speak, and to be recognized for my contributions to U.S.-Mongolian relations.

My flight from South Korea aboard MIAT, Mongolia's international airline, arrived in the capital, Ulaanbaatar, at midnight, where I was met by a very nice man and woman in their twenties, English-speaking members of the intelligence service who would look after me throughout my visit. After a few hours' sleep, I was up, standing at a window in my hotel suite watching—to my dismay—heavy traffic creeping through the streets in a smoggy morning rush hour. Ambassador Bold received me in his office for a formal one-on-one lunch. CNN was broadcasting on a large TV screen opposite his desk. The schedule called for me to deliver an address at the Ministry of Foreign Affairs that afternoon, following which I would be awarded an honorary doctorate by the Institute of the General Intelligence Agency. There would be dinner at one of the best restaurants in town that night. The next day, my young guides would take me out into the countryside to one of their national parks for sightseeing, camel riding, and Mongolian eating and drinking. On the third and last day, I would deliver another speech at the Ministry of Defense. There would be a formal dinner hosted by Bold at the prime minister of Mongolia's guest house, following which I would be driven to the airport for a 3:00 a.m. departure for Japan, en route to Atlanta, Dulles, and Annapolis—a grinding thirty-six hours.

I enjoyed myself and received high honors throughout the stay. Bold's farewell dinner was dressed by musicians in costume entertaining on

Mongolian stringed instruments. At its conclusion, Bold presented me with a *morin khuur*, or horsehead violin, with strings and bow strings made of horsehair, and with a small bronze plate attached commemorating the visit. The academic robe, hood, and cap were spectacular: royal blue, cardinal red, and white silks, with a Genghis Khan cut to the cap. My first camel ride added to the adventure. Minus the camel, all else was packed up to be shipped to the college.

My own research, writing, and speaking—to wit, the speeches in Mongolia—were a continuing, important part of my role as college president. I valued the intellectual and substantive exercise. It was important to lead by example with my faculty. And I welcomed the opportunity to represent the institution and promote it on the national and international stage. I had, of course, been writing and speaking since my Antarctic exploration days—my publications included many published essays, the novel *A Death in Geneva*, and two hardcover works of nonfiction, *Our World in Antarctica* and *With Presidents to the Summit*. In 2000, the director of the college's Writing Center edited a softcover book called *Clift Notes: Intelligence and the Nation's Security*, a collection of my essays and speeches, which included the prize-winning article "The San Cristobal Trapezoid," which John Hughes and I had published in 1992. The volume had been inspired by a letter from the president of Hampden-Sydney College, Lieutenant General Samuel V. Wilson, USA (Ret.), who had praised two of my speeches and urged publication, noting that mine was a light that had been too long under a bushel. A second edition of *Clift Notes* appeared in 2002, with the inclusion of several newer speeches and essays.

In 1995, I had added a much-valued editorial side portfolio to my professional life, accepting an invitation from David Gries, chairman of the editorial board of the Central Intelligence Agency's peer-reviewed scholarly journal *Studies in Intelligence*, to become a member of the board. *Studies* was created in 1955 as a result of a monograph published by the CIA's legendary chairman of the Board of National Estimates, Sherman Kent.

"Intelligence," he wrote, "has become in our own recent memory, an exacting, highly skilled profession, and an honorable one." But, he continued, "As long as this discipline lacks a literature, its method, its vocabulary, its body of doctrine, and even its fundamental theory run the risk of never reaching full maturity." *Studies* was published quarterly, primarily at the classified level. Indeed, the 1992 issue carrying my article on the Cuban Missile Crisis was the first unclassified issue.

I looked forward to receiving and reviewing manuscripts submitted for publication, and I welcomed the editorial and intellectual give-and-take among the members of the board at its quarterly meetings. It recharged editorial skills and thinking, preparing me for a future assignment that I could not then be aware of, and it took me back to my days as editor of the Naval Institute's *Proceedings*. During my fifteen years of service on the *Studies* board, I several times had occasion to invoke the independent, challenging-common-wisdom approach of *Proceedings* in urging my colleagues to accept good writing that might ruffle a few bureaucratic intelligence feathers. My role also figured positively in that of president of the college, giving me insights as I worked with students and faculty on their research and its publication, giving me new ideas on how best to publish our own monographs and create our own college press, and unveiling a new cast of talented characters—the *Studies* authors—as possible college speakers and conference participants. *Studies* would publish more of my works, including a book review and an essay on intelligence in the digital era, "From Semaphore to Predator," based on a speech I gave at a conference at Yale. In the fall of 2000, the board surprised and honored me by publishing a forty-fifth-anniversary special edition of *Studies* that included "The San Cristobal Trapezoid" as one of the ten best articles of the first forty-five years.

Research and writing continued on other fronts. In 2005, I had the pleasure of being a coauthor of the five-volume work *Strategic Intelligence*, edited by Professor Loch Johnson of the University of Georgia (Praeger Security International). My chapter was titled "The Coin of Intelligence Accountability." I again coauthored with Loch in 2010, with a chapter titled "The Evolution of International Collaboration in the Global

Intelligence Era" in *The Oxford Handbook of National Security Intelligence*. This speaking, publishing, and networking led to a surprise contact from the provost of Robert Morris University in the early spring of 2009: Would I consider being the university's commencement speaker?

I gladly accepted, and opened my May 9 address thus: "If I may borrow from the late, irreverent Kurt Vonnegut, thank you for being educated. Some of you may have heard of a graduation speech Vonnegut gave many years ago. He was introduced, rose, moved to the podium, adjusted the microphone, adjusted his robes, looked out over the faces in the vast auditorium and said, 'Things are very, very bad. They are going to get worse. They are never going to get better. Thank you.' He then turned and took his seat again." Robert Morris honored me with the Honorary Doctor of Laws degree.

A month later, on June 10, 2009, I was onstage at the Kongresshotel overlooking Lake Templiner in Potsdam, Germany, to give the keynote address to the Bundeswehr Intelligence Conference, the first foreigner ever invited to address this major annual assembly of Germany's intelligence officers. The head of German military intelligence had extended the invitation following our discussions during his weeks as a Visiting International Intelligence Scholar at the college. The subject of my address was international cooperation in the era of global intelligence. I titled it "International Cooperation: I Think It Would Be Good," borrowed from Pakistan's ambassador to the United States, Husain Haqqani. When lecturing at the college a few months earlier, he had been asked, "What do you think about the U.S./NATO strategy in Afghanistan?" The ambassador replied, "I think it would be good." I had put a great deal of thought into my own speech. When I concluded, several officers came up to chat. One offered his hand and said, "What a pleasure it is to hear someone who can think and speak, just imagine, forty-five minutes—I timed it—without a single PowerPoint slide."

My German host very kindly provided me with a car, driver, and escort during my stay. The weather was good, and the touring was excellent. I had a day and a half following the speech before my flight to Sofia for the next Black Sea / Caspian Sea Conference. The hotel, with its

Restaurant Zeppelin, was worth touring. The exterior, set in shoreline woods, was in the shape of three Zeppelins tethered to the ground. Its interior had been constructed with lightweight metal and wood fittings along the lines of those in the weight-conscious German Zeppelins. The shores of Lake Templiner had been one of the building sites for the airships.

My one request was quickly accommodated. I had asked to cross the Glienicke Bridge over the Havel River between Potsdam and Berlin. We parked, and as I stood on the walk at the middle of the span, I imagined the famous Cold War 1962 U.S.-Soviet spy exchange of Rudolf Abel for Francis Gary Powers.

The invitations continued. The head of Romanian military intelligence wrote to invite me to be the keynote speaker at a conference later in the year marking the sesquicentennial celebration of the service. I was separately and informally advised that the president of Romania would wish to present me with a high award for my contributions to U.S.-Romanian relations at the highest levels over several decades. I would make the trip to Bucharest in early November 2009, deliver my address, and receive Romania's highest national decoration for a foreigner, Knight in the National Order of Merit, from President—and merchant mariner—Traian Băsescu.

As these events were unfolding, I was already preparing for the next professional chapter in my life. I had taken the decision that fifteen years as college president was enough. In fact, I had been repeatedly questioning myself about continued service after about the twelfth year—bearing in mind that normal senior executive tours in the executive branch are three years, give or take a few months. Now, in 2009, the new curricula, faculty, provost, dean, and head of college operations; the three centers; and the fresh ten-year reaffirmation of accreditation were all in place. The college was in great shape. The moment was right. I attached importance to giving the DIA director time to establish a search committee to find the best possible successor. In April, I sent an email to the faculty and staff advising that I would depart the college at the end of September. While all were slightly stunned, myself included, the work of the college continued apace.

Prior to my announcement, I received a casual invitation from a member of the college's Board of Visitors. Soon after we had created the BSI degree, I had set about recruiting a good senior member of the enlisted services for the board, to bring good insights to the academic program for our new enlisted students. In the process, I discovered Master Chief Petty Officer of the Coast Guard Vincent W. Patton III. Vince was serving as senior enlisted adviser to the commandant of the Coast Guard. His academic credentials, to say the least, were overwhelming—four college degrees, including a doctorate of education from American University, with a master's in theology from the University of California, Berkeley, soon to follow.

In our first meeting at the college, he told me how he had pulled plunging Coast Guard recruiting into a positive, steep climb. He had recommended to the commandant that the Coast Guard focus its recruiting ads on television coverage of professional wrestling. Several senior officers had ridiculed him, chewed him out, and worse. But the commandant had said to give it a try . . . and up the recruiting numbers went, almost immediately. What was the secret to his success? He had quietly noted what his teenage daughter and her friends were watching on television.

In early 2009, Vince Patton was a member of our board. He was also serving as chairman of the U.S. Naval Institute's editorial board. Not knowing of my plans to leave the college, but knowing I had been *Proceedings* editor and had long been an active Institute member, he invited me to meet with the editorial board to share my observations on the Institute's current work and on best editorial practices. The meeting, in early April, was a great success. The Naval Institute's offices were on the Naval Academy Yard, only a mile and a half from my home. My brain whirred. In the spirit of the best 9/11 Commission guidance, I began connecting the next career here-to-there dots. At that point, I was seventy-two years old.

CHAPTER 16

Full Circle

U.S. Naval Institute, 2009–2023

Major General Tom Wilkerson, USMC (Ret.), the Naval Institute's chief executive officer in 2009, invited me for a chat following the editorial board meeting. He was pleased to have me exploring the possibility of returning to the Institute, given my years as *Proceedings* editor and the many highlights of my federal career. That said, the Institute was running on almost an empty tank in terms of funding. The financial crash of 2008 had done damage to its endowment, and all staff were on a voluntary 5 percent pay cut. He did not have ready operating funds sufficient to offer me a salary.

We continued our dialogue over the summer. I had made up my mind that I would really enjoy returning to the Institute. Shortly before my end-of-September departure from the college, Tom said he would have a nice office ready for me. We agreed that I would start with the title of counsel, working initially on a pro bono basis, while he worked on finding my salary. The prodigal son was returning after wandering for forty-three years—and would in time become vice president for planning and operations. This time I stayed at the Institute for fourteen years, until October 2023.

As talks with Tom continued, I was also immersed in the detailed, tedious, necessary work of attending to all aspects of my departure from the federal government. There were endless forms to be filled out with DIA and the government's Office of Personnel Management, the new home base for my pension. There was Medicare, insurance, and on and on it went.

I was not involved formally in the work of the search committee for my successor, but I would receive a quiet call from time to time from one or more members of the committee, with ideas and names to be tested. In the end, a good choice was made. Rear Admiral David Ellison, USN (Ret.), PhD, a Naval Academy graduate, had academic experience as superintendent of the Naval Postgraduate School and head of the New Mexico Military Academy.

Gretchen, Alex, and Ty came with me to the change-of-command ceremony at the college on September 30, 2009. The auditorium was packed. Good words were said. I was awarded the Director of National Intelligence Distinguished Service Medal. Of far greater meaning to me, I was awarded the permanent title of president emeritus of the college, complete with an elegant engraved parchment. Gretchen was presented with flowers and a handsomely matted and framed citation commending her for her service as first lady of the college.

The next morning, October 1, 2009, I was A. Denis Clift of counsel, surveying room 410 in Beach Hall, U.S. Naval Institute. My new space was a twenty-by-twenty-foot, high-ceilinged, top-floor, corner office with six large windows on three sides and a fifteen-foot-long floor-to-ceiling bookcase on the fourth. Beach Hall sits on a rise known as Strawberry Hill on the Academy Yard. To the east, I looked out across the historic cemetery with its stately trees; across Sherman Field and Dorsey Creek to Rickover, Nimitz, and Alumni Halls; down along the Severn River; and out to the Chesapeake Bay. The view to the north was straight across the Severn River. To the west, I looked up Dorsey Creek, past Hill Bridge and Hubbard Hall, home of the Naval Academy's crew; past the King George

Street Bridge to the boathouse and campus of St. John's College on the Rowe Boulevard Bridge, and beyond. The State House Capitol dome and the cupolas of St. John's McDowell Hall and the State Treasury Building were tucked in the treetops. I would be able to walk to and from home.

The cedar-shingled house that Gretchen and I bought in 1971—and together, year after year, repaired and renovated—now has a distinct grace and stature. Built by architect Philip Cooper in 1911 as his dream home, it rises more than three stories high, with a white lintel running beneath the line of the pitched roof and two great brick chimneys. Its large white double-hung windows with wavy antique glass are green-shuttered in the front, framing white pillars and capping the arch of the front entrance. Leaded-glass windows dress three sides of the house, including the west-side bay window, with more than four hundred panes. A two-story wing on the east side has near-continuous double-casement windows on each floor beneath the white lintel.

The American flag is centered above, flying from a twelve-foot, eagle-topped flagpole. The house is located in Wardour Bluffs, a peninsula jutting into the Severn River. In the early 1900s, landscape artist Frederick Law Olmsted Jr. designed the bluffs' curving roads and property boundaries. Looking to the east, whether from the veranda or the east wing, the view runs for miles beyond a long, rectangular lawn with bordering garden, down the Severn River, with the Naval Academy on the right and the Naval Station on the left, out beyond the outer harbor of Annapolis, and across the Chesapeake Bay to Kent Island.

While quietly marveling at my good fortune, I moved ahead in my renewed career with the Institute. There were some shocks. In the 1990s, lawyers had decided that active-duty admirals and generals could no longer serve on the private sector Naval Institute board of directors. On my return in 2009, a number of senior business types were now serving, and they were trying to change the mission from a private, nonprofit, educational service and publishing house to a lobbying role! As the months unfolded, Dame Fortune intervened.

Vice Admiral Peter H. Daly, USN, was about to retire as the deputy at U.S. Fleet Forces Command. He was a *Proceedings* reader from childhood, a life member, and a *Proceedings* author, and he had served on both the editorial board and the board of directors. As he now prepared to retire from the Navy, he threw his hat in the ring and was selected as the new chief executive officer. At his urging, Admiral James Stavridis, USN (Ret.), who had just been Supreme Allied Commander Europe and was now dean of the Fletcher School of Law and Diplomacy at Tufts University—also an Institute author and life member—agreed to serve and was elected as chairman of the board. Good change after good change would follow. The Institute ship of state was on course again.

In the meantime, the college was thriving, as I was confident it would. Lieutenant General Jim Clapper, now retired, was named director of national intelligence by President Barack Obama and confirmed by the Senate in 2010. In early 2011, he sent me an email advising that he had taken the decision to name the National Defense Intelligence College the National Intelligence University—that it was, in fact, the community's degree-granting seat of higher education and research. He thanked me for all I had done to make this possible. On August 29, 2011, I returned to the college for the convocation of the university.

Following the keynote address by DNI Clapper and the Provost's Charge to the University, I was called to center stage by President Ellison: "Mr. A. Denis Clift," the provost read from her place at the podium:

> For more than 50 years you have dedicated yourself to service to the Nation and its future leaders, beginning with active naval service during the Eisenhower and Kennedy administrations.
>
> You have served in military and civilian capacities in the administrations of 11 successive presidents, including 13 years in the Executive Office of the President. You have served on the National Security Council and as the Assistant for National Security Affairs to Vice President Walter F. Mondale. You have long and dedicated service as a U.S. Commissioner on the U.S.-Russia Joint Commission on Prisoners of War / Missing in Action created by President

George H. W. Bush and President Boris Yeltsin with the goal of accounting for servicemen still missing from past conflicts.

From 1994 through 2009, you served as President of the National Defense Intelligence College, and on your retirement you were named president emeritus. From 2000 through 2005, you served as a Commissioner on the Middle States Commission on Higher Education.

In recognition of your extraordinary achievements, the National Intelligence University proudly confers upon you the degree, Doctor of Strategic Intelligence, Honoris Causa.

With this humbling recognition, my college president's mission was completed. As I now returned to the Institute with fond memories of my role as editor in the 1960s, the organization was in full press forward on all fronts into the digital age. I jumped in and out of various projects as I worked to get my Institute sea legs back under me.

On one important front, the pages of our archived print copies of *Proceedings* going back to 1874 were brown and starting to crumble. Some of the print photographs in the Institute's very large and valuable photo collection were cracking and starting to fall apart. The Naval Institute's oral histories, some 250 strong, by Navy and sea service officers and enlisted personnel with distinguished careers, were languishing with the audiotapes holding the interviews—and in danger of crumbling.

Working with contractors, our technical staff began the digitizing. We had a question to answer. How would we know at a quick glance what the issue-by-issue, year-after-year digitized substantive contents of the *Proceedings* and the histories were? With the CEO's concurrence, I took on the marvelous challenge of reading every issue of *Proceedings* from 1874 and writing a four-to-six-line summary of each article: title, author, and contents. In the contents, as I soon discovered, were superb course-setting, milestone essays capturing the history and shaping the future of the Navy.

Just a few examples: In 1874, in the very first issue, Captain Stephen B. Luce called for better Navy enlisted and merchant mariner training.

Congress acted on his recommendations. Lieutenant Ernest J. King, future five-star Fleet Admiral, won a gold-medal prize in 1909 for his essay on the need for better shipboard organization in the new steel and steam Navy. In 1912, Lieutenant Chester W. Nimitz, future five-star Fleet Admiral, authored a detailed, professional, prescient essay on the submarine as a weapon of modern warfare. Lieutenant Hyman Rickover, future four-star admiral and "father of the nuclear Navy," wrote an essay in 1935 on the need to update international law to deal with submarine operations. With submarines attacking merchant ships, one could no longer expect submarines to first board, inspect, and give safe harbor to crews.

After two years, with the enormous *Proceedings* summarizing task completed, I turned to skimming each of the thick oral histories and finding particularly enjoyable, instructive passages for our press staff to pull from the audiotapes and add to our oral history advertising.

With both of these projects completed, my brain and files were replete with the contents of our publications and the contributions of the Naval Institute over the decades. Long ago, as *Proceedings* editor, I had guided the production of a ninetieth-anniversary issue in 1963. Now the Institute was approaching its monumental sesquicentennial anniversary in 2023. We needed a published history. After many broader staff discussions, Vice Admiral Daly turned to me, knowing of my publishing background, and said, "Denis, you know that history. You write that history."

I created decade-by-decade chapters to tell the story, from the post–Civil War advent of the Institute through the 1870s and on into the 2020s. *The Pen and the Sword* offers a rich, detailed history, with quotes from so many who have contributed to the publications, and who have helped in their careers to shape the Navy and sea services' history. The Naval Institute Press had already, in 2014 after my return, published a second edition of my novel *A Death in Geneva*, and in 2018 had further honored me by publishing my new novel, *The Bronze Frog*. But the Institute's history is my Naval Institute capstone contribution. Mission accomplished; relieve the watch.

APPENDIX

Staff Schedule, Nixon and Pompidou in Iceland, 30 May–1 June 1973

Author's note: A detailed schedule for summit travel such as this, termed the "bible," provided all essential information for staff members.

The White House
Washington
Abbreviated Staff Schedule
Trip of the President
to Meet President Pompidou
Reykjavik, Iceland
May 30–31, and June 1, 1973

The final detailed schedule will be distributed on board 26000 upon boarding at Andrews Air Force Base on Wednesday, May 30, 1973.

Weather Forecast: For May and June, the average high temperature is 50 degrees, low overnight 30 degrees. More than half the days during these months are rainy, windy and overcast.

BLACK TIE will be required for dinner guests Thursday, May 31, 1973.

WEDNESDAY, MAY 30, 1973

9:45 a.m. EDT   26000 departs Andrews AFB en route Keflavik, Iceland.
               (Flying time: 5 hours, 15 minutes)
               (Time change: +4 hours)

10:00 a.m.   S '76 departs Andrews AFB en route Keflavik, Iceland.
                              (Flying time: 5 hours, 15 minutes)
                              (Time change: +4 hours)
                              NOTE: S '76 will fly over volcanic eruption on Westmann Islands.
7:00 p.m. IST   26000 arrives Keflavik
7:30 p.m.   S '76 arrives Keflavik
Advanceman: Dewey Clower

Arrival ceremony
9:00 p.m.   The President meets with President Eldjarn at State Council House.

Participants:
United States   **Iceland**
The President   President Eldjarn
Secretary Rogers   Prime Minister Johannesson
Dr. Kissinger   Foreign Minister Agustsson

9:30 p.m.   Talks conclude

OVERNIGHT

THURSDAY, MAY 31, 1973

9:40 a.m.   Staff motorcade departs en route Kjarvalsstadir.
9:53 a.m.   President's motorcade departs en route Kjarvalsstadir.
9:58 a.m.   Arrive Kjarvalsstadir (Head-to-Head Meeting Site). The President greets President Pompidou on his arrival.
10:00 a.m.   Meeting begins. Counterparts meet separately.
                              Foreign Policy
                                  United States
                                  Secretary Rogers

	Assistant Secretary Stoessel
	Ambassador Irwin
	Denis Clift
	Economic Policy
	United States
	Secretary Shultz
	Under Secretary Volcker
	Deputy Special Representative Malmgren
12:00 Noon	Meetings conclude. Return to residence/hotel.
	PERSONAL STAFF TIME
	2 HOURS, 44 MINUTES
2:50 p.m.	Staff motorcade departs for Kjarvalsstadir.
2:54 p.m.	President's motorcade departs en route Kjarvalsstadir.
2:59 p.m.	President arrives Kjarvalsstadir.
3:00 p.m.	Meeting begins. Same counterparts meet separately.
	PERSONAL STAFF TIME
	2 HOURS, 20 MINUTES
7:30 p.m.	Staff motorcade departs en route President Eldjarn's Residence.
7:40 p.m.	President's motorcade departs en route President Eldjarn's Residence.
	U.S. Dinner Guest List
	The President
	Secretary Rogers
	Secretary Shultz
	Ambassador Irving
	Ambassador Irwin
	Dr. Kissinger
	General Haig
	Mr. Ronald Ziegler
	Under Secretary Volcker
8:00 p.m.	Reception begins.
8:30 p.m.	Dinner begins.
	Toasts.

250 APPENDIX

11:00 p.m.　　　　　　Dinner concludes. President and party return to residences.

OVERNIGHT

FRIDAY, JUNE 1, 1973

9:50 a.m.　　　　　　Staff motorcade departs en route Kjarvalsstadir.
9:53 a.m.　　　　　　President's motorcade departs en route Kjarvalsstadir.
10:00 a.m.　　　　　Meeting begins. Same counterparts meet separately.
11:30 a.m.　　　　　Meetings conclude. Presidents, followed by their counterparts, proceed to plenary session.
12:15 p.m.　　　　　Bus will depart Loftleidir Hotel for those not participating in the meetings en route Keflavik Airport.
12:35 p.m.　　　　　Plenary session concludes.
12:40 p.m.　　　　　Motorcade departs en route Keflavik Airport.
1:25 p.m.　　　　　　Arrive Keflavik Airport. Departure ceremony.
1:35 p.m.　　　　　　S '76 departs Keflavik, en route Andrews AFB.
　　　　　　　　　　　　(Flying time: 5 hours, 50 minutes)
　　　　　　　　　　　　(Time change: –4 hours)
3:25 p.m. EDT　　　　　　S '76 arrives Andrews AFB.
3:40 p.m.　　　　　　　　26000 arrives AFB.

ABOUT THE AUTHOR

A. Denis Clift served as president of the National Defense Intelligence College, the flagship degree-granting education and research institution in the U.S. Intelligence Community, from 1994 to 2009. In 1999, in parallel, he was elected to serve as a commissioner on the Middle States Commission on Higher Education for the 2000–2002 term, and then reelected for the 2003–5 term. From 1992 to 2009, he also served as a presidential commissioner on the U.S.-Russia Joint Commission on Prisoners of War / Missing in Action, created by President George H. W. Bush and President Boris Yeltsin, with the goal of accounting for servicemen still missing from past conflicts.

Mr. Clift was born in New York City. He was educated at Phillips Exeter Academy (1954); Stanford University (BA 1958); and the London School of Economics and Political Science, University of London (MSc 1967). His academic honors include honorary PhD degrees from the Institute of the General Intelligence Agency of Mongolia (2008), Robert Morris University (2009), and the National Intelligence University (2011). He is a veteran of two Antarctic expeditions, including the 1961 Bellingshausen Sea Expedition. From 1963 to 1966, Clift was editor of the U.S. Naval Institute *Proceedings*. He rejoined the Naval Institute in 2009, serving in senior leadership as vice president for planning and operations.

Clift began a career of public service as a naval officer in the Eisenhower and Kennedy administrations and served in military and civilian capacities in the administrations of eleven successive presidents, including thirteen years in the Executive Office of the President and the White House. In 1971, he joined the National Security Council staff. From 1974 to 1976, he was head of President Ford's National Security Council staff for the Soviet Union and Eastern and Western Europe. From 1977 to 1981, he served as assistant for national security affairs to Vice President of the United States Walter F. Mondale. From 1991 to 1994, he was chief of staff, Defense Intelligence Agency, following service as deputy director for external relations of the agency.

Clift attained the highest Senior Executive Service rank, SES-6, in 1993.

His awards and decorations include the National Order of Merit, Rank of Knight, Romania's highest national decoration for a foreigner, awarded in 2009 by President Traian Băsescu; the President's Rank of Distinguished Executive, awarded by President George W. Bush in 2001; the President's Rank of Meritorious Executive, awarded by President Ronald Reagan in 1986; the Department of Defense Medal for Distinguished Public Service; the Department of Defense Distinguished Civilian Service Medal; the Director of National Intelligence's National Intelligence Distinguished Service Medal; the Coast Guard's Distinguished Public Service Medal; the Secretary of Defense's Meritorious Civilian Service Medal; the Secretary of the Navy's Commendation for Achievement; the Oceanographer of the Navy's Superior Achievement Award; and the Director of Central Intelligence's Sherman Kent Award and Helene L. Boatner Award. He directed the production of the film *Portrait of Antarctica*, screened at the Venice Film Festival. Clift's books include the novels *The Bronze Frog* (Naval Institute Press) and *A Death in Geneva* (Random House), and the nonfiction works *Our World in Antarctica* (Rand McNally), *With Presidents to the Summit* (George Mason University Press), *Clift Notes: Intelligence and the Nation's Security* (NDIC Press), and *The Pen and the Sword: The U.S. Naval Institute, 1873–2023* (Naval Institute Press). He also coauthored *Strategic Intelligence* (Praeger) and *The National Security Intelligence Handbook* (Oxford University Press).

The Naval Institute Press is the book-publishing arm of the U.S. Naval Institute, a private, nonprofit, membership society for sea service professionals and others who share an interest in naval and maritime affairs. Established in 1873 at the U.S. Naval Academy in Annapolis, Maryland, where its offices remain today, the Naval Institute has members worldwide.

Members of the Naval Institute support the education programs of the society and receive the influential monthly magazine *Proceedings* or the colorful bimonthly magazine *Naval History* and discounts on fine nautical prints and on ship and aircraft photos. They also have access to the transcripts of the Institute's Oral History Program and get discounted admission to any of the Institute-sponsored seminars offered around the country.

The Naval Institute's book-publishing program, begun in 1898 with basic guides to naval practices, has broadened its scope to include books of more general interest. Now the Naval Institute Press publishes about seventy titles each year, ranging from how-to books on boating and navigation to battle histories, biographies, ship and aircraft guides, and novels. Institute members receive significant discounts on the Press' more than eight hundred books in print.

Full-time students are eligible for special half-price membership rates. Life memberships are also available.

For more information about Naval Institute Press books that are currently available, visit www.usni.org/press/books. To learn about joining the U.S. Naval Institute, please write to:

Member Services
U.S. Naval Institute
291 Wood Road
Annapolis, MD 21402-5034
Telephone: (800) 233-8764
Fax: (410) 571-1703
Web address: www.usni.org

www.ingramcontent.com/pod-product-compliance
Lightning Source LLC
Chambersburg PA
CBHW021952160426
43209CB00001B/15